The Tri-Angel Way

A woman's journey of spiritual development

In-Formation

Moments of Realization

Joanna Infeld

Printed in the United States of America

Kora Press is a registered trademark.
ISBN 10: 0-9760512-4-9
ISBN 13: 978-0-9760512-4-4

Cover painting by Karina Edwards

KO
RA

K O R A
P R E S S

Kora is a type of pilgrimage and meditation by movement in
the Tibetan Buddhist tradition. A kora is performed by walking
around a mountain, temple, stupa, or other sacred site.

The Tri-Angel Way

A woman's journey of spiritual development

Level 1

In-Formation

Moments of Realization

Joanna Infeld

From the Publisher

Kora Press is proud to present the first book of the trilogy *The Tri-Angel Way* by Joanna Infeld entitled *In-Formation; Moments of Realization*. This trilogy is another in a series of publications dedicated to human development, the search for truth and the human story. In this first book the usher, or teacher, is a clairvoyant grandmother who instructs a young woman seeking for answers to questions concerning the reasons for living and her unique part within this earthly journey.

The main character of the book is questioning her purpose and mission in life and decides to undertake a search for knowledge and truth. To her surprise, she finds what she is looking for within her own family, but her quest leads her to more questions than answers. She discovers that a real journey into the mystery of life is like that: it will always produce a further hunger to find out more …

The other parts of the trilogy are titled *In-Tuition; Moments of Awakening* and *In-Sight; Moments of Being*.

If you enjoy *In-Formation; Moments of Awakening*, you will probably want to check out other books by the same author from Kora Press (available online from *www.Amazon.com, www.BarnesandNoble.com, www. Borders.com* and other book sellers):

Rainbow Woman (written under the name Joanna Francis)
Unmasked; Spirit Flares (written under the name Joanna Francis)
Dear Gabriel; Letters from a trainee angel.

Contents

Foreword

In-Formation; Moments of Realization, the first in the trilogy of books titled "The Tri-Angel Way," tells the story of one woman's spiritual journey at the first of three progressive levels of understanding. It is more a parable than a factual relating of events (though many real experiences did take place). I do not want you, the reader, to be distracted by places and real names, so suffice to say that the action takes place "somewhere in America at the present time."

The main emphasis of the story is upon the main character's inner journey and development throughout one year. So I am not concentrating on external events, as would be the case with a more traditional autobiography. The narrative traces the growth of awareness and development of consciousness of a young woman, Barbara Faye. It points in the direction where the real heart of human action takes place. So this is not an autobiography in the traditional sense but rather a spiritual journey in parable form, written from the standpoint of the protagonist, Barbara Faye.

I hope you enjoy this journey of discovery. The first chapter of the Level 2 book in the series—*Intuition; Moments of Awakening*—is added at the end of this volume for your reading pleasure.

Joanna Infeld

This book is dedicated to all those who have never known their grandmother, so that they may learn from the wisdom of mine.

from Barbara Faye

Chapter One

Clairvoyance

"You have to let me go," my grandmother said as I sat by her bed, holding her hand and praying for a miracle that would save her from this specter called death that we had all been fearing, except her, it seemed, for the last weeks during her debilitating illness. "It is time," she added and as I looked into her eyes, made large and glassy and intense by illness and suffering, I thought she looked much better—there seemed to be color in her cheeks and a renewed energy, as if she were gathering together all her remaining strength and vitality, in preparation towards that final journey that awaited her. I felt she was waiting for my permission to exit and that I should not keep her from departing any longer. I remembered that often before death came a final summoning of strength and lucidity and that this was a good moment to die—with consciousness and mental faculties intact. There was something else which caught my attention in those final moments—I felt another presence in the room, as if someone had entered and was standing at the foot of her bed, waiting for her to join him or her; I was not sure which. I looked at the spot where I felt this odd presence, but could see nothing. I looked back at my grandmother's face and saw that her eyes were focused on the very place where I had attempted to detect the unseen being. Her dry mouth seemed to relax into a gentle smile as she said to someone who was not there, "I am coming. I'm ready."

Those were her final words. Suddenly her entire body went limp as her open eyes continued to stare in the same direction, frozen like a statue's eyes, peering into another world.

This was my final encounter with my grandmother who had also been my best friend, mentor, adviser and teacher. She was a wise woman who had lived through a world war and had survived hunger, terror and fear. I knew I would miss her but within the six weeks of her illness I also understood that her departure meant that I needed to now become my own guiding light and that the time had come to claim my independence and begin to take up greater responsibility for my own actions and thoughts. I had depended on her wisdom and knowledge for too long. It was time to become a grown-up and make decisions for my own life.

Since I had left home and had gone to live with my friend Alice and more recently my grandmother, it seemed that I was putting off the time of taking up the challenge of life. It had been two years of living within a cocoon of security and it was time to spread my wings, whatever that might come to mean. The stage was set and I was ready, though I was not yet sure, for what.

Ever since I was a child I seemed to have a gift; at least that was what my mother used to call it. "That child has a gift," she used to say to her neighbors and friends, and they all used to look at me differently, as if I could see into their hearts and souls. Well, I couldn't, at least not then, when they expected it and not on demand. What my mother was referring to as my gift was my ability to predict the future or see the past. However, this was not something I could turn on or off at will; it would come upon me unexpectedly and unpredictably and out of my mouth would come a statement that I had neither preconceived or attempted to make, and whenever that happened, I came to know, and so did my mother, and in time others who knew me, that it would come to pass. It was as if someone else would speak through me and no one would be more surprised than I.

I remember when it first happened. I was only six or seven years old and my mother was dressing my brother and me for school. Even today I can see her tying a red scarf over my snowsuit, getting us ready to meet the school bus in time. I was not thinking of anything in particular, there was no image that appeared in my head (images came later); I just blurted out in a high-pitched voice, full of unexpected anxiety, "Don't send us to school. Not today. Today we should stay home."

"Whatever made you say that?" my mother asked, bewildered. She looked at me inquisitively and touched my forehead, checking whether I had a fever. But the moment had passed and I was just as surprised as she was. I saw her concerned look and my brother in his navy blue coat, staring at me with his mouth open, as if he was seeing me for the very first time.

"I don't know." I shrugged my shoulders and picked up my lunch box from the kitchen table. "Let's go," I said, somewhat embarrassed, taking control of the situation, wanting to leave the incident behind me, as if nothing had happened, and the three of us walked through the door into a cold winter morning.

During the morning at school I thought of that moment a few times and wondered about it, but soon dismissed it as I became engrossed in the work of the day and playing with my girlfriends during the breaks. My brother ran up to me once during the lunch break and imitated my morning outburst, "We should stay home today, we shouldn't go to school today," he taunted, as he made faces and soon ran away again to play with his mates.

I blushed as my girlfriend Eva, who was standing with me at the time, asked what that was all about.

"Oh, nothing," I said. "It was just something that happened before we came to school today. He's just being silly." And we continued with our game of hopscotch.

Steve soon changed his attitude when we were on the school bus riding back home that afternoon. It was at the crossroads when the lights turned green and the bus started to move forward—a truck that was coming from the left at full speed kept going through a red light and onto the middle of the crossroads. The driver of the schoolbus slammed his foot on the brakes, but it was too late and the oncoming truck hit the school bus on the left side, pushing it towards the right side of the road until it abruptly came to a stop at a right-hand angle to the direction of the oncoming traffic amidst the sound of broken glass and bending metal. All the children screamed as we were thrown forward, hitting the seats in front of us or being thrown out of our seats altogether. When I realized what had happened, I found myself on the floor of the bus with my knee badly hurting and a piece of glass embedded in my forearm. There was noise, crying, screaming and commotion all around me, and I was hearing all this noise as if through a haze. Then strangers entered the bus and began helping the children disembark onto the pavement where they waited for the ambulances to arrive. All of us were taken in groups of four or five to the hospital where our wounds were seen to and hurting limbs X-rayed. Steven had bashed his head against the seat in front of him but luckily, nothing serious had happened to any of us, as the bus was not going very fast, having just started up at a green light. Only the driver and Mrs. Shawn, the new gym teacher who was standing on the steps next to the driver were badly hurt. Mrs. Shawn had to stay in hospital for several days due to internal bleeding. We all signed a card for her the next day and a few of the older children even went to see her in the hospital and took her a bunch of flowers from the entire school.

Mother came to the hospital to pick us up, as she and the other parents were notified about what had happened. She had hurried from work to take us home as soon as we were released from hospital. I still have a scar on my right arm to remind me of that fateful day.

That evening at dinner, Mother remembered what I had said in the morning before school, and she told Father the whole story. Verbally he seemed to dismiss the incident as insignificant, but nevertheless, he did give me a peculiar look, as if to probe the depths of my soul in search of the truth about my perception ability or gift, as Mother began to refer to it. Steven in the meantime concentrated on eating his soup and never even looked in my direction. He did, however, stop teasing me from that day on.

Nothing more was said about the incident, except that we found out later that the brakes of the truck had unexpectedly failed that day. My wound healed, my bruise disappeared and everything went back to normal, with the one exception that we heard that the truck driver had been badly hurt in the accident as well. The gym teacher, however, was fine and was back at school after a short absence.

The next time I predicted the future, it occurred a couple of years later when I was on holiday with my mother and my friend, Tina. We were at the seaside and had spent the day at the beach swimming, sun bathing and playing with a big red beach ball that Mother had brought with us from home. We were just packing up our things to go back to the hotel for dinner, when I suddenly exclaimed, out of the blue, "Auntie Daisy needs to talk to you." My mother looked at me, astonished. Aunt Daisy was my mother's younger sister and she lived in England, having married an Englishman. She only used to phone my mother on her birthday and at Christmas, and although they were friends, as well as being sisters, or so they claimed, they only saw each other when my parents traveled to England to see my father's family. So when I told my mother that Auntie Daisy needed her, she at first was going to dismiss my claim as unreal, but then stopped herself, as she no doubt remembered what had happened with the school bus. She knelt down, right there in the sand and put her hands on my shoulders.

"What do you know, darling?" she asked, looking concerned.

I shrugged. "I don't know. I just know she needs you now. She needs to talk to you, that's all." And then the moment passed. But my mother heeded my cry and, as I learned later, she actually phoned Aunt Daisy and found out that her sister had been frantically looking for her, not realizing that the three of us were away on holiday. Her husband, uncle Alex, had been missing for two days and Daisy was upset. It was not the first time, because Alex was a drinker and a gambler and sometimes he would just disappear without telling Daisy where he was going. So this was one of those occasions and Daisy needed a shoulder to cry on, or rather an ear to cry into.

After that, the family tended to listen whenever I had one of my "turns." And they knew I wasn't faking it because during these episodes my voice would change and it was as if someone else was speaking through me. During such an event I myself would listen with astonishment to what I was saying, mostly not believing a word of it, but over the years learning to pay more strict attention.

I remember one time it happened when my friend Elizabeth got engaged to be married. She phoned me up and asked if I wanted to be a bridesmaid. It was quite funny actually, because one moment I said, "Yes, I would love to," and the next moment I was shouting down the phone: "Don't do it! You can't marry him! He will make your life a misery!"

Elizabeth was silent for a moment and then started laughing. As the moment passed, I started laughing too, embarrassed that I had caused such consternation and contradiction. The episode was soon forgotten as we started talking about wedding dresses and ceremonies, and of course she married her fiancé and of course I was a bridesmaid and everything seemed to go smoothly until soon after the wedding, when he hit her for some small "misdemeanor." A few months later she confided in me that he had been regularly beating her up in attacks of unfounded jealous rage. However, she did not have the courage to leave him until finally, two years later, having given birth to a child and having watched him physically punish both of them for crimes they had not committed, she took her baby daughter, went back to live with her parents and took out a court injunction against him. It was only then that she and I both remembered what I had said to her before the wedding. It was at this point that Elizabeth introduced the nickname "The Oracle" and both my friends and my family adopted it and it stuck to me like used-up chewing gum. In a way I was proud of the fact that I did have a special gift that made people respect me and somewhat fear me, though it wasn't really me that they had a trepidation about; it was that voice that seemed to adopt me from time to time, especially when some misfortune was about to strike and affect someone I knew.

I didn't need to know a person well to be able to warn them of an impending disaster. At one time I walked into a jewelry store to buy a new battery for my watch and as I looked at the lady behind the counter, before I had a chance to ask her for what I wanted, I found myself saying, to her and my astonishment, "Be careful, this store is too accessible and you shouldn't be here on your own. You might be robbed."

She looked at me curiously, hesitated for a moment and then replied with a polite smile, as if to say that she would indulge my interference in her affairs, "Oh, no, this is a good neighborhood. Nothing bad ever happens here." And then she added, with a professional courtesy, "How can I help you?"

Well, I read it next day in the local paper—the store was robbed that very night and everything was taken, while she was held hostage at gunpoint. That really scared me. I did not want to spend the rest of my life going around predicting disasters. I needed to understand better what was happening to me and how to make use of this dubious gift for the benefit of myself and others.

I never had any visions or premonitions about my own fate and future. The only time I was in any way affected by my own predictions was that very first time when I announced that we (my brother and I) should not be sent to school—the day the school bus crashed.

It was completely a different story when I was able to read the past; it did not matter whether it was a disaster or a happy occurrence—I would suddenly get a picture in my mind and when I put the person I was talking to to the question, it would invariably turn out to be true. Sometimes embarrassing for both of us, I would nevertheless feel it was my duty to check out the veracity of these images, as they appeared in my head, not censoring or altering their content, even if it was quite personal (and it most often was).

That started one day when I was still at school and the teacher walked into the classroom late, apologizing for her tardiness.

"I had to take my daughter to the dentist," she said as she sat down at her desk at the top of the class, while opening the class register and putting on her glasses.

In my mind I saw her in her bedroom with a man and I could distinctly hear her saying, "It's all right. I'll go in late today," as the two embraced.

"No you didn't. You were home," I said and needless to say, she got very upset with me.

"Are you saying that I am lying?" she asked with a false indignation in her voice.

"No." I replied, "I just know where you were and what you were doing."

Following that exchange I was sent to the Principal's office where I received my punishment: I had to stay at school until six in the evening that night, helping some of the older children who edited the monthly newsletter prepare the latest issue for print. That was always one of the main punishments at our school, short of suspension or a call to the parents. Even the cleaners took pity on me and were asking what kind of heinous crime I had committed, but I just said I had answered back to a teacher, rather than telling them the whole story, which I did not think they would believe anyway.

And so every now and again an image would appear in my head and I would know with complete certainty what the person I was talking to had been doing that day, that week or even that hour. It was a complete read-out, in color and detail, with sound and sometimes even smells, like when I spoke with my friend Billy and instantly could smell fish, even though the picture that went with it turned out to be five days old. I saw him on a boat, fishing with his brother and I saw several buckets of fish they had caught; I could even feel the breeze on that trawler. Although I knew at the same time that he had just returned from a trip, I had no idea where he had gone.

I remember one day when I was out shopping with my mother—I must have been seven or eight at the time—we were in a mall and my mother decided to try on some shoes—she loved shoes and already had quite a collection. As she was attended by the sales assistant, I wandered off between the racks of shoes. I noticed a man holding a pair of sneakers and I walked boldly up to this stranger, pulled on his sleeve and asked, "Who is Gary?"

He looked down at me with great surprise and answered, "Gary is my brother. How do you know?"

"Tell him to be more careful on that bike," I said, as in my head I had a very clear picture of a man falling off a motorbike.

"Well, you're damn right he should be more careful," he said. "Gary is in hospital with two broken ribs and a dislocated shoulder after he took a spill from his bike two days ago." He replaced the sneakers on the shelf and added, "How do you know about Gary?"

"I don't," I replied and turned away, skipping my way through the maze of shoe racks back to where my mother was trying on a pair of navy pumps. The man followed me, obviously curious about what I had said. As we approached, my mother looked up, clearly surprised to see me being followed by a stranger.

"Is this your daughter?" the man asked.

"Yes," my mother replied. "Is something wrong?" She sounded worried.

"No," he said, "but she told me about my brother Gary who has recently had an accident and I want to know how she knows about him."

My mother put her hands on my shoulders, as she always did when she had something serious to say to me and looked into my eyes. "You heard what the man said," she said. "Is it true?"

"Yes, I saw a picture of a man called Gary and I knew he had fallen off his bike." I shrugged my shoulders as if this was the most normal thing to have happen. "Can you let me go now?"

My mother took her hands off my shoulders and turned to the man.

"This happens to her from time to time," she said, "and it always checks out. Sometimes she sees the future, sometimes the present and sometimes the past."

The man muttered something and walked away. I couldn't tell whether he believed my mother or not.

That evening I was lying in bed when I heard voices coming from the living room. I was curious what was going on, so I got out of bed and crept down the hallway towards the living room, making sure no one could see me. I recognized the voice of my grandmother—she was talking with my parents. They all sounded very serious and concerned.

"It is a gift of clairvoyance," my grandmother was saying and I realized she was talking about me, even though I did not understand the meaning of the word clairvoyance at the time. I started listening attentively. "It means clear sight and it says that she can tap into a person's aura or energy field," my grandmother was explaining. "We all carry all our experiences with us, in the form of minute energy signals. Some people can read these signals and tap into a person's history, often in an unconscious, undirected way. Barbara can obviously do this occasionally, though she has not yet learned how to control or direct this ability."

"Well, that would explain her ability to read the past, like she did today. But what about the present? Sometimes she knows what is going on at the same moment, like when she told me I needed to phone Daisy and it turned out Daisy had been frantically looking for me all over the place."

"That can be explained as well with some understanding of the unseen worlds of energy and power," my grandmother replied. "Energy can travel faster than light and sometimes a person who is on the same frequency, for whatever reason, can pick up another person's actions, moods or needs. For some reason Barbara connected to Daisy's desperation that day and responded. After all, they are both Aquarians, aren't they?" she added with a laugh.

My mother was obviously thoughtful and spoke slowly as she posed her next question. "I can understand the past and even the present, but what about the future?" she asked. "How can anyone predict the future?"

"The future has been and is being predicted all the time. One of the reasons this happens is that people normally do not heed warnings and continue to act according to their character, desires and history. If Caesar did not go to the Senate that fateful day during the Ides of March, perhaps he would have died an old man in his bed. And the reason it was possible to predict his assassination is because it had already been planned, therefore the thought of it already existed, even though it had not happened yet. If you had kept Steven back from school that morning when Barbara warned you about the school bus crash, perhaps the day would have turned out differently. She could predict the future because the brakes on the truck were already beginning to fail, the route was prepared by the school beforehand and all the ingredients for the accident already existed. I think fortune telling is possible because people tend to be predictable, treading on familiar paths and seldom veering into new territory. However, I also believe we can change our patterns, but we must consciously decide to do so, otherwise we become victims of our already established circumstances. It is a bit like a script that has already been written. We have the ability to become the director and change the script, but only if we decide to undertake that responsibility. Mostly we behave in old familiar ways. We act out our part, rather than writing the script."

"I think I understand," my mother said. "I can carry on in my own established ways and continue to be who I am with nothing different or better becoming of me …"

"Or you can decide to become a different person—" my grandmother completed her thought process for her, "better or worse—by, for example, educating yourself or deciding to take on a new role."

"But people do this all the time, don't they?" my father asked.

"Yes, they do and each time they change, they create a new role, which can then continue along newly established patterns or it can be added to again and again. But mostly people become comfortable with their identity and don't know how to or don't want to change. So an abused woman will continue to enter abusive relationships and an unreliable person will continue to be unreliable until they make a conscious decision to break the pattern. Rare is the person who really takes themselves on as a project and sets their feet upon the path of a development journey. That's why it is usually not so difficult to predict the behavior of other people—just extend their current situation and ways into the future and the future will be revealed."

At the time I did not understand what they were saying, but I remembered their words, which puzzled me for years. It was many years later that I managed to ask my grandmother about it and she explained that some people do possess the gift of seeing into the present, past and future and that this is a gift that I must use only to help people and never for self-gain. By helping others we accumulate a very special energy substance that we will need when we come to the end of our days, for it will help determine what will become of us after we die.

I then heard Grandmother explain about the gift of clairvoyance. She told my parents that it often jumps a generation and she was not surprised that it had turned up in me.

"Barbara will need to understand how to use her unique gift," Grandmother said. "I will help her through her growing up years by offering guidance and by making sure that she does not feel isolated or at less, just because she can connect to subtle energies from the past or from the future." And so my grandmother kept her promise and from time to time she would explain what I was feeling and give me ways and means to gradually understand and harness my abilities so that I no longer would become scared or worried that I was some kind of freak.

So, having built up a connection and endearment with my grandmother over the years, when she was taken ill, I said to my parents that I would look after her because I knew she was going to die and I wanted her not to die alone or neglected, but for her to be able to stay in her own home where everything was familiar and as she liked it. So rather than placing her in a home, they employed me, on her behalf and with her willing consent, to look after her, prepare her meals and do whatever needed to be done to make sure she was comfortable. At first I don't think they believed me that her illness was terminal, but as time progressed and she was not getting any better, my family realized that yet again I was right and that this wise patriarch was indeed preparing to move to another world.

So there I was, in my grandmother's bedroom, with my mother sitting on the other side of the bed. In the last two weeks before her departure we had employed a nurse to help with the daily tasks of looking after her, because she had not left her bed and needed constant care. The nurse came in and out of the room, professionally and discreetly, so as to give us the privacy and space for these final moments.

"She's gone," my mother said and she leaned over to close her mother's eyes. We had both seen this done in the movies and knew that this was the thing to do.

"I'll call the doctor," she said. He had been to see her the previous day and had confirmed that she was nearing the end. He had also told us what to expect and that we should call him as soon as the end came.

I was still holding her hand when he arrived. I could not believe she was actually gone. She had accompanied me all my life; she was always there for me, even more so than my own parents who were always busy and working all hours of the day. And more recently, within the last months and during the weeks of her struggle with her illness, I had grown closer to her, as she had guided me in my search for meaning and illumination, and taught me how to better understand and use my gift.

Chapter Two

What Do You Want?

My grandmother was a strange woman. She knew things, and nobody understood how or where she had learned them. She had a knowledge of herbs and astrology and she could tell a lot about a person just by looking at them. She was definitely a healer, because I remember the day she healed me back to health in one session. It was just a couple of months after I had left home and was renting a room from my girlfriend Alice. I was at a crossroads and had no idea what I was supposed to be doing or where I was going. I was picking up odd jobs here and there, house-sitting for friends, cleaning houses of my parents' acquaintances, standing in for secretaries on maternity leave, even teaching in an emergency situation when my friend John who was a teacher became ill. It was at this time that I discovered a small lump in my breast and hastily booked in to see my doctor. He took one look and made an appointment for me to see a specialist.

"They'll probably want to do a biopsy," he said, "to find out what it is."

"Does it look like cancer to you?" I asked.

He would not commit himself. "It is impossible to tell," he said. He booked me in to see the specialist, but she was not available for a whole fortnight; 14 days of waiting with this anxiety and fear gnawing at me incessantly! I didn't want to wait, so I decided to go and see my grandmother instead.

That night I went to see Grandmother and she could immediately tell that something was the matter.

"What is it?" she asked as soon as I had walked through the door. "It's no use trying to hide from me. Tell me what's up."

And so I did, and in no time she had me lying on the couch and was running her hands above my body, making strange sounds while she did so. My grandmother had always claimed that her grandmother was Cherokee and that she had learned all she knew from this wise old clan mother. No one in the family had ever seen any documentation or photographs to prove that this was so and quite frankly, I did not believe her for one moment either, but the fact was that as I was lying there she was making incantations in some strange language which I had never heard before. She also burned incense and candles and continued to wave her hands over my body and in particular above my breasts. It lasted for about an hour and afterwards I felt totally exhausted, but as I lay there resting before going home, I could not find the little lump, which had been the size of a pea.

When I went to see the specialist in two weeks' time, she could not understand why my own doctor had sent me to see her. She could find nothing and ordered a CT scan, just to make absolutely sure, but I never went because I knew that the lump had gone.

This whole episode made me consider my own mortality and my feelings about being alive on planet Earth. I wondered about my purpose in life and whether I would be able to find that special something that I was meant to do and be. I started reading and researching and visiting various groups that claimed to have access to special knowledge, ancient ceremonies and healing rituals. This journey took several months and I met many interesting people, as I practiced yoga or dowsing or a number of healing techniques. But in the end I felt that none of these were right for me, and I ended up approaching my grandmother and asking her if she would take me on as a student and teach me everything she knew. I now know how assumptive and inconsiderate I had been, making such a huge demand, but it was done from authentic admiration, ignorance and appreciation for her skill. At first she was reluctant because I don't think she thought I was serious enough and she presumed that my intention and interest would soon wear off. But she was wrong and when I approached her with my request for the third time, she agreed to meet me and talk it over.

"When you come, make sure that you know exactly what you are asking for. You must decide what it is you want; otherwise I will not be able to teach you."

We agreed to meet on a bright April Sunday morning and as I walked through her front door, it was a very different woman from my usual friendly grandmother that I encountered. She looked serious and her severe attitude made me hold back; rather than giving her the usual embrace and kiss, I bowed my head and awaited further instructions from her. She led me into her living room where she had set up two chairs opposite each other in the middle of the carpet. The sweet scent of sweet grass and sage lingered in the air and the room felt different than I had remembered it—somehow larger, emptier and full of an atmosphere that made me feel more as if I were in a church than an old woman's living room.

She indicated one of the chairs and I sat down, awaiting further instructions.

"If I am to teach you," she began, "there need to be some rules and disciplines that you must agree to before we begin. Is that clear?"

"Yes, it is. I'll do whatever you want." I was a little bit intimidated by this new aspect of my grandmother, but there was also an excitement in the air, because I felt that whatever she had to offer would be challenging, but real and most probably life changing.

"First of all I need to tell you that there is no way I can teach you everything I know, because that would take me seventy-five years, which is as long as I have been alive, and neither you nor I have that much time at our disposal. So that's the first thing I wanted to say to you.

"Next, so that we do not become dispersed over a hundred subjects, it is for you to decide what you want to know and what you want to become. Have you thought about it, as I asked you to? Do you know what you want? Do you now know what you want to be when you grow up?" She half smiled at the joke, because she knew that I was already over twenty years old, having graduated from secretarial college and having been through a couple of more or less serious relationships. Also, we had already discussed this very question when I was twelve years old, but clearly I no longer aspired to be a film star or a famous prima ballerina.

I had my answer ready for her. "Yes, I have thought about it a lot," I said, pleased that I was prepared for her question. "I want to understand human behavior. I want to know why people do what they do and how I can help them understand their own psychology and the behavior patterns of those they deal with."

My grandmother smiled. She had combed her hair up in a bun on top of her head, which gave her an unusually severe look.

"That is a very big question and one that I will not be able to fully answer, because even after all these years and after studying hundreds if not thousands of people and their behavior, I am still continuously learning about behavior and psychology. A lifetime is not enough because every human on planet Earth is unique and different with their own idiosyncrasies and individual approaches to life."

She fell silent for a moment and I waited for her to continue. She thought for a while and then spoke again. "I'll tell you what I'll do. I'll meet you for a series of lessons, far deeper than the exchanges we have shared before, which will give you a good grounding in the subject and then you can choose to either continue with another teacher, take a university course or simply carry on with your life. It can't hurt for you to know a few deeper things about life and how to have a successful interaction with people you meet. So you will be in tuition not to me but to the energies and gifts that I have connected to during my 75 years on Earth."

Another moment of silence and she continued to lay down some rules, which she expected me to obey and adhere to. "I might give you some homework to do when we meet and I will be asking you to make a payment for my time and effort. Not necessarily in monetary terms; it will vary from week to week, but you must be prepared to give of your time during the week so that you can be better prepared to receive the lessons when you come here. People don't value what they receive for free and I want you to appreciate and work with the information I will be giving you, so that it comes alive as you apply it and helps you on your way. This way you will pay for your tuition time. My time is limited and therefore it is precious. You might think you have a lot of time because you consider yourself to be young, but I tell you, your clock is ticking too and already the physical aspect of you is declining, though you might not feel it quite yet. And even if you do have another fifty or sixty years, they will be gone before you even realize it. Remember to respect time and do not waste it, because you can never recapture it. I know you know this, but you will really know it when you are older. Now it can only be an interesting concept for you, but one day it will become real."

She then proceeded to give me my homework. "Next time we meet, I want you to bring a list of all the things you want in life. Don't limit yourself; give yourself free range. We all want so many things, at so many different levels. Write down everything you can think of that you want, from the most obvious to the most obscure; from the small things to the big dreams and even to your fantasy wishes. You will need to know this if you wish to embark on this journey with me, because only then will you have a clearer view of where you are going. It all starts with what you want."

The task proved to be much more difficult than I initially thought, because it made me realize that I was not at all sure what I really wanted in life. I made many attempts to write down my desires, but I always felt that there could be more, though I wasn't sure where to find it or how to define it. I tried to let my imagination roam free and started with the physical aspects of my life, then moving to all other surrounding circumstances. So, first, did I want to live where I was? Or did I want to move? I felt that I was at the right place at the right time, because being in tuition to life and life skills with my grandmother was exactly what I wanted to be doing, above all else. But then I tried to look beyond the present into the future and all I could see was myself teaching someone the way my grandmother was teaching me. Perhaps I should open a school? This was odd because I had never thought of this possibility before, but now it seemed like the right thing to do. Anyway, I wasn't going to make any decisions in a hurry, but just wondered about this new image and view of the future that was appearing before me. Of course I also wanted to earn enough money to be able to afford a place of my own. That went without saying and it did not take too much of an imagination to picture a house in the country, but not too far away from the city; a car, and, yes, a partner who would share the same interests and ideals. I could see myself being very busy and popular, teaching, writing, traveling around the world, signing books, saving lives and …

At this point I had to stop because I felt I was running away with myself. There was so much more that I needed to know and do before I could even begin to embark upon this path, or any other path for that matter. I had to smile to myself. At least I felt I had something to go back to my grandmother with.

I was nervous and excited before visiting my grandmother for the next "lesson," which I realized was such a funny word because it implied an offering of less, not more. I tried to make up a word from the combination of the words more and on, but it sounded too much like moron, so I just chuckled to myself and gave up.

As soon as I arrived, my grandmother invited me in and offered me a seat. Without any preamble, she started to speak in a tone of voice which was new to me but I began to recognize as her teaching tone.

"All right, young lady," she said. She tended to call me a young lady when she was serious and somehow wanted to accentuate her seniority. "Before we continue, there is something we need to look at."

"What is that, Grandma?" I tried to look surprised and innocent.

"Well, you should know the answer to that question, because I gave it to you as your homework last time we met. The question is, what do you want?"

"I do remember, Grandma, and I have a whole list of things I want," I said proudly as I produced my notebook out of my bag.

"Well, let's start from the top," she said.

"I want to be happy," I read out, and I was getting ready to continue to the next item, but she interrupted, "What does that mean?" she asked.

"I don't know," I shrugged. "Everyone wants to be happy. I guess it means content, satisfied, fulfilled …"

"Hang on a minute. Satisfied comes from the Greek word satis, which means full, satiated. Fulfilled is full-filled or filled to the brim and content means filled with content. Do you think happy means full, not needing more? And if so, how long can such a feeling last?" she asked.

"It never lasts," I confessed with a sigh. I thought of a few rare occasions when I had felt happy. After a date or when I had bought some new clothes that made me look pretty. How long did that ever last? These were fleeting moments and the happiness associated with them was short-lived, too.

"We are always changing," my grandmother said, "and human nature is to change. Therefore if happiness is a state that depends on external circumstances, then it will never last."

"Are you saying that there can be different kinds of happiness, and that there is a happiness that is triggered by one's internal state?" I asked.

"Yes, it is possible, but very few attain it."

"Tell me more about it." I wanted to know.

"People these days seem to be always in pursuit of something and usually this something is outside of themselves—a new relationship, a new house, a car, a career, fame, appreciation, money, power. But real happiness comes from an internal serenity, a value for life itself. It radiates with an inner glow and has no demands or expectations attached to it. It is to be content to be who you are and where you are. There is a fullness and a satisfaction, but not the kind that follows a good meal or good sex, for it is a constant companion and stems from the very fact of being alive."

"That sounds great, but clearly I have a long way to go. How can I achieve that kind of happiness?"

"The secret is not to want anything for yourself and never to think something is missing from your life."

I looked at her and suddenly I understood, as I could feel a certain equanimity radiating from her and enveloping me in its warmth and feeling of protection.

"Grandma, are you happy?" I asked, although I already knew the answer, because I felt she had been speaking about herself.

"Yes, child, I am," she replied softly and for a moment there was silence between us, but that silence spoke to me louder than many words ever could.

"All right, let's continue," she broke the silence first.

"Well, as I look at my list, it all seems irrelevant now," I said, looking at my piece of paper and thinking that my wants seemed to be quite trivial and predictable now.

"Being happy or unhappy does not mean that you can't want things, too." Then Grandmother added, "There is a difference between wanting something for yourself and wanting things for a reason. The reason why you want it makes all the difference."

"So do you want things?" I asked, not knowing how to reconcile her description of happiness with her admission that it does not necessarily exclude wanting something.

"Yes, I want many things," she replied with a smile. "I want you to be happy, for example," she said, "which in my world means you finding and being close to your life's purpose. But that doesn't mean that I will be unhappy if you decide to screw-up your life. After all, you are a free and independent individual. But if I can help you, I will. You see, like you, I have been given many talents and skills, some of which I have had the privilege of developing and working with throughout my life. I want to continue to improve and to use these skills to be able to help and heal others. So, while I am still alive I do want to be useful. When I want something, I make sure I want it for a reason that is greater than myself and includes other people, the ecology, the family, the Earth. For example, I want there to be peace and I want your future children to have a future." Another moment of silence passed between us before she asked me again to carry on with my list.

"I think I need to think this over again," I replied. "But all right, here it is. I want to have a meaningful relationship that will last. I want to be able to understand why I can sometimes read the future. I want to have a place to live so that I am not always dependent on others for my livelihood. I want to know better what I want." I fell silent.

"Well, that's a start," my grandmother said. "You have to always know what you want, or you will never get it," she said. "And be sure to want enough to fill a lifetime. Otherwise you might end up with nothing more to want, and a human that does not want is a dead human."

"What do you mean, Grandma?" I asked.

"Well, imagine that you find a man and you are in a good relationship. Imagine that you have a place to live and that you do understand why you can sometimes predict the future. Then what? All this could happen to you by next year, or even by next month. If you fulfill all your wants and there is nothing left for you to want, you will feel empty and purposeless; you will be used up. Trust me, I know. You need to learn to think big so that you will never catch yourself up. All right, so what else do you want?" she asked. She saw that I was looking through my list and was ready to read from it.

"There is a lot I desire," I said, wondering if I wasn't being greedy. "I want a boyfriend, a job and a place of my own."

My grandmother smiled. "Yes, we already know that. What else?" she asked.

"I want security; I want to know that I can pay my way and not have to worry each month whether I can pay the rent and the bills."

"Well, that's a practical start," she said. "You first need to take care of the basics before you can start helping other people. So I suggest you get a regular job first. And the way to do it is to write down everything you want from a job and then go out and find it." She made it sound so simple and I had no doubt it wasn't going to be that easy. But I decided to agree with her and do as she had suggested.

Grandmother than added a further recommendation: "I suggest you re-look at your list and make sure you have some big wants in there. For example, what's wrong with wanting there to be no war in the world? Perhaps, if enough people seriously wanted peace, then it could happen. Who knows? We need to consciously want if we are going to make a difference in this world. What is wrong with wanting all children to never be hungry or lonely or sick? I know there is not much you personally can do about the state of the world, but you do have the freedom to want and that is a good beginning."

I walked out of my grandmother's house with my head spinning. There were so many new thoughts coming and going through my brain, I felt someone had given me permission to think in a new way and I was not sure whether I was capable of maintaining this bigger view. I realized I had been quite selfish and parochial in my thinking and I was glad to know that not everyone in the world was as limited as I had been. I was grateful to my grandmother for sharing her thoughts with me, but I was also worried that I would never be the same as before, satisfied with my small victories and simple pleasures.

So next morning, in keeping with my grandmother's advice, I wrote down all the things I wanted from a job—good pay, an interesting and challenging activity requiring at least some concentration, a short commute and easy access, as well as a locality that would be near to shops, restaurants and a gym. I also wanted to meet some interesting people and make friends to boot. I looked at my list and smiled at the improbability of what I was asking for. I then made it even more improbable by heeding Grandmother's advice and adding my desire for world peace to the original list of wants.

I then went out, bought the local paper and phoned the numbers of businesses that were advertising jobs that seemed appropriate for my level of skill, education and experience. Unfortunately, all positions had been filled before I even dialed the numbers. The same routine was repeated the next day and the day after that. Every evening Alice would return home from work, ask me about my progress and restate the fact that she could not let me stay on indefinitely if I found that I could not meet my obligations as far as paying my share of the rent and utilities was concerned.

Chapter Three

Energy Givers and Takers

On the Friday I phoned a company that produced and sold kitchen gadgets and utensils. They were looking for a receptionist and when I phoned up, the woman at the other end of the phone asked if I could come over straight away. Full of hope and intention, I quickly changed into a suit, put some make-up on and was out the door in less than twenty minutes. As I approached the building where the business was housed, I realized I was entering a warehouse in a rough part of town, but I decided not to be deterred and to think positive, so as to portray a competent and cheerful persona.

As I entered up a small flight of stairs, I saw there was an older woman behind a desk in the cramped lobby. She was talking on the phone and as soon as she saw me, she gestured for me to wait. It took a while, so I had time to look at the posters on the brick walls advertising various kitchen utensils, pots and pans. Finally, she put the phone down and asked, "Are you here about the job?"

"Yes," I replied. "I think I spoke to you on the phone."

"That's right," she replied. She had a really deep voice. "I am leaving and we need a new receptionist. Can you type?"

"I finished secretarial college with honors," I replied, ready to produce my diploma. She waved her hand, indicating that she didn't need to see it. "That doesn't mean a thing," she said and repeated, "Can you type?"

"I can type 75 words a minute. Is that sufficient?"

"That will be fine," she said. "You'll be typing addresses and press releases," she gestured at a stack of paper on her desk. "Nothing complicated," she added. A man in a brown UPS uniform walked up the stairs with a large package on his shoulder.

"Where does this go?" he asked.

"Just turn right and go straight through to the warehouse," she replied. They're waiting for it in there." The man turned right and walked through the door.

"Can you start Monday?" the woman asked.

"Sure, that would be fine," I replied, but something in me was trying to tell me that would not be fine. I decided to ignore the little nagging voice.

"Then go in and see the boss," the woman pointed to a glass door on the left. "First door on the left. I'll tell him you're here." She picked up the phone and I could hear her saying, "A young lady is here for the receptionist job," as I walked through the glass doors and found myself in a dark corridor with a couple of light bulbs dimly illuminating the grey walls and the four doors on either side. I knocked on the first door on the left.

"Come in," I could hear a man's raspy voice from within. I opened the door and peered inside. A middle-aged man with a large pot belly and a tie that didn't reach his waist was sitting behind a desk covered with files, papers, newspapers, magazines, photographs, envelopes and other assorted items.

"So you are here for the receptionist's job?" he asked as he leaned back in his chair and started looking me over. "Can you type?" he asked.

"Yes, I can," I replied.

"We need someone to direct the traffic that comes into this building all day long. We need someone to type a lot of envelopes, ad campaigns and press releases and to take messages and keep track of the salesmen and other employees. You would also be opening and redirecting the mail as well as any phone calls that might come in. Can you do all that?"

"Yes, I think I can," I replied.

"Well, how about starting Monday and we can check you

out," the man smiled. "We can discuss the salary and benefits on Monday."

"What time should I be here?" I asked.

"Come in at eight thirty," he replied and just at that moment the phone started to ring. He picked up the receiver and as he started talking, he waved for me to leave the room. I turned around and walked out. As I passed the receptionist, who was now typing at her desk, I said, "He told me to be here at eight thirty on Monday."

"I'll see you then," she said and she didn't even look up from her typing. After that brief encounter I felt drained and tired. I couldn't understand it—I had done nothing that day and yet all afternoon I was dragging myself around, as if I had been ill for a week.

On the Monday I was standing at the bus stop, waiting for the bus to take me to my new job. I was somewhat worried that I had neither a contract nor any information about remuneration or holidays, but I was going to give it a try. It was drizzling slightly and the sky was overcast, and the bus was late with more and more people gathering at the bus stop. Next to the bus stop there was a kiosk selling newspapers, cigarettes and candy, and for some reason I decided to buy the local newspaper. I scanned the front page, and the moment I opened the paper to look inside, there on page two I saw a picture of my future boss. It appeared that he had been arrested that Saturday for embezzlement and obstruction of justice. On the photograph he was being led from his home to a police car, and he was in handcuffs. I immediately understood why I had felt so drained and unwell after my interview on Friday and I decided on the spot that I was not going to go into work that day.

The next day the agency I had been temping for phoned me up and said they had a temporary job for that week, so I was working for the next four days and managed to earn my rent money for the month. I phoned my grandmother and told her what had happened, and she agreed to see me again that Sunday.

On Sunday, as soon as I arrived at my grandmother's house for our next session, she sat me down and started explaining, "If you want to understand human behavior, there are several things you will need to know. First of all, you will need to look at human interactions as an exchange of energy. When you speak to another person, and they speak to you, every word is a wrapping, just like a candy paper, inside of which is a package of energy. And there are many, many kinds of energies: some are invigorating, some healing, some are harmful, some debilitating. When you speak with someone, ask yourself the question, 'How do I feel, having spoken to them? Do I feel better or worse? Am I in a different place in myself now? What am I prone to think about? And what was I thinking about before we spoke? Has it shifted? If so, how? And how do I feel about myself, having had this conversation?'

"Did you catch those questions? Did you write them down? I want you to remember them and to practice asking yourself these questions after every encounter and exchange. Start today and when you come back in a week's time, be sure to have some answers for me. I want you to begin to feel and understand the many forms that human manufactured energy can take. We exude energy all the time, not only in our language, but in our postures, movements, gestures and intonation. I can say 'I love you' and make it sound sentimental, sincere, ironic, jesting, mocking, habitual, matter-of-fact, imploring, begging, even threatening." She demonstrated what she meant and it made me think that she would have made a great actress.

"How did you do that?" I asked.

"You can do it, too," she replied. "I was not acting," she added, as if to contradict my thought process. "I simply reached for the feeling which accompanied each statement inside myself, pulling it out of the memory banks and displaying it for you to hear. We are all custodians of many forms of expression that we have learned and stored during the years of our life. Whether we can access them or not is another matter; it is a question of practice and belief and, of course, purpose."

We sat for a minute in silence, and I then replied, "I can see that if one had a powerful reason to convey one's feelings to another person, then one would be more inclined to practice speaking with such sincerity."

"I am not sure what you mean. Can you give me an example?" she asked.

"I think so," I replied. "For example, if you need to plead with someone for their life, because they are about to commit suicide, then you will reach for any argument that might work and you will find in yourself the sincerity with which to present it."

"Yes, as long as it is genuine and based in real compassion," my grandmother acknowledged. "Sometimes it is too late to attempt to be compassionate when such a situation presents itself to you, if compassion is not part of your make-up. Some feelings are impossible to fake and will always sound false if they are simply acted out and not real."

There was another moment of pause and I looked at my notes. "I want to ask you about one of these questions," I ventured.

"All right. Which one?" she asked.

"The one about how a conversation makes you feel about yourself. I would have thought that how you feel about yourself is an internal process and not something that is influenced from outside."

"Oh no, on the contrary, though it does depend on who you are and how firm are your convictions and beliefs. For example, if someone criticizes you for something, then even if you don't believe what they say is true, you might feel demolished by their remarks. Or it could be even more subtle than that. Simply by how a person treats you, you might feel large or small as a person. So if someone is respectful and mindful of your needs, asking whether you need help or assistance, offering to support your efforts in any way, you will feel enhanced and uplifted, even if the person offering is not a friend or an acquaintance. Think of two salesgirls or two waiters: one is courteous and remembers your order accurately, and the other is slow, forgetful and obviously doesn't care. In fact, he makes you feel as if you have interrupted his valuable rest time and that he is doing you a favor by serving you. Which restaurant would you rather go to?"

"The one where I am served promptly and courteously, of course" I replied.

"Exactly. Every one and everything we encounter in life either adds to our wellbeing or takes away from it. You can come out of a restaurant tired, angry and annoyed, simply because you happened to sit at a table that was served by a rude waiter. Is that not so?"

"Yes, it is."

Another moment passed before she started speaking again. "Each person has within them an entire storehouse of experiences, feelings and qualities that they have either inherited from their family or acquired throughout the course of their lives. Most of these lay dormant until we need to call upon them. They can be activated when a situation arises that calls for their assistance. Just as the memory of how to ride a bike becomes reactivated as soon as your feet reach for the pedals, so do feelings, skills and emotions become powered with repetition and usage.

"The secret of success lies in the ability to remember them and to practice that which you wish to retain," she added, as I sat in silence, still marveling at her skill. "It also depends upon how well you know yourself."

"So are you saying that a person who becomes angry is more likely to get angry again?" I asked.

"Precisely. This can escalate until it can become difficult to break the trend and the anger controls the person, rather than the person controling their anger. It is true that we are creatures of habit and once we find a routine that works for us, for whatever reason— whether promoted by comfortability, ease of process or because it enables us to do what we enjoy, or what we perceive our duty to be— the more we do it, the more difficult it is to break the habit. Thus the person who stops working will still wake up at the habitual time and someone who is used to picking a fight with their partner at the slightest disagreement, will find it very difficult to start acquiescing without so much as a word of protest."

"Yes, I can see that. There comes a point where you can expect certain behavior patterns from people as you get to know them. You can anticipate how they will respond to, say, a present or a proposition or a request for assistance. This in turn will promote you to turn for help to those that you expect to be by nature helpful."

"That's true. So if we want to appear helpful to others and build that image about ourselves, we should start behaving in a helpful way, offering our assistance wherever we see it is needed. That way you can paint your own portrait, deliberately and thoughtfully, rather than waiting to see what your reaction will be when someone happens to ask you for help. Build the character you desire that you want to have and to be."

"So although we are creatures of habit, does that mean that we don't necessarily need to be subject to our habits?" I asked, trying to think of an example.

"No, of course not. That's what free will is for. But remember that some habits are more difficult to break than others. For example, someone on drugs might find it very difficult to simply stop taking them without professional help. Some people have a strong will and some people are weak. But will can be built and developed over time. It all depends on what you want. And how much you really want it."

"So I guess it is important to know what you want first."

"Exactly. That is why I first asked you to write down a list of what you want in life. It was important to start understanding the power behind everything you do. What you want is your spur, your urge and your potential power. It all depends on how much you really want it. As mentioned last week, your reasons for wanting what you want can be the deciding factor in whether you achieve what you want or not. The more deliberate and thought through the reasons, the more chance of success."

So I had another task to fulfill during the week—to observe my interactions with other people and then ask myself the questions my grandmother had given me, following each encounter. That proved to be simple enough and I soon developed a catalogue of phrases and adjectives describing my feelings subsequent to the many dialogues that ensued during the week. Filled with new ideas and concepts, I was eager to share them with my friends, but soon found out that few people were interested. Mostly I was treated with polite tolerance, as if my friends were humoring me and politely listening to my theories without becoming involved themselves.

I bought myself a small notebook and started jotting down my impressions. This proved to be a very revealing exercise and I even developed a scoring system from one to ten defining each encounter that I considered, later adding up the total results scored by each person I had spoken with.

When the day of my visit arrived—Sunday—I knocked upon Grandmother's door, notebook in hand and once inside her living room, I proceeded to explain to her about my list of people and my marking system, categorizing the perceived flow of energy from others to me and from myself to others, which I had registered and felt as I encountered friends and acquaintances.

She listened attentively, obviously pleased that I had come back with some concrete examples and then, after I had finished speaking, she replied, "Very well, but that is just the beginning. You must continue with your list. As the days pass, extract from your notes the names of the people that you meet and talk to on a repetitive basis and begin to check out trends. So, if you notice that you feel drained after dealing with certain people again and again and again, then you must start to find ways to avoid them or find ways to make the relationship more constructive. The only exception will be if you deliberately decide to help them by giving them your energy and taking theirs in return. If you do this philanthropic act, then you will have to find ways to replenish your own energy once you have finished dealing with them. This is something that I will teach you how to do.

"You will find that some people take away your energy and they may feel enhanced from doing so, but unless you specifically intend to help that person who might be going through a crisis or a difficult time, then you must begin to protect yourself and deny them their customary fix. On the other hand, if you note that there are others who make you feel well and invigorated and inspired, then these are people who you should seek out and cultivate. But beware, and begin to take note if you can, whether in fact you are feeding from them and thus causing a weakening and energy debilitation in them. Because if you do, then sooner or later they will want to avoid you, whether they decide so consciously or simply instinctively realize that they need to do so for self-preservation and defense. The best relationships are those where both parties inspire and enhance each other, thereby drawing in extra energy into the relationship and not costing each other at all. It is like having an investment that grows. Energy is very much like having savings. There is definitely a limited amount of it to go around and we must protect our investments and try to make them grow. That is why, as a person grows older, they are more protective of their energy and time and are less willing to spend these two treasures foolishly. When you are young there is time and energy to spare and waste, or so you think, and it takes time to realize what takes away and what adds to our wellbeing. That is why this exercise is so valuable; it will show you where you are expending your energies unnecessarily. It will save you time and help preserve your health for when you will need to rely on it in the future as you grow older. I wish I was given this advice when I was younger. My health would have been so much better—old does not need to mean ill or weak. It all depends how you look after yourself throughout your life." She stopped for a moment, clearly reflecting upon her past.

She then added, "You can also take this exercise and apply it to the various activities and tasks you perform during the day, as well as to the people you meet and encounters you have. Each tasking will inspire you or take you away from inspiration, thus giving you food for thought or causing a dulling of the senses."

Chapter Four

Blame

Since I left home my mother would call me every week and ask about my personal life. She tended to get emotional when she felt that I was not doing something she would approve of. She sometimes would urge me to come back home or tell me I should get a job. She didn't understand that one of the reasons I left home was to get away from her incessant nagging and attempts at managing my life.

That Sunday morning was no different. When she heard I had not taken up the job which I had told her about two weeks earlier, she really got upset and proceeded to tell me how important it is to earn a living and fulfill my obligations and save for the future. She told me I was irresponsible and would probably never amount to much. I replied that I was twenty-four years old and could look after myself; I ended up putting the phone down.

When I went to see my grandmother that afternoon, she immediately detected that something was wrong. I could never hide my moods from her and I always ended up telling her all about my latest problems.

"She is so difficult," I said. "She expects me to be responsible, wise and self-sufficient within a couple of weeks. Doesn't she know that it takes time to find a job? I can't imagine she was independent and earning a living at my age. She ..."

My grandmother soon interrupted my barrage of words and accusations. I thought she was just chatting to me, but I soon realized that she had taken what I had said and was turning it into a lesson. I made a mental note that I should be more conscious about what I say during future encounters.

"Let's move on to the lesson for today," she said and I pulled out my notebook, which I had prepared, ready to take notes.

"Today we are going to look at blame," she began, "and how it affects relationships. I see that this is the current need in you. Have you noticed how, when someone gives you reflections concerning a project you had done and you are faced with criticism, you might find yourself desperately trying to escape from this uncomfortable situation by thinking—who else was involved in the project? Who can I blame? It is then that you might realize that blame is like an entity that is very insidious and perfidious. Blame is the averting of responsibility for one's actions and it is an escape, running away from a lesson or a challenge. It temporarily relieves pressure but as a result it distorts reality and bends the facts to support its claim. With blame at the helm of our consciousness, what lives in the unconscious will not match the conscious perception of reality. Have you noticed how two sides of a story are never quite the same and how some details are conveniently forgotten, while others are accentuated and acquire added importance and weight? Have you noticed how isolated sentences are remembered out of context, while the mitigating circumstances are forgotten? The whole incident then gets written under the heading of that one sentence which forever more is waved about like a banner and an example of uncaring, selfish or mean behavior.

"No one can remember all of the circumstances surrounding an event—our memories are selective. We remember what we want to remember and we remember what supports our theories concerning other people. To study reality and the truth, one needs to be interested in both sides of the story, in order to rise above both and become an exponent of what we will call the third view. Blame locks one into the two extremes of the law of polarity and keeps one away from what is real. Rather than blaming people, try thinking this—influences do things through people. The third vector view is not personal; it is not targeted against another person and thereby it is not detrimental to one's dealings with others. On the contrary, it has the ability to reveal an unbiased opinion and another way of going on that is objective and unselfish.

"Just look at the word itself. Blame says that there is an inherent weakness in the person's constitution, or their will is lame, and cannot handle the truth. It is as if the two words—*be* and *lame*—have been shortened down to one word—*blame*. The cure is to strengthen the character by knowing who you are, knowing what you are like and knowing what you want.

"Another situation in which blame occurs is in the way of an ongoing complaint where one sees another person (or people) to be responsible for the predicament one is in. This often appears under the guise of a statement or sentence beginning with 'they,' whereby these elusive 'theys' are always guilty, irresponsible and downright stupid. Somehow 'they' never seem to get it right.

"Finally, to conclude this excursion into the realms of blame, we will briefly take a look at the blame that goes to all those who have messed up our lives at various times, whether in the area of upbringing, education, relationships, finances, work or family. How many are there? In looking back, doesn't it seem as though these mysterious people deliberately had set out to harm and hurt us? And yet that is not so; it is only how we have written the past to ourselves so as not to have to draw the painful lessons from those experiences. In other words, our misfortunes were not everyone else's fault, because those people who we consider to be the culprits were doing what they thought was right for them at the time, even though it did not meet with our approval, did not match our expectations or was not up to our standard. And what about all those things that we have done to hurt other people—those things we would rather forget but others perhaps blame us for till this very day? As the therapist says to the person who is blaming others for his misfortunes, 'Somewhere in the world sits someone in a therapist's office blaming you!'

"When you find a flaw in the behavior of another or spot a mistake or see clearly how they could have done something better or more effectively, do you make fun, criticize and judge or do you pass on your suggestions without a feeling of superiority and satisfaction attached? If blame is going to retreat from your aura, you need to face your own mistakes, which probably aren't so bad, after all, on the one hand, and accept that others will have different ways of doing things than you on the other.

"Love the truth as a first principle because the truth is what is and it is not tainted by personal bias. Thus the saying 'God is with us' used throughout history by various fighting factions is proof in itself that that side had departed from the path of truth. For if you live, God is with you. The question is, are you with God?"

My grandmother paused and I put my notebook down.

"That was quite a delivery," I said, admiring her eloquence. "I have never heard you speak like that before."

She smiled wistfully and replied, "There are many things about me that you do not know."

"Like what? Give me an example."

"No, not today. I am tired. Another time. All in good time."

She got up and I saw that as a signal to leave. I gathered my belongings and followed her to the door.

"See you next week," she said as she closed the door behind me.

The next morning my roommate Alice and I were having breakfast together when she casually announced that there was a job opening at her place of work—Versatile Furniture—and that perhaps I would like to apply for the position of dispatcher. She worked for an office furniture factory and showroom as receptionist and I knew from her stories that she enjoyed the environment and the people she worked with and that it sounded like a fun place to be.

I had already decided that I needed a stable job as my finances were becoming more and more limited every day, so I felt that I needed to do something with my life to put it in order and give it more of a direction. The lessons with my grandmother had confirmed the conviction that somehow my destiny was wrapped up in this affair of exploring human behavior and finding ways of mastering my own energies, their causes and manifestations. I expressed my interest, as I poured myself another cup of coffee.

"Yes, that would be interesting. How do I apply?"

She smiled and I could tell that she had planned the whole thing.

I wouldn't put it past her that she had already spoken to her boss about me.

"Funny enough, I have an application form right here." She reached for her briefcase, which was sitting on the kitchen counter, packed and ready to accompany her into work. She pulled out a form and handed it to me across the kitchen table.

"If you get a picture taken today and fill it out, I can take it in tomorrow," she said.

"No need to wait. I'll fill it in now," I said, thinking that haste would convey eagerness to my prospective employer and give me an edge above the competition. "I already have a spare photograph. I had several taken when I renewed my passport last month," I added.

I got up and fetched a pen from one of the drawers. I started to fill in the form.

Alice stood up. "This is going to take longer than you think," she said. "You're going to have to describe your entire work history. It's OK, I'll take it in tomorrow. I have to go now."

She got hold of her briefcase and walked out the door. "See you later," she added as she closed the door behind her.

She was right. It took me most of the morning to fill in the questionnaire and to present myself in a favorable light, so that I would appear fit for the job. This was not easy to do, as I really did not have any dispatching experience, but I felt I could do it, because I was a good organizer, having at times helped my father organize his time schedule by arranging appointments, demonstrations and conferences. By early afternoon the form was complete and I was quite proud of myself. I tried to look at it with the eyes of a potential boss and interviewer and felt that they definitely should at least want to see me and talk to me. The picture was a strong asset—I looked warm, efficient and mature, with a hint of playfulness in my smile. I felt no one could resist that image, added to which was the consideration that they would not have to pay an agency's fee for hiring me.

I was right. The very next day Alice called me from the office. She was excited and pleased. "They want to see you," she said. "I took the form in this morning and they told me to arrange an appointment."

"Great. When can I come in? Tomorrow?"

"Sure. How about tomorrow at two?"

"That will work well." I felt things were going my way for a change and I found myself wondering whether my lessons with Grandmother had anything to do with it.

Chapter Five

Confidence

I walked in the next day, having coached myself to be confident and to exude reliability, punctuality and efficiency. In fact, I had written these four words—confidence, reliability, punctuality and efficiency—on the mirror in the bathroom with my lipstick and gazed at them last thing the previous night and first thing in the morning, attempting to bring them into myself, so that they could become part of me. I realized it was not that simple, because it took time and effort to build these qualities within oneself, but if I could only act the part, perhaps I could convince them that I was indeed the very person they were looking for. I had also taken out the list I had written after my lesson with Grandmother, during which she had grilled me about what I wanted. The items on the list—higher pay, proximity to home, shops, restaurants and a gym, a challenging position and working with interesting people could all be fulfilled by this next job, especially as I wasn't being paid anything at the moment! The list was now in my wallet and I had been looking at it every day for the past week or so.

As I walked into the office, the first person I saw was Alice sitting at the reception desk. It was nice to see a familiar face, but she seemed so different with a phone receiver in one hand and the light from the computer screen illuminating her face which was marked by concentration. She looked up as I walked up to her desk.

I thought I would try to match her role and proceeded to ask in a formal tone, as if I had never met her before, "I am here to see the Human Resources manager, Mrs. Franks," I said.

She smiled at me, as she put the receiver down. "Yes, she's waiting for you. Go down the corridor and it's the third door on your right. You'll see the sign on the door. And, good luck!" Finally, she smiled as she looked directly at me.

I began to feel nervous, but I was determined not to show it. I turned away from the reception desk and ventured down the corridor that had been pointed out to me. I soon found the designated door and stood in front of it for a moment, wondering whether I should knock or not. How strange, that at a moment of pressure, even the simplest of actions seems complicated and not straightforward any more. I tried to remind myself that whoever was behind that door was human too, with human traits, worries and weaknesses.

I had just lifted my hand up to knock, when the door opened and a young man walked out with a file under his arm, went straight past me and disappeared down the corridor. He didn't even look at me and seemed preoccupied with his mission. I peered into the room through the now open door and saw a middle-aged woman in a grey suit looking straight at me from behind a pair of gold-rimmed spectacles.

"May I come in?" I asked more tentatively than I would have liked.

"Miss Faye, I presume?" She smiled as she stood up and her face lost some of that severity that was initially there.

"Yes, that's me."

"Do come in."

She stretched out her right arm and we shook hands. It fleetingly struck me what a strange custom that was and I even more fleetingly wondered where the custom had originated from. It felt quite ancient and I could distinctly feel the warmth of her flesh and the throbbing of her blood as she squeezed my hand a little too hard, as if she wanted to demonstrate her strength.

"Please sit down," she said as she sat down herself. I lowered myself into the chair that was positioned in front of her desk.

"I see you applied for the position of dispatcher and that you are a friend of Wonderland Alice." She opened the file in front of her. I was surprised she had called Alice by her nickname, which I knew was how she was known at work.

"Yes," I replied. "She told me about it a couple of days ago. She's my roommate."

"Well, I see that you don't have a lot of dispatching experience," she said as she looked up at me. "But that doesn't really matter so much, as long as you are open to learn."

"Oh yes, I certainly am."

"All right. Well, before we go any further, I want you to take this aptitude test. She handed me a sheet of paper with a series of questions. "Take your time and try to answer the questions as accurately as you can." She handed me a pen and swung around on the chair to face a computer which was located on another desk behind her, so that she now had her back facing me.

The questions were not difficult. With a basic knowledge of geography, mathematics and a bit of common sense, I managed to do quite well, or so I thought. I think I dispatched the trucks (on paper) in the right direction, with the right amount of cargo and personnel on board. When I handed the completed sheet back to Mrs. Franks, she applied a grid from her drawer to the answers and seemed quite satisfied with the results. Satisfied enough to continue, anyway.

"Would you be OK with having a boss who is not much older than yourself?' she asked.

"Sure. I don't mind."

"Well, you just saw him. He was leaving as you entered the room," she said. "Brian is the boss of all the dispatchers."

"How many are there?" I asked, somewhat surprised that I would not be the only one.

"At the moment, five. One for each route." She pointed to a map of the area that was hanging behind her desk. Each area was filled in with a different color.

"This one would be yours," she added. "Providing, of course, that you get the job."

She was pointing to the northern sector of the city, which was, in fact, where I was currently staying and where my grandmother's house was."

"Oh, good," I said. "That's where I live."

She then said that she would be in touch, once she had seen the other candidates and if I were successful in the 'preliminaries,' I would be invited to a second interview, during which I would meet my prospective boss. She then sent me on my way.

I thought the interview was short and did not hold much promise. She never asked me any in-depth questions about me, my interests, habits or opinions. Despite the fact that I thought I had done well with the questionnaire, I was quite sure that I wouldn't get the job. On the way out I made a face at Alice who was talking to a delivery boy as I managed to catch her eye. She smiled, shrugged her shoulders and went back to the task of signing for a parcel which was being placed in front of her on the reception desk.

"See you later," I said and went for the door. As I exited into the warm spring air, I felt disappointed with myself. "Well, that was a waste of time," I concluded, as I walked through the car park towards the bus stop.

A week passed and I was back to scanning the papers, making the odd phone call, registering with a couple of agencies and beginning to wonder whether I should move to a different location. It was a Monday morning when Alice called from work.

"Can you come in today?" she asked.

"Yes. Now?"

"Yes. Come now if you can. You will meet your prospective boss."

Forty-five minutes later I was there, knocking on Mrs. Franks' door.

"Come in," she said and when I entered I noticed she was picking up the phone. She gestured for me to sit down as she spoke into the phone. "Brian? Mrs. Franks here. Can you please come to my office to meet Barbara? Thank you." She put down the receiver and looked at me. "We have short-listed the applicants and you are one of the five successful ones. If you are selected, when can you start?"

"It depends on when you make your decision."

"Oh, we need to decide by tomorrow or the next day at the latest. The man who is doing the job now is leaving at the end of May. And we were hoping to have at least two weeks for you to learn from him before you take over."

Now this sounded more promising and I began to feel more confident and optimistic. The door opened and I turned around. In walked the same man I had seen the first time I came in for my initial interview. He was tall and slim, with brown curly hair and glasses, with an intense look on his face. He was probably in his late twenties or early thirties. He seemed serious and preoccupied. He walked up to the desk and held out his hand.

"You must be Barbara Faye."

"That's right," I said and we shook hands. He sat down in the chair next to me. "I am in charge of the five dispatchers, covering the five areas of the city. It is their job to process orders on a daily basis, to make sure the trucks are loaded and the paperwork ready for the day's deliveries. By each Friday morning you will have prepared a delivery schedule for the next week and you will requisition the number of vehicles you need as well as the appropriate number of installation personnel. It is my job to then coordinate the five schedules according to availability of resources. Here is a sample of a schedule prepared by one of our employees. In fact it was done by the guy whose place you would be taking, if you are to be successful."

He handed me a sheet of paper with five boxes on it, marked with the five work days of the week, filled with writing—numbers of trucks, addresses, deliveries, names of accompanying personnel and order numbers. Brian looked at me questioningly, with what appeared to me to be doubt.

"Do you think you can do this job?" he asked.

"Yes, I am sure I can." I replied, putting on a convincing, self-confident voice.

"All right then. What I require is punctuality and reliability above all else," he added. "When there is a deadline and an important delivery to be made, there is no room for error."

I could tell that he was a demanding boss, but he also had the aura of someone who doesn't ask for something he is not prepared to do himself.

"I like working under pressure," I added.

"Well, we'll see." He turned to Mrs. Franks: "If you don't need me, I'll get back to my work."

"Yes, that's fine, Brian. Thank you."

He got up and walked out the door, the look on his face indicating that mentally he was already somewhere else.

"So, do you think you will be able to get on with him?" Mrs. Franks asked.

"Yes, he seems very nice."

"He works very hard. When there is a major delivery, he might ask you to come in on a Saturday as well. Can you manage that? We do not pay overtime; just for the work getting done."

"Yes, I can do that. I'm not married and I don't have children."

"Well, not yet, anyway," Mrs. Franks said with a smile. "All right. We'll let you know." She stood up and I followed her example. We shook hands.

"Thank you for coming in."

I smiled, not quite knowing what to say. "Thank you," I finally said, with the emphasis on *you*. And so that was that. I went back to Alice's house and made myself a cup of tea. If I get this job, it will change my lifestyle, limit my freedom and keep me occupied morning to night, I was thinking as I sat down in the comfortable living room armchair. But then I will be earning enough money to be able to enjoy my life better and to fill the little free time I would have left with study and research. I was becoming quite intent on pursuing my newfound path of learning and discovery with more diligence.

I only had to wait two days. Mrs. Franks called me early in the morning, while I was still eating my breakfast. Alice had already gone to work and I was beginning to plan my day when the phone rang. "I'm phoning about your job application," Mrs. Franks said. Of course I knew why she was phoning. "We have a decision and your application has been successful. Can you start work on the fifteenth?"

"Yes, I can," I replied. I was delighted to have been successful. Suddenly life seemed to be flowing in the right direction and I was pleased and grateful that I would be able to pay my way.

Mrs. Franks continued, "You will start, like everyone else in this firm, on a trial basis for the first three months. During the probation period you will not have any holiday entitlement, but after six months you can start taking your holidays. For the first three years you will be entitled to 14 days of holiday leave."

"That's fine," I said.

I phoned Alice straight away.

"Have you heard?" I asked. "I got the job! We'll be working together! Isn't that great?"

She sounded distant and not as pleased as I thought she would be.

"Well, I'm very glad for you," she said and added, "I'll see you later." She then put down the receiver. I couldn't understand why. After all, it was her idea in the first place! Why was she being so cold and indifferent? I thought it would be an excellent excuse to celebrate and go out together. I felt very disappointed and when she came back from work, I told her so.

When I did, she became defensive and denied that she was cold. She insisted she was simply busy at work and didn't have the time or mind space to express her satisfaction at the fact of my having got the job. After all, it was her initiative that got me the interview, so why was I being so sensitive? I had to agree with her, though some doubts did linger.

That Sunday my grandmother decided to brief me about confidence. As we sat down, she started to explain, "Confidence is a quality that everyone should have and that you need if you want to be successful at whatever it is that you decide to do in life." She then proceeded to give me a lesson about the many kinds of confidence that exist. This surprised me because I had assumed there was only one. I mentioned this to her.

"That's the problem with your reasoning," she said in reply. "You and most of the human race think that everything is flat, two-dimensional and easily definable. But I tell you, no, everything has layers and levels and dimensions. That's what makes life so interesting." She smiled as she considered what to say next. "A dictionary definition is a fossilized description, arrested in time and, like a butterfly in an entomologist's collection, pinned to the page. But language is alive and moving and developing all the time, changing with the times and acquiring new subtle meanings and nuances."

She took another pause and started speaking about the different aspects of confidence, beginning by explaining about conception and the uniqueness of each life. "Out of millions and millions of chances, you were the person who was given life and has had the privilege of being born on planet Earth. First, your parents had to meet. Out of over three billion possible women, your father was attracted to your mother and she was attracted to him. Then they had to get together and create a circumstance within which they were able to bring a baby into the world. Then, they had to make love at exactly the time when that one particular egg produced by your mother's ovary was traveling down her fallopian tube and was ready to be fertilized by your father's sperm. Then, out of the millions of sperm that your father's body produced daily, that one sperm that had an extra X gene, actually made it up the right fallopian tube and managed to fertilize your mother's egg. Then, the pregnancy had to be carried to term, because apparently about fifty percent of pregnancies don't make it and often women don't even realize that when they menstruate they actually might be losing a fertilized egg.

"So your birth was a miracle, just as every birth is a miracle." Then my grandmother continued to explain, "You have managed to survive into adulthood, overcoming several childhood illnesses and encountering germs and dangers on a daily basis."

She then took a calculator out of her desk drawer and proceeded to count up the planet's investment in my wellbeing, calculating how many loafs of bread, chickens, cows, fish, lettuces, vegetables and fruit I had eaten in my lifetime, how many pints of milk, water, tea, coffee, juice and sodas I had consumed and how much air I had breathed. As she pointed out, this was a huge investment and must have happened for a reason.

"The first reason to have confidence is the very fact that you are alive, despite all the pitfalls on the way and thanks to the huge investment in your wellbeing by the planet and all those people who have looked after you and helped you since birth. So, having acknowledged the fact of your uniqueness, let's look at the three kinds of confidence that you need to learn about to become more effective and successful in the world. The first is expressed in how you hold yourself and how you behave." Together we compiled a list of attributes that confident people exude and radiate—such things as walking tall, holding one's head up high, smiling, looking directly at the person they are talking to, speaking clearly and loudly enough to be heard, dressing with an easy elegance, having a firm handshake, believing in themselves. Grandmother then asked me to walk around the room, embodying as many of the symptoms we had listed as I possibly could. I found my gait had changed—I was walking straight and smiling and shaking Grandmother's hand with a direct look in the eye and a firm handshake. It felt good to do and I wished I could feel that confident all the time.

"You can," Grandmother said. "Sometimes you can simply act confident and a confident energy will recognize the behavior pattern, and it will come and enhance your day. I think this is what you are feeling right now," she added as she observed my walking around the room.

"It's true," I said. "I do feel more confident."

"You see, there is a lot of confident energy in the world," Grandmother explained. "It is exuded all the time by confident people everywhere. So why not take advantage of that fact and connect to their manufactured frequency to enhance your behavior?"

I paused and came back to sit beside her. "That was easy," I said, pleased with the result.

"The second kind of confidence comes from acquired skills and knowledge," Grandmother continued. "A confident person knows what they know and they are prepared for any situation, trusting that they will be able to handle themselves. Theirs is a self-reliance and an ability to adapt to change. The more a person knows, the more they can do and above all, the more they know they can do, the more confident they become.

"So it's not enough to be able to do something, it is also important to know that you know how to do it." Grandmother noticed my quizzical expression, so she explained further, "For example, how about all the things you have learned to do in your life but have taken for granted ever since?" she asked.

"Like what?" I couldn't imagine what she meant.

"Like walking, tying your shoelaces, writing, riding a bike, playing the piano, boiling an egg, swimming … Do you get the idea? It took a lot of effort to learn those skills, but do you give yourself credit for all that learning?" she asked. I had to admit that indeed, I did take it for granted.

"And what about speaking a language?" she asked further. "It took you three years to speak properly and yet you don't give it a second thought. Did you try to learn a foreign language in school?"

"I did—French and German," I replied.

"And to what result?" she asked further.

"I still can't speak either properly," I replied. "It's too difficult; too many words to learn."

"Exactly," said Grandmother. "And yet you speak English with such ease. Don't take it for granted." She took a moment and then continued. "The third kind of confidence is the result of qualities that you radiate. A person who knows for sure that they are reliable, hard working, persistent, fair, caring and kind, will also radiate confidence. Thus I recommend that you set your feet upon the path of acquiring both skills and attributes, not necessarily so that you may use them, but so that you may have confidence in your ability to succeed."

I then asked her for an example, and she explained further, "If you had a car and knew how to change a tire, then even if someone else changed it for you, they would feel honored to help you, rather than pressed into that situation by your inability to help yourself. It is very different doing something for someone who can do that task for themselves but want you to help them, rather than feeling blackmailed into doing it because they are helpless and lack confidence in their own abilities. Also, you would feel much better about yourself if you asked someone to help you, even if you did not need their help, but simply wanted them to accompany you in your efforts to perform a task that needed to be done."

Walking out of my grandmother's house that day I could swear I already felt more confident and ready for my new job. I also made the decision to take on the building of confidence as a deliberate quest and exploration, necessary for my future.

Chapter Six

Punctuality

My life had acquired a new routine. Up at 7:30am, breakfast at 7:45am and off to the office at 8:00am for an 8:30am start. I had forgotten how busy rush hour traffic could be. However, it was fun sharing the drive in with Alice and telling each other the stories and gossip from the day before. We now were acquainted with the same people and every time she mimicked someone, I was soon able to recognize who it was. She really had a talent for taking on other people's personas and I enjoyed her tomfoolery as we journeyed together, taking turns to drive.

For two weeks I dispatched furniture to stores and installation sites with George who was moving out west and was so preoccupied with his impending move and his wife's pregnancy that he didn't really care much about the job. He was in his forties and he swore a lot—every item on the site was a piece of shit and the names he called people I don't like to use in print, but underneath that rough exterior he appeared to be a caring individual, though his care was selective and no longer included his daily duties in its domain.

The first day we went out together he was helping with the installation of five office suites in a large building belonging to a local government office. He wanted to make sure that the installation would go smoothly, that he had the right number of installers with him and, I suspect, he simply wanted to get out of the office, as well as to show me how an installation worked.

He walked through the offices, taking notes and passing on instructions to the installation team. As they started carrying in the desks, bookshelves, chairs and other furniture, he turned to me and said, "Let's get out of here. Let's go and have a coffee."

This certainly sounded like a great idea to me; after all, he was the boss. I did worry for a moment about his motives but quickly talked myself out of it, as he seemed to be a respectable married man without a hidden agenda. Besides, it was broad daylight in a busy city neighborhood. Also, he had spoken about his wife in such endearing terms that my doubts soon passed and I felt quite settled as I accepted his invitation.

We walked to a small coffee shop down the street; he had left his car in the government car park.

"Be careful with Brian," he said as the coffees were served. "He's single and he has been out with several women in the office already."

I wondered why he was saying this. "I'm sure he'll invite you out as well. But be warned, it never lasts."

He then added after a moment of quietly sipping our coffees, "Don't tell him I told you."

That evening after a chicken takeaway dinner, Alice and I settled down to watch a rental video together. I tried to sound casual, but the truth was that I really wanted to know.

"Did you ever go out with Brian?" I asked, trying out the best nonchalant tone I could muster. We were sitting on the sofa facing the television screen, when she abruptly turned towards me, her eyes blazing.

"Whatever gave you that idea?" she asked, her tone unusually sharp.

"Nothing, I just wondered." I still tried to sound casual and disinterested, though I felt my composure slowly crumbling.

"Absolutely not!" That *not* was very emphatic, I thought. It seemed to me that she was protesting too much, but I decided not to say anything more. She seemed to calm down and after a few minutes of silence, she added, "He's been out with quite a few girls at the office. It's best you know. So don't have any expectations; it never lasts long."

"So I'm told."

She turned to face me again.

"Who told you that?"

"George. The guy whose job I am taking over."

"Oh, him. Yes, he would know. He was going out with a girl called Emilia. That was a few years ago. Brian came along, swept her off her feet and then dumped her two months later. Poor George was quite heartbroken, you know. Of course now he's married and has probably forgotten about the whole affair."

"I don't know about that. He seemed pretty determined to warn me about Brian."

"Well, I guess that's office politics. Everyone knows everyone else's business."

"What about you?" I asked. "Did he ever try to go out with you?"

"Me?" I could see her blush in the dim light of a lamp. "Well, he tried, but I would never go out with him. He's not my type. He did ask me, though."

"When was that?"

"Oh, about a year ago. I can't remember now."

Her voice sounded casual. Then she added, "OK. Shall we watch the movie now?" And with that she clicked the remote, as if to end the conversation and started the film, which had been set up earlier, ready to go.

Slowly I was getting to know my colleagues and the ways of the company. I was even beginning to make friends with a couple of the girls, though I did not enjoy going out for a drink during the lunchtime, because if I did, I would feel sleepy and lethargic in the afternoon and unable to concentrate, and the job required me to be focused and exact. Once I took over from George I became responsible for the deliveries within my area. Some days would be slack and there would be time to think ahead and plan for the next week, but some days would be so busy that I would hardly have time to go for lunch, and I would have to grab a sandwich at the corner delicatessen and eat it at my desk in between phone calls, emails and delivery specifications.

Each of the five routes were handled by a different dispatcher and when one of us was not as busy as the others, we helped each other out, with Brian orchestrating the entire department, including two secretaries, five drivers, two warehouse managers and ten installers. It was a big operation, as far as my previous office experience was concerned, and I had to learn fast to keep ahead of the game.

I believe it takes about six weeks to become acclimatized to a new job and indeed that is how long it took before I knew everybody's names and stopped confusing Marylin from Accounting with Marylou from the sales office.

I was also getting to know the larger clients, those who would place orders repeatedly and expect preferential treatment. I soon established a good rapport with the delivery teams as well and began to feel quite pleased with myself as I struggled to keep up with timetables and delivery schedules.

On Sunday I overslept and by the time I arrived at my grandmother's house, I was twenty minutes late. She was waiting for me and I knew I was in trouble when she sat me down and looked at me with that intense look I came to know so well.

"Let me explain to you about punctuality," she said and I immediately became defensive.

"I am sorry I am late," I said. "I was so tired after a week of work, I overslept. It won't happen again, I promise."

"This is not about you," my grandmother said, and then she added with a smile, "Not everything is about you, though you might find that difficult to believe."

I didn't reply to that, because I felt that anything I would have said at that moment would have come out all wrong.

"So the lesson today is about punctuality," my grandmother continued. "Not your punctuality or lack of it, but punctuality in general. I will explain to you why the difference between two minutes early and two minutes late is like the difference between respect and rudeness.

"An arrangement to meet someone is a contract and I am sure you would like to be the kind of person who not only keeps their contracts, but also has a reputation that says that you adhere to your commitments." I nodded in agreement.

"A mutually beneficial contract can be the beginning of future contracts which can in turn lead to profitable deals, joint ventures, new friendships and so much more. But apart from the obvious benefits afforded by a courteous and respectful relationship, there is the effect that being early or late has on you, as well as your partner or the person you have an agreement with. If you are early for an appointment, it means that you have time to settle in at the place of the meeting, so if it is a restaurant, café or other public place, it will give you the time to find a suitable table or place to sit, to buy a cup of coffee, go to the bathroom and make sure that none of your valuable meeting time is wasted. It means that when you do meet another person or people you are calm, collected and ready to engage. It also means that you are demonstrating to yourself as well as the other person that you are reliable and professional, a person who is more likely to be trustworthy and a good partner. On the other hand, if you are late, you will arrive rushed, heated and in no position to engage straight away. You will need time to settle, to cool down and to gather your thoughts. What a difference between these two scenarios! And sometimes ten minutes can make all the difference."

"You are right. I can certainly confirm what you are saying because today I had to really rush to get here twenty minutes late and it hasn't helped my self-image one bit. Not to mention the fact that I caused you to wait and wasted your valuable time."

"Exactly," confirmed my grandmother. "People often blame the traffic or unexpected events for being late. But if you expect the unexpected and give yourself an extra ten or fifteen minutes to deal with heavy traffic, a last minute phone call or any other business, then you will not be late. Some people are always late and some people are never late. Now why is that, considering that we all have unexpected events and demands in our lives?" she asked.

"I guess it is all to do with planning."

"It's all to do with your mindset," said my grandmother. "Simply decide that you want to be the kind of person that is always on time and honors their contracts, and you will soon see what you need to do in order to create that kind of image of yourself. And the first person that you need to educate about who you want to be is you. Everything else will follow."

She made it sound so simple, though I already knew that it would take time and effort to be able to rearrange my brain synapses to build an image of myself as someone who is confident, punctual, full of serenity and self assurance. Nevertheless, I liked the idea and decided to give it a try.

"I want to be like that," I said. "I want to be reliable and respectable, someone you can really be proud of."

Grandmother smiled. "I believe you do," she said and smiled again. "I believe you do," she repeated.

I was sitting at my desk, trying to work out how to manage two urgent deliveries at the same time, both due to go out the next day. I managed to book an extra installer from the southern route, but there was no truck available, so I thought I would ask my friend Jeff who owned a truck and was without work to help me out. But I needed Brian's permission to employ someone from outside and spend company money.

His office was behind the warehouse, to give him easy access to the warehouse managers and installers who were all based there. I didn't go there very often, because I was usually busy at my desk in the front part of the building, on the second floor.

I felt a bit nervous as I approached his office, probably because I had hardly spoken to him over the past six weeks, having been instructed and coached by my predecessor, George.

I knocked and listened for a reply. It was very noisy in the warehouse, with truck engines running outside the loading bays and the sound reverberating through the large space, with men shouting at each other and with the drivers and installers shifting boxes and packages, getting ready for the morning deliveries.

"Come in," I finally heard from behind the door, so I opened it, peered in and went in. Brian was sitting behind his desk, which was absolutely covered with paperwork. Next to his desk was a table with a laptop computer on it and on the walls were maps of all the delivery routes, the city and the locality, next to lists of addresses and delivery schedules.

He looked up from his writing and asked, "How are you getting on? What can I do for you?" His pen still in his hand, he obviously was not expecting to spend much time with me—he didn't even ask me to sit down.

"I have a question," I said.

"Yes, go ahead."

"I am organizing two urgent deliveries for tomorrow. Can I hire an extra truck from outside?"

Now he became a little bit more interested and put his pen down.

"Who are the deliveries for?" he asked.

"Century Oil and Safety First," I replied.

"Oh yes, if you can get a reasonable rate, do it. We must keep those two happy at all costs."

"Thank you, Brian. That's all I needed to hear."

I turned around and started heading for the door, when I heard him say, "Well done for thinking of it."

I looked back at him and smiled. I thought he looked really handsome and somewhat vulnerable at that moment. His back was resting against the chair; he was smiling and looked quite relaxed. He smiled back and I said, "Thank you," before leaving his office.

It was lunchtime and I needed to coordinate the two urgent deliveries. I decided to stay in the office and work through my lunch hour. There were phone calls with enquiries concerning deliveries and schedules and time was moving fast. I had just completed a list of all the items that were needed for the next day's deliveries, so I went down to the warehouse to make sure that all items were in stock. I had built a good rapport with Sam, the warehouse manager; he always was very careful to check all the boxes and crates before loading the trucks. He took the lists and promised to make sure everything would be ready for the morning in preparation for delivery. "Don't worry about a thing," he said.

I thanked him and was heading towards the stairs when Brian came out of his office and started walking towards me. He stopped as I was passing close to him and asked casually, "How is it going? Are you ready for your important deliveries tomorrow?"

"Yes," I said. "Sam has been very helpful in organizing the inventory."

"Good, he's a great warehouse manager. No one knows the products like he does."

"Yes, that's true." I was glad that Sam got a mention. He was always such a great help. I was just about to walk past Brian when I thought my hearing had failed because I heard him say something else. "Do you want to go out for dinner tonight?" he asked, or at least that was what I heard him say. I spun around and looked at him. I hesitated very briefly.

"Yes, thank you," I said before I could even think it over. I could have kicked myself for responding so quickly.

"Very well, I'll pick you up at eight," he said. I hesitated for a moment; something was missing here.

"Do you know where I live?" I asked.

"Of course I do," he replied as he looked back up at me briefly. "You are staying with Wonderland. See you at eight."

And that was it. He went back to his work and I headed for the stairs to my office, my head spinning.

All through the afternoon I found it difficult to think about anything else but my evening date. I was surprised to be so excited and I even admonished myself mentally by saying, 'Don't be silly, haven't you been on a date before?' It was difficult to concentrate, but I needed to, because the afternoons were usually dedicated to organizing next day's deliveries, and I needed to be alert because of the two deliveries to Century Oil and Safety First.

I walked past Alice a couple of times during the afternoon, but somehow refrained from telling her my news. I thought I would keep it to myself until our return journey home. Finally, five o'clock arrived and I grabbed my jacket and purse and went to the front desk to collect Alice, but she was in the middle of typing addresses on envelopes and didn't look at all as if she intended to leave.

"Aren't you coming?" I asked.

"No, I can't. There's a meeting at six and they asked me to stay, so I'll probably be here till nine. I can do with some overtime. Why don't you go home without me and I'll catch the bus."

"OK. I'll see you later. I'm going out, so don't wait for me."

"OK, have a good time."

I tried to sound as casual as I could. She didn't seem to suspect anything unusual. After all, I did sometimes go out. It could be any of the exciting things I sometimes would do—go to the movies, meet a girlfriend, late night shopping. It didn't matter; I would tell her later.

Back at the house I had a lot to do. I first had a bath and attempted to relax, but kept looking at my watch, which I had put on a chair by the bathtub. The hands were zooming ahead. I got out of the bath at 7:05pm and the first question arose—what should I wear? I had no idea where we were going, but I wanted to look my best. I investigated my closet and couldn't find anything suitable. I went back and forth through all the dresses hanging on the hangers—there were plenty of them—summer dresses, winter dresses, long dresses, short dresses—but nothing quite suitable for what I had in mind. I wanted to look elegant, sophisticated, yet not too dressy or loud. What I really needed was a black dress; that would be perfect. And then I remembered—Alice had exactly the right kind of dress. I was sure she wouldn't mind, but I decided to phone and ask first. We did wear each other's clothes from time to time when the need arose, but we did always ask. I phoned the reception, but there was no answer. I looked at my watch. It was 7:30pm and she was probably serving coffee in the boardroom or perhaps she had gone to the bathroom. Who knows? I thought I would try again in a few minutes and dashed into her room. I opened the closet and stopped for a moment to admire the order and care with which she had hung up her clothes. They all looked so fresh and neat and new. I spotted the dress and pulled it off the hanger. I tried it on and it looked great, as I admired myself in the long mirror on her closet door. 'Yes, this will do nicely.' Although I still remembered to phone again as I went back to my room to look for my black shoes and evening bag, I must have forgotten by the time I went into the bathroom to comb my hair and put some makeup on. When I finally checked my watch, it was 8 o'clock. I walked up to the phone and started dialing the office number, when the doorbell rang.

I opened the door and was surprised at how different Brian looked. He seemed relaxed, confident and much more handsome than his usual preoccupied work image. And yes, he wasn't wearing glasses, which made his eyes look more penetrating; they were the main feature that struck me as he looked at me and I looked at him. He looked somewhat surprised as well, as if he was seeing me for the first time.

"You look lovely," he said and the word lovely sounded a little bit strange and old-fashioned. I couldn't remember anyone calling me that before.

"Thank you." I picked up my jacket and purse. "Where are we going?" I asked.

"That's a surprise," he smiled endearingly.

We drove out of town, as he explained that he was taking me to the seaside, to a little restaurant overlooking the sea. The days were long and it was beginning to get dark by the time we got there, but the waxing moon was out and it illuminated a silver path from the horizon towards the beach which was visible below.

"So how are you settling in?" he asked and it felt a little bit awkward at first, talking about work. I felt neither of us really wanted to but that is what we knew we had in common.

"It seems to be going fine," I replied. "I'm getting used to the routine, I know most of the clients I have organized deliveries for and I think I have seen or ordered most of the items that we sell."

"Yes, I've noticed that your route seems to be running quite well. I guess George did a good job of passing on the ins and outs of the system."

"Yes, he did." We were sitting in an enclosed porch overlooking the sandy beach. The seagulls flew by screeching, as if hoping for food and calling through the glass windows.

The food was delicious and we drank a couple of glasses of wine.

We had moved away from talking about work and were sharing stories from our childhood. Brian was brought up by two teachers and they had expected him to become a teacher too, but he was always interested in healing and had spent a couple of years traveling and studying various belief systems and methods of energy work in India, Australia and South America. However, he was not qualified to set up a practice and needed to earn a living, so he at first applied for the very same job that I was currently fulfilling. After three years of organizing deliveries, he was asked whether he wanted to take on the function of dispatch manager, which he had been doing ever since.

"I knew there was something different about you," I said. Do you practice healing?" I asked.

"Yes, I do, privately," he replied. "I've had some amazing results. I work with the energy of the body." He then proceeded to explain to me about the human aura and how he sometimes saw lights around people and from that he could tell where the trouble lay.

"Can you see mine?" I asked.

"Well, I'm not trying to at the moment. It's a different way of looking and I need to concentrate," he said. "I try to reserve that faculty for my healing work."

I was intrigued and interested. It made me think of my grandmother. Maybe one day I would introduce Brian to her.

The evening passed very quickly and the staff began clearing the tables before we felt ready to go. Brian paid the bill and reluctantly I said it was time to go back to the city. As we got up I upset my wine glass and spilt wine down the front of my dress, but I made light of it, as I didn't want a small incident like that to spoil the evening.

When I got back, Alice was in the kitchen, making tea. I tried to sneak into my bedroom, but she came out of the kitchen and walked towards the door, as soon as she heard my key in the lock.

"Where have you been?" she asked and as she did, she noticed the dress and just stood there with her mouth open. "What are you wearing?" she exclaimed.

"I'm so sorry. I tried to phone you, but there was no answer and I spilt wine down it. I'll replace it," I blurted out, before she had time to realize what I was saying. But slowly she was getting the picture.

"How could you?" she demanded. "You are staying here as my roommate and then you start going through my things and next thing I know, you've destroyed my best dress! You can't replace it; it's one of a kind. Didn't you notice the designer label?" She was really upset now.

"I'm sorry," was all I could think of saying.

"Sorry won't fix it. You're so selfish. I can't believe you did that. You always think of yourself first."

"And you always dramatize everything," I replied. "And no, I didn't check the label," I added.

"So why was it so important that you had to wear my best dress?" she asked after a moment.

"Because I had a date," I said but I decided I would not tell her with whom, despite her continuous interrogation. It went on like that until she eventually got tired and went to her room and slammed the door.

Chapter Seven

How to Argue Successfully

The next day I didn't see Brian at all. I heard from the man who was the dispatcher for the eastern route that he had gone to help with a delivery in the central area, the territory that contained our most influential customers. I knew this because Sacha was looking for him to help solve a problem he was encountering with his installers and he came to my office asking for Brian's cell phone number. When I gave it to him, he phoned Brian from my office and was sorting out his problem right there in front of me. I pretended I wasn't listening as I opened the filing cabinet and started going through my files, but I did hear every word. Brian would be back in the afternoon and he would talk with the men. In the meantime Sacha was to carry on with his work and load the trucks for tomorrow. I saw how Brian's will and authoritative way had a calming effect on Sacha who went back to his work with reassurance and confidence.

I phoned Grandmother that afternoon. "I had this big argument with Alice," I said, "and I don't understand why. She says that I am selfish and always think of myself ..."

"Now hold on, I see that I need to explain to you the rules of arguing effectively," she replied. "Come over and we'll go through some ideas for future use."

This sounded interesting. So I left Alice a note telling her that I was going over to Grandma's to learn to argue effectively, so that both sides can win and feel heard. It turned the whole thing around, from being a disturbing experience to becoming an opportunity to learn something new.

The first thing my grandmother said to me as she led me into her small living room was, "There is nothing wrong with a good old-fashioned argument. You cannot expect never to have them. They clear the air and allow a person to really see what the other person is feeling and thinking. So be glad that someone cares enough about you to be prepared to argue. Only people who don't care about each other don't argue."

She then put the kettle on for a cup of herbal tea, so I had a moment to think about what she had said. As we sat down, with cups of tea in hand, she continued, passing on what later turned out to be one of the most important lessons of all.

"Above all, in an argument, you must not use two words, and those two words are *always* and *never*. For two reasons: firstly because they are simply not true. In a relationship nothing happens always and never is also very unlikely. But in the heat of an argument, these are very tempting words and people will often use the word *always* to describe an action that perhaps had happened a few times, or they will use the word *never* to express their hope for an action to take place in the future. There is something very final about these two words, whereas a successful argument needs to remain open-ended. You said that Alice had said that you always think of yourself first. Well, you can point out to her that this would simply be an impossibility."

I smiled, because I could see Alice's face, if I could only get her to listen. I didn't feel logic was her strong point, but I was resolved to try.

"And what is the second reason?" I asked.

"The second reason why you should never use the words *always* and *never* in an argument is because an argument should be only about one specific incident and not about the past, or grievances that had never been aired and resolved before."

"What are the other rules of arguing successfully?" I asked, as I took out my notebook and pen and sat poised, ready to take some notes.

"Oh, there are several," she said, as she took another sip of her tea. "Let's go through them one by one. First, you need to state your value for the other person, so that they don't feel devastated by the experience or that your whole relationship is in jeopardy because of one mistake. Second, as I already mentioned, an argument or misunderstanding should be about one incident and not an entire relationship, or a whole string of issues. It is a clash of two points of view or two frequencies and is proof that you are trying to find ways to move forward that you both can adhere to.

"So always start by saying that you value the fact of your friendship and that you believe it is a successful relationship. The argument is about fine-tuning or correcting a misunderstanding, but in no way does it undermine your value for each other. This will give you a good foundation from which to begin. If you can manage it, it is best to argue without heat, but, of course, that might not be possible, as emotions tend to flare and a person can become defensive when something is being pointed out to them. The more light, the less heat there will be and by the same token, the more heat, the less light. I am sure you would want more light in your life."

"Absolutely," I confirmed.

"What were you arguing about?" she asked.

"Well, nothing, really. The argument started because I wore her dress and I spilt wine all over it, so that it is ruined. But I think she really might be jealous because I went out on a date." I was not going to mention Brian at this point, at least not yet and not in this context.

"So it sounds like one thing led to another."

"Exactly."

"Well, in future, try to argue about one thing at a time. Decide what you are going to argue about and keep to a single item or subject. In other words, argue about the dress, solve that issue, and then move onto the next subject. So if she brings in the fact of your dating a man she doesn't approve of, you can politely let her know that she had drifted away from the subject of the argument."

"Yes, I do see that, though she doesn't know who I was out with. I think it is simply the act of dating that she disapproves of."

"You see," Grandmother said, "very often an argument is sparked by actions or words that are the end result of a whole process. For example, if you get annoyed because someone keeps leaving their rubbish on your desk, but you don't say anything, when you finally do tell them that it annoys you, you will probably explode. So prevention is better than an argument. Indeed, when you prevent something, it is often because you pre-vent it, that is to say, like a pressure cooker, you let off steam before the explosion has a chance to occur. So tell the people that you deal with how you feel before it gets loaded with anxiety or anger. Of course, in this case the argument was sparked by an action that was not a repetitive occurrence."

She looked at me and noticed me taking notes. She then said, "So, to recap, there are seven important rules that will ensure you have a successful argument that can lead to resolution and ensure that the argument is not destructive. Point one is to state your value for the other person. Point two is to never say *never* and never say *always*. Point three is to argue about one subject at a time and it is best to agree what that subject is, because sometimes it is unclear or an argument can easily escalate from one subject to another. A person can argue about a dress, but really they are driven by jealousy, for example. So before you know it, the argument is arcing from one subject to another without ever mentioning the real issue and the real cause of the problem.

"Point four is to exhaust a subject. This is important, because by listening to the other person and trying to understand what happened to spark the argument, you can get another perspective and look at the situation from the other person's point of view. Everyone is different and the person you argue with will have different needs, insecurities and anxieties. Learn to walk in their shoes and don't be stubborn in your insistence that you have the right idea of how things should be done.

"An argument is an excellent opportunity to learn about yourself—what is it about you that annoys people? Do you tend to argue about the same old thing over and over again? Why is that? Do you have a blind spot concerning an aspect of your character? An argument is a challenge, a test and a learning. Do not give up halfway through, before the other person can feel that they are heard and have had adequate time to express their emotions. Statements like, 'What do you want me to do?' are not helpful because they surrender responsibility. You can argue and still maintain your dignity and self-stature.

"Point five is don't attack or counter-attack. If the other person is at fault, it might be difficult for them to see it or admit it, just as it would be for you to admit to a mistake. I know that about you."

She looked at me with her steely grey eyes and I could feel myself blush. She smiled indulgently and continued, "Sometimes when a person is accused of something, they will counter-attack. So, for example if someone tells you you are late, you might be tempted to respond by saying that they are sometimes late themselves. And this takes us back to point three, which is to stick to the issue at hand.

"Point six is to state your feelings correctly. So if you feel let down or hurt, say so, don't diminish the truth by trying to make it sound less hurtful or less extreme. There is no substitute for honesty and the truth. Half-truths are difficult to deal with and they will not clear the air; the unexpressed feeling will linger and will inevitably come up another time.

"And the final point is, never walk away from an argument. If you do, you will leave the other person hanging, unfinished and even more frustrated than before you started. So have the courage to see it through to the end, so that there is resolution."

Armed with such advice, I went back to the house to talk it over with Alice. She was there, sitting on the sofa and reading a book. I asked her if she wanted to talk and she reluctantly agreed, as she put her book down. I told her that I had just learned to argue effectively and that I wanted to share my knowledge with her. At this she became interested, so I took her through the lesson my grandmother had given me, point by point.

"You see," I said, "you did say I was always selfish, which simply cannot be true. No one is always selfish. And if I were, I am sure you would not continue to be my friend."

"That's true," she admitted. "But you said that I always dramatize everything, which also cannot be true. I don't always make a drama out of everything." She had a point and I realized I had conveniently forgotten that I had said that. At that moment I could clearly see that my memory was indeed selective.

"Well, then we're even," I said.

"Well, not entirely. I am still upset about the dress," she pointed out.

"I guess you have a right to be," I admitted. I had an idea. "I'll tell you what. Why don't we go shopping tomorrow and I'll buy you a new dress?" I had just been paid and felt glad I could afford to make such an offer.

Yes, Alice liked that idea. After all, a dress is only a dress and a friendship is far more precious. You can't buy a real friend. I had to promise not to take anything of hers or go into her room without her permission, unless there was some emergency that would require it, and the same would apply to my possessions and my room.

The next day was Saturday and we were sitting in a coffee shop at the mall. Alice had chosen her dress, which although expensive by my standards, was not so expensive by hers. I could see that she had compromised and had chosen something that was reasonable. I therefore felt both relieved that it was settled and glad not to feel guilty any more that I had destroyed her dress. I was hoping to get the spot cleaned and to keep the dress, so I thought it was quite a good deal all round. We had spent several hours going from shop to shop and we both had bought a few extra bits and pieces—I had purchased a belt and a new lipstick with matching nail polish; she had splashed out on some expensive perfume and a couple of new bras. So there we were sipping our cappuccinos, glad to be talking on normal terms again, tired from the shopping, but pleased with our purchases. I was off guard, relaxed and open, when Alice suddenly looked at me with a steady gaze and put me to the question in a slightly demanding kind of voice. I knew that voice and the posture: Alice was a Taurus and stubborn with it; when she wanted to know something, she would keep on asking until she got her answer.

"So who were you with last night? What date was so important that you needed to borrow my dress without asking?" I knew there was no point withholding or avoiding the answer; she would find out anyway. Best she found out from me. Besides, I didn't see any reason to keep it a secret and thought that I had been selfish and foolish to withhold this information from her so far.

"I was out with Brian," I said.

"Oh," she said and that was all she said. She went quiet after that and stopped talking for a moment. I thought she would be pleased, but then I remembered how she had warned me that Brian had gone out with several girls in the office. I thought I should reassure her.

"He was very nice," I said. "We simply went out for dinner." I was trying to make light of our date, but felt that that was not how it was being received.

"Well, that's all right. You're grown up, you know what you are doing. Just remember that I have warned you."

"Yes, I remember," I replied. "It was just a dinner date. Nothing happened." I don't know why I said that; I felt I needed to convince her, or maybe myself, that it wasn't serious. Not yet, anyway.

Chapter Eight

Assumption

On Monday I didn't see Brian, even though I had to go to the warehouse a couple of times to supervise the loading of the truck for the next day. I don't think he was in his office because I couldn't hear him on the phone and there was no light on in there. The following day we were supposed to be delivering and installing furniture in a downtown showroom. They had ordered very specific, custom-made shelving and two units had not arrived with the rest of the consignment. This always made things difficult, and especially in this case, because they were expecting to have a grand opening in a few days. It also meant that the truck would need to make two deliveries, not one, that their buyer would be upset and that in turn meant that I would need to come up with a solution fast. I decided to send in two other units that matched the rest of the furniture on a temporary basis, to tide them over and to go into their showroom to placate the owners and make sure that the delivery boys would not be given too hard a time.

The following day I spent most of the time out of the office. I needed to go into town to the showroom where we had delivered the wrong inventory. The owners demanded that I come to see how awful the substitute shelves looked; they neither fitted the space nor matched the other units which had been custom built and painted to match the modern décor of the showroom. Well, there was nothing I could do and it was not my fault that the factory had not fully fulfilled my order, but there is no substitute for the human touch, so I went to the showroom, expecting a row and remembering my grandmother's advice concerning successful arguments.

As soon as I arrived, Mrs. Preston, the store owner, was the first to approach me. Probably in her late thirties, she had a statuesque figure, tight blonde curls adorning her oval face with blue, almost watery eyes and full, very red lips. Her heels made a "clip clop" sound across the tiled showroom floor and I could tell I was in trouble.

"Are you Barbara?" she asked. I nodded. "Come with me, let me show you something." There were workmen milling around the showroom, hanging up pictures, dressing the windows, adding final touches to the displays, carrying in furniture. She was definitely agitated and I obediently followed her across the showroom floor.

"Look at this," she exclaimed as we reached a group of men standing by the substitute shelving units. Two of the men were in overalls—one was our installer with an orange V emblazoned on his pocket, and another was no doubt their employee or contractor; the third man was wearing white slacks and a silk tee shirt. I thought he must be Mr. Preston—young, successful, with dark Mediterranean looks.

"It just doesn't fit. It's too small and the color is all wrong. We specially ordered those units to fit in with the overall concept."

Mr. Preston turned to me. "Ah, you represent Versatile Furniture, do you not?" he asked. "Well, how versatile is that?"

"Half the display doesn't even fit!" Mrs. Preston added, pointing to a pile of cardboard boxes on the floor.

"I apologize for this delay," I started feebly.

"But we are opening on Saturday," Mr. Preston cut in. The unit was indeed too small and I quickly realized that we could probably find a larger unit to fit the space. I turned to the installer and asked, being that he was more experienced than I was, "Don't we have a larger unit that could fit this space?"

"Yes, the Alpine would fit in there quite nicely." He pulled out his measuring tape from his overalls pocket and checked the space. "Yes, it would be just fine, but of course it comes in pine, oak or black only."

"No, that's not good enough. It's got to be white!" exclaimed Mrs. Preston. "You always mess us around. It needs to be white, like everything else here. Just look around. White for innocence, purity and marriage. It shows off the merchandise so beautifully!"

At that moment I had a complete read-out—she had the money and Mr. Preston had married into wealth, but was brought up in poverty. Not that it mattered to my current predicament, but it did cause some contradiction seeing him giving out orders and issuing complaints, as if he had built the company with the sweat of his brow.

"I'll see what I can do, Mrs. Preston," I replied as politely as I could muster, addressing the woman who I now knew to be the rightful heir to the family's fortune. I then turned to Mr. Preston, and remembering Grandmother's lesson, I couldn't resist adding, "And we don't *always* mess you around. We really try to accommodate your requirements. This was a special order and we are late in delivering, but deliver we will." I smiled my sweetest smile and noticed that Mrs. Preston was standing there, with her mouth open, ready to make a reply, when I turned around on my heel and walked out of the showroom. At least I can change the unit, I thought, as I walked towards the company car, feeling upset by the unfortunate incident.

The next morning I went to see Brian to sort out the mess from the previous day. This was difficult for me, because I was seeing him professionally and didn't want him to think that the showroom disaster was only an excuse to visit him in his office. If we were going to have a relationship, I felt it needed its time and its natural rhythm; I wished I didn't work for the same company as he did and even began to contemplate the possibility of looking for another job. But then that seemed silly and premature, being that there was absolutely nothing between us and we weren't even going out together. Funny what tricks your mind starts playing after one date! I thought that this must be a female trait—extending one encounter into a future of possibilities.

All this was going through my head as I walked across the warehouse floor to his office door. I hesitated in front of it and finally knocked tentatively.

"Yes?" I could hear the voice from within. I opened the door and put my head through the crack, still hesitating whether to go in or not.

"Have you got a couple of minutes?" He was looking at me and smiling encouragingly. "Yes, of course. Come in," he said as he waved his hand, gesturing for me to enter.

I walked in and closed the door behind me. I had the file of the showroom in my hand, trying to look as professional as I could. I walked towards the middle of the room, hesitated and stopped at a point where I felt comfortable—a professional distance; not too intimate and not too distant. He peered at me through the lenses of his glasses.

"What's up?" he asked and it sounded friendly, relaxed and at ease. Totally different to how I felt.

"It's the Preston showroom," I said as I looked into the file, not wanting to hold his gaze any longer.

"What about it?" he asked.

"Well, I placed the order and when the delivery came, two custom ordered shelving units were missing. I phoned the factory and they won't be ready for another five days. Their opening is Saturday." He shrugged his shoulders and said, "Well, you can loan them a couple of other units until the order comes in."

I was pleased he was confirming my actions. "That's exactly what I did," I said. "But they're not happy at all. The size is wrong and the color doesn't match anything else they have."

"Well, you could go down there and explain it in person ..."

"I did. It didn't help. I think I just made it worse."

"Hmm." Clearly this was becoming more of a problem than he had anticipated. "Sit down. Let's see what can be done." I sat in front of his desk. He held out his hand and I passed him the file. He looked at the order and said, "How upset are they regarding the wrong dimensions of the units?"

"Oh, I think they could settle for a larger size, like the Alpine, if we sent it to them for their opening. It would fit quite nicely in the space. But the real problem is the color; that's what they are really upset about."

"It seems that the rest of the furniture they ordered was in white. So the oak shelving you sent along will not match the rest of the showroom."

"That's exactly right. They want white and won't even consider anything else. I had to bring the oak unit back to the warehouse. They didn't even want to talk about it."

He thought for a moment and then said, having made a decision, "I'll tell you what you do. You get a couple of men in the warehouse to paint the larger unit and send it over tomorrow, so they can prepare for their opening. Then when the shipment comes in, do the exchange at no extra charge."

Wow, that's what you need a boss for—to make decisions that no one else would dare make. After all, we might end up with a second-hand, painted unit that no one would want. On the other hand, the Prestons' showroom had a prestigious address and was an important free advertising venue for the company's furniture. It was essential everything looked its best; the Prestons had a large clientele base and there were bound to be references and further sales.

"Thank you, Brian. That is an excellent solution."

"OK, now we've solved that little issue, how about coffee tomorrow after work? I'm swamped right now, but I can manage a quick coffee on the run."

"Sure, Brian. See you tomorrow."

We were having coffee at a café a couple of blocks from the office. There was a Starbucks closer by, but neither of us wanted to be seen by our colleagues. Perhaps because of the time limit, the conversation seemed a little bit strained, but it was also strange and fascinating at the same time, as Brian turned his attention and mine to his inner thoughts.

"Do you know what goes through my mind every time I get up in the morning?" he asked. I shook my head; I had no idea. "That by standing up on two legs I am confirming and solidifying the process of human evolution. It somehow adds significance and meaning to that simple act. Isn't that bizarre?" he asked, mixing his coffee a little too loudly and a little too long.

"No, it isn't," I replied, but I was lying, because I did think it was bizarre. He was a curious man; he seemed to come up with the unexpected. He continued, "You see, it reminds me that as a representative of the human race, I have evolved. That makes me want to make better use of the faculties that I've got and develop the ones that are still dormant. I don't believe that we are the final model."

"So what still needs developing?"

"Everything! Our thinking, our sensitivity, our intelligence. There is so much more that I want to do and be."

That was when I had one of my turns and a vision appeared inside my head. I could see him healing the sick—dozens of them. They kept coming and he was passing his hands over them, and they were getting up and walking away—cured and happy. I must have looked as if I had seen a ghost, because Brian looked concerned.

"What's the matter?" he asked. "What just happened?" I looked at him and my vision seemed to return to normal.

"It's all right, I'm OK," I reassured him.

"Let me walk you to the car," he said. "You don't look at all well."

"I'm fine," I protested, but as I got up from the table, I wobbled on my feet and Brian grabbed my arm to steady me. It was at that moment that I felt a powerful surge that manifested like an electrical charge running through my body and I could feel the blood returning to my face.

"I feel much better now." I paused for a moment and Brian confirmed, "Yes, you do look better. Anyway, let's go."

I phoned Grandmother and asked if I could see her again on Sunday. She said she was busy and I felt disappointed. Having met her almost all previous times on a Sunday, I felt that this was our time and that the same time slot would have been reserved for and allotted to me, with my name on it, ready and waiting for a sign of commitment from me.

"Oh, but can't you really?" I whined. "I was so looking forward to our time together."

"But what made you think that I would be free?" she asked.

"I thought you were always free on a Sunday. I thought it was reserved for me."

"But we agreed no such thing." I began to realize that I had imagined her sitting around all day Sunday, just waiting for me to call. In my anticipation I had not allowed the space for her to have a life that would be independent of mine. How one-track and one-sided I had been in my thinking! I relented.

"Well, then, when can you see me?" I asked.

"How about Tuesday evening?" she responded.

"That would be fine." I tried to sound gracious, but I knew that the feeling of disappointment had crept into my voice.

When I entered her house and as soon as she offered me a glass of water, she came straight to the point. I could tell that she had prepared in advance what she was going to say, because it came at me with a force and without a pause within which I might have been able to respond or excuse myself.

"Assumption is a disease," she said, "and beware of its influence. Never assume that you know about another person or about how the future will turn out. You never have all the information, so better to ask questions and to assume you don't know, than to assume you do."

"Can you give me an example?" I finally had an opportunity to ask, hoping she would not bring my own behavior into the equation.

"Sure. Two people walk into a restaurant and most of the diners assume that they are a couple. Or if one is visibly older than the other, they will assume that they are looking at two generations within the same family. How many people have embarrassed themselves by referring to someone's mother or father, when they were being introduced to their husband or wife? Or, thinking they were dealing with the son or daughter, when they were really addressing the husband or wife? It happens all the time.

"Take the example of how we make decisions and judgment calls on behalf of other people all the time; when we do that we are assuming that we know better what would be good for them.

So it is one thing to say that in their situation you would have acted differently and done such and such; it is quite another to say that someone else should have done this or that. We are not in their situation, we do not have their experience or history, their belief system, their emotional make-up or their education. So we can't possibly know what would be good for them.

"As far as planning the future is concerned, there is always the chance or even the possibility that nothing will go according to plan because likely the sequence of events will spark off other events in the future, currently beyond our control, comprehension or scope. If by thinking something you can create it and make it happen, perhaps by assuming, we are causing a situation to stagnate and not change. For example, if you expect another to be their 'same old predictable self,' then maybe they will be, but if you give them the benefit of the doubt and room to grow, if you encourage them or simply ask the right questions at the right time, then perhaps they will surprise you with what they know and what they can do.

"There is a saying about the impossibility of being a prophet in one's own country. Perhaps we need to travel outside the surrounding ring of assumption to break into new territories and discover our higher selves.

"Every person is different and has their own unique needs, timings and requirements. To expect another to comply with our own expectations, standards and demands is to miss the opportunity to learn from another person's way and style and to understand their reasons for doing what they do. Therefore, at one level assumption is a reduction to a common denominator and at another it is a measurement conducted through the keyhole of one's own limited history and experience.

"To assume that anything remains the same is to deny oneself the adventure of change and new beginnings. Even when going to bed at night, we assume we will get up in the morning and that everything will be as we had left it, thus blinding ourselves to change and ignoring the newness of each passing day. If it were possible for two consecutive days to be the same, how come we can look at photographs from the 1940s or 50s or 60s and immediately note how different everything was then? Surely the change was gradual, day by day by day …"

Grandmother got up and walked to a bookshelf where she kept her photograph albums. They were all neatly catalogued and labeled, so with ease she pulled out a few of them and showed me some sample pictures from each one.

"See here," she said, opening the first one and passing it to me. "These photographs were taken during the Second World War and they show my parents. He is wearing a uniform and they are standing in front of the store that my grandfather owned. You can tell immediately that these were taken in the early forties, not only because of the uniform, but the lettering on the sign above the shop, the short pleated skirt my mother is wearing, the flat, curly hairstyle.

"Then here," she reached for the next album, "I am in my early teens. Just look at the difference! I have a pony tail and a wide skirt with a very wide and very tight belt. I've got socks on and patent leather shoes. And in the next one," she took one album from me, placed it on the floor and passed me another, "I am in my twenties and my hair is teased and piled high on top of my head and I am wearing a long skirt with a leather jacket. And that's just fashion we're looking at. But everything changed in those twenty years: morale, wealth, beliefs, hopes, everything … Just as everything has changed within your lifetime. You might not see it so distinctly as you can when you look at old photographs like the ones I have kept. But in ten years' time you will look back to today and be surprised how much the world will have changed. I guarantee it."

I must admit, the evidence of the photographs was very convincing and as she spoke I looked back in my mind's eye and I could clearly see the changes through earlier decades, as I thought of the twenties and the prohibition years and the Great Depression that followed, or as I journeyed back even further to the turn of the century and the First World War. In the meantime, Grandmother continued.

"We do leave assumption behind when we visit new places or encounter new situations, and then our faculties become alert, interested and challenged and we are ready to take in new information.

"Assumption is the killer of value and development; when circumstances change (especially to our disadvantage), we get shaken out of the blankets of assumption and value increases. There is a story of a carpet seller who offered to sell a selection of valuable Persian carpets to a lady who was looking for a bargain. He stated his final price and gave her a limited time to decide whether she was going to purchase the carpets or not. And since she was still haggling as the time elapsed, he proceeded to throw the precious carpets, one by one, onto the fire. In the end, the lady could take the pressure no longer and bought the last one for the price of the whole lot.

"At another level assumption is a closing down of the faculty when dealing with a situation, another person or a future projection caused by the juxtaposition between the imaginary model of the situation and the facts or the truth. To simplify, assumption is a closing down of one's faculty of detection due to the false premise that change is suspended and everything is just as it has always been. It says we know the score and expect continuance. In other words, someone who assumes they know about another person or can foresee their response to a situation, will cease to be alert, because they think they already know what is about to occur.

"We are changing and different all the time. No two days are the same, no two moments in a life are equal, nobody is quite the same when you meet them again—things happen to them, they change and move on. Nothing about life is guaranteed and we live inside a kaleidoscopic world, ever changing, ever increasing or decreasing, but never leveling out. Therefore we should be kaleidoscopic ourselves and acknowledge this to be so, so that we can move in harmony with the cycles, the octaves and the natural vacillations of wavelengths of energy manifesting at that time.

"Looking at it again, it could be said that to assume is to deny oneself the opportunity of progress. You are not the same today as you were yesterday. Do you realize that you are older and wiser, with more experience, than you have ever been before? You are closer to death than ever before. This is not a gloomy thought, it is a realistic thought. You have fewer days of life left than ever before. This should give you an urgency and an incentive to make this day work for you, to make it effective, to make it last by filling it up with value, real experience and thoughts that go past the local grocery store into the universe and towards God.

"We live in a changing universe on a planet traveling through space at mind-boggling speeds. The configuration of stars, suns and planets around us is never the same from one minute to the next. The universal influences affecting our lives are changing, mutating, rotating, appearing and disappearing all the time, constantly opening up new possibilities and opportunities. How can we do otherwise and how can we assume we know the complete truth about anything or that we are in control of these frequencies? To be joined to the universe is to be open and full of wonder, never knowing what will happen next and being glad that this is so. Otherwise we fix ourselves and our lives according to what already has been, thus limiting our potential and power of discovery."

I felt that was quite an important lesson and that I needed time to think about it, rather than asking questions before I had time to try and understand what my grandmother was telling me. However, I also didn't want it to end, not yet anyway, so I asked her not about the lesson but about her own journey towards wisdom.

"How do you know all this?" I asked in admiration.

"Well, that's simple. I have learned to think and I discipline my mind to open up new territories all the time. So rather than going over old, familiar thought patterns that simply reinforce what I already know, I try to challenge myself by asking questions and by doubting everything that I have managed to accumulate already."

She probably noticed my questioning look, because she continued. "For example, say you think what compassion is and you decide that it is something to do with helping others and being able to give to charity. Well, that might be one level of understanding, but every truth has several levels. And just as we looked at a number of levels to do with assumption, so there are many levels to do with absolutely everything. If you don't know that, you will lead a very limited existence, with everything appearing flat and two dimensional, more like a static photograph than a real life image. Compassion has many levels, too, and perhaps I should leave you to find out what they are.

I am sure you can have a go at finding them."

I could tell by her tone of voice that it was getting time to go. I thanked her for her generosity and got up to leave, feeling more grateful for her time than I would have, had I not had a lesson on assumption. I wondered what other levels there were and whether I would ever be able to reach for them on my own.

When I left I pulled out my notebook and wrote down the word compassion. I remembered that my grandmother had mentioned that there are many meanings and levels to the word, and I was determined to find at least one or two. To me the word had always meant understanding the plight of others and being able to walk a mile in someone else's shoes. But as I wrote down the word, I noticed that it consisted of two words—compass and ion. Ion, being an electrically charged particle, signifies energy and the passage of energy, for example from one person to another. But the word compass gives it a sense of direction, purpose, commitment. Thus, when putting the two together I suddenly understood that compassion is a deliberate passage of force from one person to another—like healing or communication.

I wrote down in my notebook: "Real compassion is directed energy, which requires discernment and knowledge." I decided I wanted to be a compassionate person. Then, looking further I realized compassion has something to do with passion and com. I wondered what com could mean and came to the conclusion that it was related to such words as commiserate and community—a feeling of unity and sharing. I wondered whether I had found another level hidden within the word itself—something to do with the sharing of one's passion. This revelation made me think about the value of language and the etymology of words. I felt there was a lot to learn about words and sensed that there was hidden power in the language, waiting to be discovered.

Chapter Nine

Keeping a Secret

The following evening Alice and I went to the movies and afterwards we decided to have a drink. I don't remember how it started, but somehow we got to talking about Brian. Maybe she sensed something, maybe she was just fishing, but I fell for it hook, line and sinker.

"So, tell me," she started, as if she had planned the whole thing. "Has Brian asked you out again?"

"Well, yes …" I was desperately searching for a way to handle this without saying too much and not appearing to be withholding anything, either.

"And …" She was visibly impatient and very curious.

"And nothing. We went out for a cup of coffee."

"Well, that's not nothing," she insisted. "How was it?"

"It was nice. We got on. I don't know what else to say. He is an interesting guy."

"So, are you going out again?"

"I don't know. We'll see. He seems to be very busy right now. I think he is studying for his business management degree or something."

"Well, don't ever say that I didn't warn you!" she concluded the conversation and I quickly changed the subject.

The next day I was sitting outside the office building, where there was a small lawn, a few trees and a couple of picnic tables for employees. It was lunchtime and there was a warm summer breeze in the air. I had packed a sandwich that morning and had bought a bottle of juice on the way to work. So I spread out my lunch fare in front of me on the table. As I took the first bite, out of the corner of my eye I saw a figure of a man walk up to me and as he stood beside me, he was blocking out the sunlight, so I looked up and saw his face. It was Brian.

"Do you mind?" he asked and I indicated with a wave of my hand the seat in front of me. He sat down and I quickly swallowed my food. He was already seated, when I managed to say, "Please do."

A few remarks about the weather and the pleasant temperatures for this time of year, and I was soon finishing my sandwich and it was getting time to get back to work.

"What are you doing this evening?" he asked, as I noisily scrunched up the empty wrapping paper and began to pick up the empty glass bottle. I paused and hesitated, but the reply came easily enough, "I didn't have any plans. Not yet, anyway." Brian smiled.

"How about dinner then?"

"Sure, that would be nice." I tried to sound casual.

"OK, I'll pick you up at eight."

"Right. See you then."

Alice was there when Brian arrived. I wished she would go out because I did not want to discuss with her every episode of my unfolding relationship with Brian. I wanted it to be my secret; I wanted it to remain private, but under the circumstances of being her roommate I didn't see how that was possible, unless I met him at the restaurant and didn't tell Alice where I was going—both of which would have been awkward to fulfill, to say the least. So, I told Alice where I was going and with whom and she just smiled, as if she knew something I didn't, but wasn't going to tell. As I rushed around the house, getting ready, she just sat there on the sofa in the living room, watching my every move—from the bathroom to the bedroom and back again.

Finally, the doorbell rang as I was putting the final touches to my hair.

"Can you get that?" I shouted from the bathroom.

"Sure," she replied and I could see her in the bathroom cabinet mirror, as she slowly arose and walked towards the door.

"Hello, Brian. Nice to see you again," she said and as I came out of the bathroom and into the living room I saw him kiss her on the cheek. Brian looked at me and smiled.

"You look great," he said. I picked up my jacket and purse and I gave Alice a kiss on the other cheek.

"Bye. See you later," I said.

"Have a good time," she said as she waved goodbye.

I felt hypocritical. I had never kissed Alice on the cheek before going out for the evening. We were friends, but there was also a distance in our relationship. Ever since we had known each other, we tended to lean on each other in times of difficulty and stress and we enjoyed each other's company, but we both knew that there were things we never talked about.

To compensate for the strange feeling of guilt that had overcome me, I threw myself into the conversation with Brian as soon as we had walked away from the front door of the house; I was doing my best to pay full attention to his comments.

The little Italian restaurant was dimly lit and the attentive waiters (two of them) seemed to know Brian and wanted to pamper to his every whim. As we were finally left alone, I asked him, displaying interest in his mental adventures, "So, have you had any interesting new thoughts lately?" My mind was arcing to our last conversation and the fact that Brian saw his standing up on two legs in the morning as a symbol of human evolution and progress.

"Funny you should ask," he replied, "because, yes, I have."

"Oh, really? What is it?" I asked, becoming genuinely interested.

"Well, I wonder about our future," he said. For a moment I thought he was talking about us, but he soon added, "I wonder whether as a race we are progressing or regressing or both."

"What do you mean?"

"Well, if you look at the technology involved in building the pyramids, modern equipment cannot even begin to match it. And then there are ancient records regarding the stars and astronomical data that we still do not have the telescopes or probes powerful enough to fully confirm. On the other hand, we do have cell phones and computers and planes and rockets and washing machines. But is that progress or is it dependency?"

"Or both," I volunteered, not sure where he was going with this conversation.

"Perhaps," he said, "we are materially well off, at least in the western world, compared with our ancestors, but spiritually poorer. Are we really still the peasant behind the button? There are so many beliefs and religions out there that it is hard to know which ones are true and which are false."

"Well, I have my own religion," I said, pleased that I could contribute to the conversation.

"And what is that?" Brian asked.

"The religion of the heart."

"And what is that?" Brian asked again.

"I listen to my heart and my instinct. If it feels right, then I go with it and give it a try"

"But what if you can't tell? Haven't you been in situations where you really don't know which way to go and both your mind and your heart are silent? Or worse, both are pulling in different directions?"

"Sure I have. But I try to live for more than just myself and to bring compassion and generosity into my life."

"So how do you do that?"

"I don't think there is any fixed rule. But I do have little reminders that help me think of the bigger picture and not be so self absorbed."

"Can you give me an example?" As he asked that question, I realized that this was exactly what I had been frequently asking Grandmother during our sessions. I began to wonder whether I was beginning to sound like Grandmother, too.

"Certainly," I said. "Whenever a new situation arises, I try to think of it from three standpoints, instead of one. First, I look at it from my personal point of view, to see how it will influence me, my behavior and my future. Then I step back a pace, mentally, that is, and try to look at it from a greater perspective, asking myself how will it effect others or the environment and what will it appear to be like in five years' time. Finally ..." I hesitated whether to carry on.

"Yes?" Brian sounded impatient.

"Finally, I try to look back on it from my death bed. Or rather," I added quickly, not wanting to sound too morbid, "or rather from the point of view of my entire life. I try to see how useful or not useful it would be from the point of view of my life's mission."

"Oh, so you believe you have a mission, do you?" Brian successfully caught the last word and turned it into a question, having evaded the point I was trying to make.

"Yes, I do. Don't you?" I turned the question around.

"I don't know yet, I'm still trying to discover the answer to that question. But I am getting more of an idea about it."

"Oh? So what's that?"

"I think it is something to do with healing. What about you? What is your mission?"

"I think we are here to learn and to write our own history in the context of human and environmental relationships. If you look at this life as one step out of many steps on your journey, it certainly puts things into perspective. Personally I feel I need to learn to give and help others, although I have not learned yet how to do that effectively."

"It sounds like you believe in reincarnation," Brian said.

"Yes, I do," I replied.

"So where did you learn this?" he asked after a moment.

"Oh, it's just something my grandmother taught me—the fact that we are all here for a purpose, I mean. The bit about my own personal mission I worked out all by myself. Though I've got to say, it's still work in progress."

The dialogue carried on and I was pleased that we were getting on so well. I felt I had found a kindred spirit. Then, with the ice wall melted and with the sharing of laughter and warm looks across the table, I took my courage in both hands and asked him, as we were being served our coffees and were sharing a tiramisu, and there was a moment of silence between us, "Did you ever go out with Alice?" The question hung between us.

He paused for a moment and replied, with a serious note in his voice, "Yes, we went out for a while. It didn't work out."

"Why?"

He was quiet for a moment, then replied, "Please, don't tell her I told you. I know you two are friends, apart from the fact that you are living together."

"No, of course not," I assured him.

"Well, she became very possessive and wanted me to move in with her. She wanted to know where I was at all times and who I was seeing every moment of the day. It was too much for me. It became a nightmare."

"I see." Again there was silence between us. I regretted having asked, because somehow it had ruined the atmosphere, but on the other hand, I was glad to know, because I felt I would have always wondered if I hadn't asked.

When I got home, Brian took me to the door and kissed me on the cheek as he said goodnight, very much the way he did with Alice earlier that night. I let myself into the house and as I tiptoed to my room, trying to keep quiet and to not wake Alice up, I noticed that the light was on in her room and a moment later, just as I was about to open the door to my room, her door suddenly opened and she stood there, framed in the doorway, fully dressed.

"Oh, so you're not asleep," I said, standing there in the corridor in my bare feet, with my shoes in my hand.

"No, I couldn't sleep," she replied. "Do you want a cup of tea?" she then asked. That was always a sign that she wanted to talk. Well, I wasn't ready for bed, either.

"Sure," I replied. "I could do with a drink. I'll put the kettle on." We both went into the kitchen and sat down at the table, waiting for the kettle to boil.

"So how was it?" she asked, attempting to sound casual and friendly, but I could tell she really wanted to know.

"It was nice," I replied, also trying to sound casual and non-committal.

"Is that all? Nice? What happened?" she enquired further.

"Well, nothing much. We talked about many things ..."

"Like what?"

"Reincarnation, religion, that kind of thing."

"That's all?"

"Yes, that's about it. Oh, and I did ask him whether he had ever invited you out." Looking back, I really don't know what made me say that. I just wanted to stop her incessant questioning and somehow I was feeling that there was a rivalry between us here and wanted it to stop. Well, that seemed to get her attention.

"And? What did he say?" she asked as we got up and stood by the kitchen counter, waiting for the kettle to boil.

"He said that you two went out for a while."

"Really?" Alice went quiet and I was sure that she was thinking about what to say next—whether to tell me the truth or not. "Well, that's not exactly true," she finally said and at that moment I realized that she had made the decision not to tell me about it.

"What do you mean, not exactly true?" I asked.

"I told you before," she was sounding impatient now, "he asked me out, but I didn't go. I didn't want to end up being one of his menagerie of girlfriends."

"Oh, I see. Well, that's not what he says."

"Then you've got to decide who is telling the truth and who is lying," she said as she turned around to face the counter and started pouring the boiling water into our two cups. I could not see her expression as she was taking her time, squeezing the tea bags and throwing them into the trash bag under the sink. I felt there was really nothing more to say, because I could see that she wasn't going to alter her line. I quickly changed the subject and asked her about the movie we had seen the night before together.

The next day at work I was on the phone, arranging a delivery, when Brian walked into my office. He seemed upset and he stood in front of my desk and waited for me to finish my conversation. I was just discussing the placement of the desks, bookshelves and filing cabinets in the office of the director of an insurance company, which we were delivering the following day.

"Yes, we'll be there at three o'clock tomorrow," I confirmed as I put down the receiver and looked up questioningly at Brian. I knew I didn't need to ask what was on his mind, because it was coming my way, ready or not. Brian was towering over me and he put one hand on my desk, next to the phone.

"Why did you tell her?" he demanded.

"Tell who what?" I had no idea what he was talking about.

"Tell Alice what I told you last night. That we were going out together."

My heart sank. I couldn't believe that she had already found time to approach him.

"I'm sorry," I stammered. "I wanted to know the truth."

"But why? I specifically asked you not to tell her I had told you. She wanted to keep it a secret and now she's upset with me." It was true; he had asked me not to tell.

"I'm sorry, I shouldn't have," was all I could say.

"That's right, you shouldn't have," he repeated and stormed out of my office, with the door closing gently behind him. If it didn't have a hydraulic slide, I am sure he would have banged the door. I felt awful as I watched him go, and guilty and miserable, all at the same time, because I could clearly see my budding romance falling apart right at the start.

I did not confront Alice, because I decided that it would only make things worse. Instead I phoned my grandmother and asked for help. She told me to come over that same evening, and as soon as I walked in the door, she began by saying, "I need to tell you about secrets."

"About secrets?" I asked, not understanding why she would have said such a thing.

"Yes. It sounds to me like your main problem is the betrayal of trust and the fact that you told Alice a secret you had promised to keep." We sat down in the living room, this time more comfortably, as she seated herself in an armchair and indicated a space on the sofa nearby. Perhaps the comfortability of the environment was proportionate to the uncomfortability of the situation I had found myself in. No, correction! Not the situation I had found myself in, but rather the hole I had dug myself into.

"Yes, I guess you are right," I replied. "What can I do?"

"Well, that's not the place to start," my grandmother began and I sensed a lesson was about to begin. "First of all, as I've already mentioned, you need to understand about secrets."

"All right then, what about secrets?" I wished I had sounded more courteous and respectful when I said that. Somehow impatience had crept into my voice.

"Well, secrets are meant to be kept. And do you know the best way to keep a secret?"

"Sure, the best way is not to tell," I replied, tackling the obvious.

"That's right. In fact it's the only way because secrets do have this tendency to travel from person to person, each one assuming the other person won't tell. But secrets are charged with energy and often with emotions as well, so they often are the first to take flight out of another person's mouth. If you have a secret that shouldn't be told, then don't tell it, despite the temptation to do so."

"Yes, I understand that now, but the damage has already been done."

"That's true, but I'm telling you now so that you don't make this mistake again."

"I won't, really I won't." That sounded very much like a phrase brought into the present from childhood.

"Look, you need to understand something else," Grandmother continued. "Speech is energy and when someone hears a secret, they will naturally want to expend it, because we humans are processing and digesting machines, so that what comes in needs to go out. A secret, however, is energy blocked because by keeping it, you hold onto the energy. When we learn something new and interesting, something that has energy attached to it, don't we always want to pass it on?"

"Yes, we do," I decided to play along with Grandmother.

"And that is the natural thing to do. We love to communicate, women especially are good at it and will find ways to do it. That is why women are sometimes accused of gossiping; it's because we are good at sharing information. Did you know that the Shawnee had only two reasons why a person would be outcast from the tribe—murder and gossip?" I did not know, but Grandmother did not wait for an answer, but continued.

"If you tell a secret, even if the person you have told it to turns out to be discreet, there still are pitfalls in actually telling it. One is that as you tell a secret, you hear yourself telling it and the brain gets the message that it can be spoken and heard. Once a secret is told, it is that much easier for it to be told again. What a person does once, they will find easier to do again. That's how almost all drug addictions start, with a person trying something out and telling themselves that they are strong enough to do it once and not do it again. However, once they have taken an abusive substance once, it is easier to take it again, telling oneself that just this once more doesn't count. But of course, as they do so, they are weakening their own will and starting to slide down the slippery slope of needing a 'fix' to be able to face themselves, their wounded self-esteem and their addiction.

"The other reason why a secret once told becomes more prone to escape from the watchful guard of the person who told it in the first place, is because a secret represents energy. Once it is told and heard, it will attach itself to the person who told it and the person who heard it in the form of energy that sits in the aura and accompanies them for as long as they remember it and as long as it is fueled by a concern not to tell. So, for example, someone might know something about another person and they might even be very good at keeping secrets, but when they see and talk to the person that the secret is about, they might not be able to stop themselves from alluding to this new piece of knowledge in the conversation, or they might simply treat the person differently, because they know something about them that they shouldn't know."

Grandmother took a short pause and I suddenly felt the burden of what she was saying.

"And there's more. If you hear secrets and you want to keep them, then you need to remember what you are supposed to keep secret and what is all right for you to know. You might be talking to someone and during the conversation you are trying to remember what you can say and what you can't say because you had promised not to. It can really get quite complicated, can't it?"

"Yes, I do recognize that scenario," I said, remembering meeting a friend who had been diagnosed with cancer and desperately trying to remember whether I was supposed to know that he was ill or not and therefore not being certain whether it was all right for me to ask about his health in specific terms, or whether I should keep to generalisms, which in the circumstances could have appeared callous and uncaring.

"So, if someone is about to tell you a secret, you can always ask the person not to tell you, because you don't want to clutter your mind and your memory with bits of information that you are not supposed to repeat. Providing, of course, that you realize beforehand that you are being told a secret and that the person telling you has the courtesy to ask whether you want to hear it or not."

"That's great advice, Grandmother," I said, "but it wasn't like that in this situation. I asked and the secret was an answer to my question."

"Well, first of all, I think you made a mistake asking about someone's private affairs, especially if it concerned a third person who wasn't there and especially if that person was someone close to you who you will be dealing with on an ongoing basis. A good rule is to never tell or listen to anything that concerns another person, unless you are prepared to say it in front of them. But, of course, then it would no longer be a secret, would it?"

"I guess not."

"There is one other consideration that you should know about. If you or anyone else tells another person a secret, it might just be that subconsciously they or you really want the secret to be told. So when you hear someone say, 'Please don't tell so and so that I told you,' you may be sure that the information will eventually reach this third person and that something in them wants you and that other person to know. How many people throughout history have jeopardized their situation by leaving a letter in an obvious place or telling a secret to the wrong person? Perhaps consciously they did not have the courage to come clean, but something in them was looking for alternative methods to get out of an uncomfortable situation and their subconscious mind found a way to do it."

"Really?" I couldn't quite believe it, but it was as though something in me knew that she was speaking the truth. She nodded and silence fell as we sat there for a moment, each one no doubt pondering our own secrets. I did wonder whether Brian really wanted me to know that he had had an affair with Alice. Perhaps he even wanted her to know that I knew. This thought process began to become quite complicated until it was interrupted by Grandmother.

"Do you know what a secretary is?" she asked.

"No, what is a secretary?" I responded.

"Someone who can keep secrets, of course. If you put the two words together—secret and tarry, you get secretary; i.e. someone who can hold on to secrets. I laughed, but the laughter did not sound very sincere, as I was still quite upset at what I had done.

Grandmother continued, "Also, think of the word secretion, which has the same root. A secretion, according to the dictionary, is a substance formed and discharged by a cell, tissue, gland or organ, or the process of producing such a discharge. Humans secrete energy all the time, so even if we don't tell a secret, the fact of knowing a secret means that we are radiating that knowledge silently, even without speaking. That is why you can pick up things about people without them telling you—you are translating their radiation and energy patterns from their aura. That is what clairvoyants do all the time."

After another brief pause, she said, "What can be done? Well, not much at this stage. Anyway, I can't really tell you what to do because then I would be carrying the responsibility for your actions, and you are a grown-up woman and need to become responsible for yourself. What I can do, though, is tell you what I would do in your situation, and then it is totally up to you to decide where to go from here. I will not take on responsibility for your actions."

"Yes Grandmother, please tell me," I requested pleadingly.

"I would wait, maybe a few days, maybe a week, maybe longer. Then, after things had cooled down a little, I would phone up and apologize and see where the conversation took us. From there I would make a judgment call whether to leave it for another week or two, or whether to try to find a way to patch it up. What do you think?"

"That sounds very reasonable," I said and thanked her from the bottom of my heart.

Chapter Ten

Lubricants

I waited a whole week, trying not to think about Brian. We spoke several times over the next few days, but it was always purely professional, working through a delivery, an order, a schedule change or seeking advice about how to deal with a client. The days were busy and I was getting used to the pace of working in a busy office. Alice seemed sympathetic to my situation and volunteered her time to listen to my guilt sessions. She was not at all apologetic for her part played in my unfolding drama and increasing misery and, having spoken about it with Grandmother, I no longer blamed her, only myself. It did take me a few days though, to be able to confess to her how I felt and how disappointed above all with myself I was, but slowly she persuaded me that she was willing to listen.

She was still insisting that she had never dated Brian and I did not believe her, though I pretended to accept her protestations of innocence on face value. Once she heard what had happened, I felt that her mood had changed and she became more accommodating and sympathetic to my emotional plight. She also volunteered a series of opinions about Brian that seemed a little bit too knowledgeable and too intimate to have been received second hand or to be those of an objective and impartial observer, but I decided not to dwell on these matters for too long.

That first night after my ill-fated conversation with Brian, I asked her again, requesting her honesty in return, "Are you sure you never went out with him? I just don't understand why he would lie about a thing like that."

Alice just laughed and replied that he was not her type. So I asked her, what her type was like and she replied, "I prefer a man who is not so serious and likes to have some fun and a good laugh. I work hard all day and I like to relax in the evening and go out with some friends for a drink or to a movie. Brian is always talking about serious matters and trying to save the world. I think we should leave saving the world to those who have the power and money to do so."

"Well, they haven't done a good job of it so far," I commented, but Alice was unwilling to continue the discussion.

Unexpectedly the next Sunday I was invited over to Grandmother's for tea and I was looking forward to an afternoon of cakes and chats, especially as I was still feeling fragile after my last encounter with Brian and my opinion of myself was not at an all time high. I did not suspect that she was going to lecture me that bright, sunny, warm afternoon, but it turned out to be an entire new lesson, even though it was delivered in the comfort of her living room, with tea and cookies on the table in front of me.

"I think courtesy is a dying word," she started and immediately I realized I was in for a lesson.

"Yes, why is that?" I asked as politely as I could muster.

"Well, there are so many things that people used to do as a matter of course and these days no one thinks about them any more."

"Like what, Grandma?"

"Well, I call these aspects of behavior lubricants because they lubricate dealings between people and make them easier, safer and more pleasant."

"Can you give me an example?" I asked and realized that this was a question I tended to ask her often.

"Sure, I'll not only give you an example, but a series of examples, and perhaps you can then find your own."

"All right, try me."

"So the first lubricant is to be mindful of another person's time and commitments. So, for example, when you phone someone at their home, do you ask if they have a moment and give them some idea of how long it will take? For example, 'Hi, this is Barbara and I need to ask you something. Do you have a minute?' Or, 'Hi, this is Barbara and I need to go over something with you. It could take ten minutes. Shall I call you back or is now a good time?'"

"I get the picture. Sometimes I remember to ask, but mostly I don't."

"Here's another lubricant. Do you offer to pay for gas if someone offers you a lift that takes more than just a few minutes to get there?"

"When I do, mostly people don't want it."

"Yes, but by asking you give them the opportunity to say no and to feel generous. And you can feel pleased with yourself that you did the right thing. Being at peace with yourself and knowing you did the right thing, that's the first rule. Helping someone else out and making them feel good because they have an opportunity to be generous, that's rule number two. Keeping relationships clean and clear, that's rule number three.

"And here's another lubricant. We have already spoken about this one—being on time. It sounds so very simple, and yet it is a very difficult aim to achieve for many people. There is a saying that punctuality is the courtesy of kings. Are you not queen of your domain?"

"I know I was late today. I'm sorry," I said, not quite sure whether I meant it or not, but I was certain she was talking about me and taking all these examples from my life.

"And don't take everything so personally," she quickly responded, as if reading my thoughts. "That's not a lubricant, that's just simple advice."

"Are there any other lubricants you would want to mention?" I asked.

"Here's one. When you want something, ask for it. So many times people expect others to guess what they want and then get upset if they don't take the hint. Learn to be outspoken about your wishes and desires. You never know when someone who really wants to help will hear you. And if you don't know how to do it direct, get someone else to ask for you. The other side of that coin says that if someone does something to upset you, find a way to tell them how you feel, because they might not even realize that they had done anything upsetting at all.

"And here is another courteous act. If someone you don't know very well meets you, especially if they make an appointment for the first time, drop them a line afterward saying how nice it was to meet them and thank them for their time. It is surprising what a difference a little bit of courtesy will make in furthering a relationship.

"If you are invited to stay with someone, make sure you thank them for their hospitality. When you stay at someone's house, you become part of their energy system, so when you leave, there are still lines of connection between you and your host or hostess. Therefore they will wonder whether you had arrived home safely and it is a courteous thing to do to phone them when you get home or send them a thank you note, telling them how much you enjoyed your stay (if you did, of course). Also, if you stay at someone else's house, remember to offer to help, say with the dishes or by preparing the food. And always strip the bed you had been sleeping in, to make it easier for your hostess to wash the dirty linen.

"There are so many small actions that make life easier for everyone and more pleasant. If you are invited to a meal, do you ask what you can bring? And even if the answer is, just bring yourself, do you still make sure that you bring something to enhance the evening, like a bottle of wine or some home-made cookies? It really is the gesture that counts, not so much the thing itself.

"It is really important, when you meet someone, to give them your undivided attention. So I suggest you turn off your cell phone when you are with someone and do not take a waiting call when you are on the phone with someone else, unless it is really important. When I was growing up we did not have cell phones or calls waiting and long distance calls had to go through an operator, but nevertheless we seemed to manage quite well without these conveniences. I would also suggest that you turn your television set off when someone is visiting you. It can be very annoying trying to have a conversation while competing with the radio or television.

"When you ask someone how they are, are you really interested? It makes a difference whether one asks out of habit and without any real meaning behind it, or whether you are genuinely interested in another person's wellbeing.

"And above all, do you try to be true to your word and at least attempt to fulfill all your promises? Words can be cheap, but it is so important, in order to build constructive and lasting relationships, to be a woman of your word.

"You see, these lubricants simply make dealings with people feel easier and cleaner. It is always important to take into consideration the feelings of the person you are dealing with, so that they may feel good about their dealings with you. I hope these small ideas can help you in your life and in your relationships."

After that short exchange I began to look around myself for behavior lubricants and soon compiled my own list. I realized, for example, that the words *thank you* and *please* were definitely lubricants and that people appreciated hearing them. Smiling was also on my list. It was really interesting to see what a smile could do. I was also beginning to learn to talk to people, even if they did not talk to me, just to initiate a conversation. It is amazing what you can learn about people just by opening your mouth and letting something polite come out, even if it is just a comment about the weather, the day or a news item.

I started practicing at work. I began to be more polite to the drivers, the installers and other people I worked with on a day to day basis, be it photographers photographing the installations or the designers, managers or accountants. I began to see the human beings behind the role and the profession, who were mostly just trying, like me, to earn a living. And as a result, I soon found that I was making new friends and that other people were becoming genuinely interested in my thoughts and wellbeing too.

Chapter Eleven

Tugging

I decided that my relationship with Brian was a lost cause and was simply not meant to be. Although my heart would beat faster every time he entered a room, I tried my best to ignore it, throwing myself into work and visiting my grandmother as often as I could, hoping for new insights and advice. I even started going out, first with Alice and then accepting invitations from other acquaintances and friends. However, I don't think I was stimulating company, because often as the dinner or cocktail conversations unraveled, I would fall into a daydream and imagine what the current event would be like, if only Brian was there. When brought abruptly back to reality by some question or well meaning concern, I would get by with a response or a remark, at the same time wishing I was back in my room, free to do as I pleased, like stare at the ceiling for hours, attempting to read a book or watching a silly program on TV.

And so the days slipped by and I felt I was trapped in a stagnant pool within the river of life, pulled along by the current but having little influence on my environment. Just bobbing along. And then something happened to jolt me out of my hibernation. I arrived at work that morning early, mindful that I had a lot to do and needed to catch up on my paperwork before supervising the loading of a truck for a very important customer in a downtown office block. This installation was going to be photographed for a prestigious magazine and needed to be flawless, with extra touches to make it visually appealing. I was quite looking forward to a busy, demanding day that would take my mind off my personal life and Brian.

It was a cold, crispy early fall day with the last leaves being blown around by intermittent gusts of wind. There was something ominous how the breeze would pick up, swirl around and die down as suddenly as it arrived. Almost as though the wind had a mind all of its own and was playing around with people and bits of paper, as well as the leaves, tossing and turning anything that it could find in its path that was light enough not to resist.

I was standing in the warehouse, supervising the loading of a truck, making sure that the right number of desks, bookshelves, filing cabinets, screens and office chairs were being packed onto the rig. There were two men loading up with the driver standing nearby, examining the paperwork ready for delivery, clipped to a clipboard. We were all trying to speed the process along, knowing that the delivery was scheduled for noon and it was already ten thirty. We were well aware that if we were late, then that would mean that the photographers and models would have to wait, and their time was valuable and costly. So the atmosphere was getting tense and none of our small group were really paying attention to what else was going on in the large warehouse space. The loading doors were open and we could feel the gusts of wind howling through the concrete building. Next to the space where we were loading the truck, there were two other loading bays on either side and both were occupied with two other teams who were also preparing for delivery at the same time.

Suddenly there was the most heart-rending cry and we all froze and stopped what we were doing, as if someone had pressed the pause button on a video machine. We looked in the direction from which the cry was coming and it soon became clear what had happened. The driver of the truck next to ours had backed up to make it easier to load a large and awkward sofa onto the back of the truck and in doing so he did not see that one of the warehouse workers was caught between the truck and a stack of boxes and crates. In a split second the truck was beginning to crush into the man's chest until the shrill cry which had caught our attention caused the driver to slam his foot on the brake and stop the truck from causing any further damage.

The driver then put the truck in gear, drove forward and the man who had been pinned to the stack of boxes fell to the floor in a crumpled heap. It all took place within a few seconds and as soon as we realized what had happened, we all ran towards the man to see if he was all right. He was not moving and his eyes were closed and none of the people who had gathered dared to move him.

"Are you alright?" I asked, kneeling down beside him, but he did not answer. At that moment Brian came out of his office, obviously sensing that something was wrong, and ran towards us. As soon as he saw the man on the floor, he pulled out his cell phone and dialed for an ambulance. He pushed his way through the crowd that had by now gathered, and knelt down next to me beside the man on the floor. He just delicately touched the man's cheek and the man opened his eyes and looked at Brian, obviously dazed and not quite comprehending what had happened. He then looked at us and could see our concerned looks, for his gaze next turned back to Brian as he seemed to mutely question him about what had just occurred.

"Are you in pain?" Brian asked.

"My chest …" the man clearly had difficulty breathing. "It hurts when I breathe." He was obviously in pain, but we all felt relief that he was alive. Brian placed his hand on the man's chest and you would think that the extra weight would have caused additional pain, but we could all see that the man felt relief as he took a deep sigh and the blood seemed to return to his face.

"You'll be all right," Brian said as he put his arm under the man's head, lifting it up slightly. "You are very lucky that it wasn't worse. A truck like that could have crushed you like an egg." The driver of the truck had joined the group and was watching as well.

"I am so sorry, Matt. I just didn't see you there." He couldn't quite believe what had happened. Just at that moment we could hear the sound of sirens in the distance, coming nearer fast, until the car stopped right outside the warehouse loading doors. Two men jumped out of the ambulance, ran to the back, opened the doors and pulled a stretcher out. We stepped aside and made room for them as they wheeled the stretcher into the warehouse. Brian was the first one to speak, "I think he has broken some ribs," he said and the two paramedics nodded as they knelt down and briefly examined the man, asking him to move his limbs and neck.

"We are now going to lift you up and place you on the gurney," the larger of the two said, as they skillfully and quickly lifted him onto the stretcher. Matt winced but it was only a brief moment and the stretcher was then extended to full height and wheeled to the back of the ambulance.

"I'll go with him," Brian said and started walking towards the ambulance. One of the paramedics was already in the cab. I quickly followed and volunteered to go as well. Brian looked at me as if to say, "No, you stay here," but he clearly changed his mind and nodded. I called out to one of the installers, "I'll see you on site. I can get there from the hospital." Brian was already in the back, sitting next to Matt who was now covered with a blanket and strapped onto the stretcher. I got into the back of the ambulance and the door was closed behind me. I sat on a bench next to Matt. Brian put his hand on Matt's chest and the ambulance drove off, with the siren blazing. We sat quietly for a moment as the car rushed through red lights, the traffic pulling aside and making room for us.

"You'll be all right, Matt," Brian said for the second time. I wondered how he could be so sure. Matt opened his eyes and gave Brian a weak smile. "You have a healing touch," he said. "I feel much less pain now."

"Just relax. You'll be well looked after," Brian responded, all the time with his hand on Matt's chest.

We were at the hospital in no time and at the emergency entrance Matt was quickly transported through the sliding doors. Brian and I followed behind him. There was a wait before anyone could examine Matt, though a doctor and a nurse came to look at him while he was still in the corridor, lying on a gurney. No doubt they were assessing his injuries and deciding how soon he needed to be seen. It took quite a long time and while we waited, sitting next to Matt, bringing him a glass of water and asking him from time to time how he felt, we hardly spoke a word and when we did it related to Matt and his state of health.

Finally a nurse came towards us, asking us to fill in a series of forms concerning Matt's particulars and his insurance details. Having completed the forms, Matt was finally wheeled off to have his X-ray taken.

As we sat there, I took my courage in both hands and said, "I am so sorry, Brian, about what happened with Alice. I shouldn't have said anything. I am sorry." He turned towards me and looked at me with a penetrating gaze that had a sadness attached to it. "I am sorry, too," he said. "I wish it hadn't happened."

"So do I," I responded. "If only I could take it back."

"That's the thing about life," he said. "You can't take anything back." He paused for a moment and added, "But you can learn from the experience. And I sincerely hope you do."

"Oh, I will, I will," I assured him and myself at the same time. "I already have."

"Oh, really?" he sounded incredulous.

"Yes, I think I have learned my lesson. Once and for all."

"I guess time will tell." He was now looking at the floor. There was a moment of silence and soon Matt was wheeled back from the X-ray room, lying on the gurney and waiting for the doctor on duty to have a look at his X-rays. He was looking calmer now and more color seemed to have returned to his cheeks. Brian got up and walked over to the gurney and asked him how he was feeling.

"Much better, thank you." Matt was smiling now. Our conversation had been interrupted and I had little hope that we could speak again. It didn't take long for the doctor to come along and speak with us. He asked if we were Matt's family, but we explained that we were colleagues from work.

"He has two broken ribs and his chest is quite bruised," the doctor said. "But there is nothing seriously wrong with him. However, we will keep him overnight for observation, just to be sure."

A hospital orderly soon came by to wheel Matt to a room on one of the wards. We followed the gurney to the elevator and onto the third floor of the hospital. Once we were on the ward, a nurse appeared and helped transport Matt from the gurney onto the bed. Matt moaned as he was moved. He was obviously in pain. We sat with him while his chest was bandaged, and as soon as he seemed settled and relaxed, we decided to leave him, having promised to call his wife to let her know what had happened. Brian assured me that he would look after the details and speak to Matt's wife.

We left the hospital together and as we were going down to the lobby in the elevator, I said to Brian, "You really do have healing powers. It was amazing to see the change in that man the moment you put your hand on his chest."

"Yes, I know," he replied. "It frightens me. I don't know what it means."

"It means you can help people."

The elevator arrived and soon we were walking through the main entrance and onto the street. I knew what I needed to do next.

"I better go to the offices of Sterling Silver Insurance," I said. "There's a photo shoot planned and I need to make sure all the furniture is properly set up."

"All right, I'll see you tomorrow."

"All right. Bye." It was so quick. The next minute he was hailing a taxi, standing in the middle of the road and before I knew it he was gone. I felt grief, as if someone had died or some opportunity had been taken away from me. I caught another taxi and went downtown toward the imposing Sterling Silver Building. The installation was in the Executive Suite on the twelfth floor and as I arrived, the installers were still putting the various pieces of furniture together while the models were drinking cups of coffee and chatting. The photographer and his assistant were trying to set up their equipment, while various Sterling Silver employees were coming in and out of the office, no doubt curious about what was going on. Everything looked like a mess and as it was already getting late, I could see that the whole day could easily be wasted if something wasn't done immediately.

I first approached the three installers and asked them to move all their tools from the two offices that were complete, or at least looked complete, according to the plans. I then asked for some help from the Sterling employees in cleaning the place up. I next got the installers to move to the other end of the office suite to leave us some room to operate in. I got the photographer and his assistant to set up the lights and cameras in the first office and finally I got the models and their agent and make-up artist to get ready. It is amazing how quickly the atmosphere changed from chaotic to organized, from a sense of anything goes to industrious and working towards a result. I got the models (two women and a man) to sit behind the three desks in the first office and very soon the first photographs were being taken. I had to go to the next floor down to find some genuine files, books, magazines and those little objects that people who work in offices bring from home to make their workplaces more individual. A few pictures, plants, calendars, pens and mouse pads added a bit of color and so we were in business.

It was funny, but the models sitting behind desks just did not look genuine enough, so as the pictures were being taken, I went scouting for some other people who would look good in a picture. I went back to the eleventh floor and knocked on the first office door I could see. The name on the door said "Andrew Johnson, Sales Representative."

"Come in," he said and as I opened the door I was looking straight at him. He was perfect. He looked like an office worker, but he looked good at the same time. He had taken his jacket off and he was sitting in his shirt and tie, with the sleeves of his blue shirt rolled up.

"Can I borrow you for a moment?" I asked. He just sat there, not comprehending. "We are taking some photographs upstairs for a magazine and I need someone to sit at a desk."

"Oh, all right. But it better not take long, because I need to go and see a client."

"No, just a few minutes. Please." He smiled and got up, pulling his jacket off the back of the chair as he did so. He started walking towards the door at the same time putting his jacket on.

"So where are we going?" he asked as the door closed behind us.

"Just one floor up," I said.

When we got to the Executive Suite on the twelfth floor, I introduced him to the crew, as if I had known him for a while. "This is Andrew Johnson," I said, "and he is going to help us. Let's have Andrew sit at the desk by the window. He'll be the boss and you two girls can sit over there and be his assistants."

"What about me?" the young male model asked, disappointed to have to give his desk up to an amateur. I had it all worked out. "You can be a petitioner. Come and stand here by the first desk. You are asking for an appointment."

By five o'clock we had over a hundred pictures and a whole variety of angles, combinations and pieces of furniture recorded. We were all exhausted, but the installation was finished, except for a few minor details that needed to be corrected the next day. The place looked great and I was feeling really pleased with myself. At ten past five, just as I was getting ready to leave, having had a final look at the place, an older gentleman walked into the room, came straight up to me as if I had been waiting for him and introduced himself as vice-president of Sterling Silver. He said he had come down from his office specially to have a look around.

"Nice job," he said, as I took him on a guided tour of the seven offices that comprised the twelfth floor. "It really does look good. I want to thank you in the name of the company."

"Don't thank me," I replied modestly. "The thanks should go to the company I work for. It's their designs, their workmanship and their installation."

"Yes, of course, but I heard how you came in and sorted everyone out. That was your work. I don't believe we would have had an office that is ready to be moved into, if you weren't here. And I have movers coming in here early tomorrow bringing in computers, files, books and everything else that will be needed to start our workday on Monday morning. If it wasn't ready, we'd be in trouble and we would lose some precious work time, which means loss of money. So, to cut this speech short, I would like to thank you in the name of the company and in my own name, too."

"Well, in that case," I conceded graciously, "I accept your thanks."

"So, as a way of saying thank you, please allow me to invite you to our Halloween party which will be held next week. Here is an invitation." He reached into his jacket pocket and pulled out a printed white card. "I look forward to seeing you there."

"Thanks a lot. Thanks," I said. He started walking towards the door. I put the invitation away, gathered up my things and followed him out the door. By the time I got to the corridor and the elevator, he had gone.

On Monday, as soon as I arrived at the office, people started asking me about Matt. Apparently news had gotten around about his accident and miraculous recovery and people were beginning to say that Brian had healing hands. I tried to ignore the rumor and certainly decided not to add fuel to the fire, but also realized that there was a whole group of people who saw him lay his hand on Matt's chest, as Matt was lying in pain on the warehouse floor, and also saw how Matt's face had changed and relaxed, literally within seconds. So when anybody asked how Matt was doing, I simply responded, "Remarkably well," and told them that he had been released from hospital the next day.

That afternoon Brian walked into my office. He didn't call, he didn't knock, he just walked in, as if he owned the place, straight up to my desk and said, "Thank you for taking care of the Sterling Silver installation on Friday. I hear you really sorted it out." I looked up at him and smiled. "Just doing my job," I said modestly.

"Oh no, I think it was more than that. I am sure that after what happened that morning, it was the last thing you wanted to do. And you did a very good job. I've got pictures to prove it."

It was at that moment that I noticed he was holding an envelope in his hand. He opened the envelope and pulled out a bunch of photographs and placed them on my desk. He took the chair that was in front of my desk and brought it to the other side of the desk and sat down beside me.

"Have a look at these," he said. "Jeremy brought them in first thing this morning. We had a meeting with the advertising department and we sent three of them to the Office Furniture magazine." I started looking at the pictures. They did look good, but the best ones were the ones with Andrew, the sales representative in the foreground and the models in the background.

"Are these the ones you sent to OF?" I asked.

"Yes," he replied. "Who is this guy? He looks great. He's a natural."

"Oh, just a sales rep from Sterling Silver, who happened to be around," I replied. I could feel Brian's presence so near to me and it was quite hard to concentrate on the pictures that were lying on the desk in front of me.

"They are talking about you at the office today," I said, as he started to gather up the pictures.

"Oh, what do you mean?" he asked.

"They say you have healing hands. They saw what you did with Matt on Friday."

"Well, it's true." He was holding the pictures in one hand and the envelope in the other, as he suddenly swiveled his chair around, leaned over and kissed me. He really caught me unaware of what he intended to do, but after the first shock, unsure of what was going on, I relaxed into the kiss, as I felt tingles all over and a burning sensation running through my entire body. My arms were soon around him and his arms, while still holding the pictures, were around me as we embraced for what seemed like a long time. Finally, he tore himself away and said, "I didn't mean for this to happen."

"But it did," I said, desperately wanting to hold on to the moment.

"Yes, it did," he admitted. "We'll talk later."

"When?" I needed to know. He was already getting up. "I'll pick you up tomorrow at eight and we'll go somewhere quiet." He picked up the chair and replaced it in front of the desk.

"All right. I'll be ready." He walked out of the office, gently closing the door behind him. I sat there for a moment, unable to concentrate, unable to move or think. I felt my whole world had changed in that moment and would never be the same again.

I went to see Grandmother that evening and she was looking fit and ready for another session. Her first comment, when she saw me as she opened the door was, "You look really well. Alive and vibrant. What happened?"

"I met someone at work," I replied.

"Who is he?" she asked.

"He's a colleague," I said, and then I corrected myself, "He's my boss."

"Is he anything more than that?" she asked, looking intensely into my face, as if trying to read something subtle that might have been there.

"Not yet," I answered, "but we've been on a couple of dates and I'm going out with him again tomorrow night."

"Is he the same guy that you were so upset about some months ago because you repeated something he had told you in confidence?"

"Yes, that's him. You see, you advised me to wait and now finally we are going out together."

"Well, he is certainly doing something to you because you look more alive than I've seen you for a long time."

"In what way?" I asked.

"Now you're tugging," she said.

"What do you mean?" I asked.

"That's a good subject for tonight," my grandmother said. "Tugging. People do it all the time. Let me explain.

"All dealings represent a flow of energy—it passes from us to others and from others to us. Usually there is an exchange both ways and mostly there is not much difference in a person's energy levels before and after. This is the casual conversation, the brief encounter, the business call. But even in these circumstances there are those we prefer to deal with and those we would rather avoid. As I explained to you before, there are energy givers and energy takers, though mostly we are both. Sometimes we meet a person who means more to us than an average acquaintance and they represent food. Perhaps a friendship is formed or a more lasting relationship and we spend time with those who provide us with energy food. But if we feel our food supply is getting low, or our self-esteem is calling out for a boost or our ego needs confirmation, we will set out to get some extra energy and this is done in many ways.

"Everyone needs confirmation and most people do not get enough of it. The world trades in insecurity and lack of confidence, and to counter-balance this we have developed subtle ways of a practice that I call tugging. For example, think of times when you have used phrases like, 'Tell me more,' 'Do you really like it?' or 'What else did he say?' These are examples of expressions asking for more food—it is not even the information that we seek, but the transmission held within the words. Sometimes we will even pretend we do not hear, just to be able to hear something again. A man says to a woman 'I love you,' and she hears him perfectly well, but she can't help herself tugging for more, so she says, 'What did you just say?'"

I had to smile because I suddenly remembered how that very afternoon Brian had said that we would talk and I was very quick to ask him when, thus tugging to receive a commitment. It occurred to me that women are especially good at tugging.

"Another example of tugging is making someone ask you to do something more than once, by saying 'no' the first time, even though you know perfectly well that you are going to do it in the end. Complaint and grudging are other examples of tugging, aimed to solicit sympathy or guilt. Have you ever heard someone say something like, 'You just go off and enjoy yourself while I stay here and do all the work,' even though they don't mean it and say it to cause an opposite effect?" I had to admit that I had.

"How about someone asking, 'How come I always end up cleaning up your mess?' There can even be extreme cases of tugging when a person makes themselves sick, just to get attention. This can either be done consciously, in which case the person pretends to feel worse than they really do, or unconsciously, because the brain obligingly produces the disease to match the person's wish.

"One of the greatest symptoms of tugging is jealousy. Jealousy is born of possession and it implies that one person has a claim to another, to their time, or that they have the right to dictate their behavior. Our language allows a person to say, 'my friend,' 'my husband,' 'my girlfriend,' but no one can possess another person—each human is born free and if they choose to spend time with another, it should be because they want to.

"Each person is unique and no two fingerprints are the same. Each spirit life represents a bit of God and with an exchange between people webs of connection can be established that are not possessive, but enhancing, not marred with jealousy, but graced with gratitude that another person exists. Behind all life is the Creator and to love one person in a possessive way is denying the other person their freedom. To be jealous is to limit one's possibility and blind oneself to the beauty of all life.

"The greatest gift anyone has to give is the gift of their time. Be glad that another person wants to offer you this gift and if you want more from them, make sure you have so much to offer in return that the other person would want to spend time with you. Do not demand. If a woman is free to leave at any time and has the means to do so, the man she lives with can be sure that she is with him out of choice, not economic necessity, which will give him a great security and continued satisfaction. The most successful relationships are those within which both partners want to be with each other, where every moment is fresh and new and where both have the freedom to be themselves and develop in their own unique way.

"The other side of tugging is giving. Have you noticed that when someone gives, you soon want to make a return? It works the other way as well. When you give to another, they will want to pay back as well. Give to receive. Rather than tugging and demanding, learn to be generous first. Life pays the giver back, perhaps not immediately, and perhaps not the way you might expect, but, you will see, it works in the end—when you learn to give, you will receive.

"Surprise your friends and acquaintances with acts of kindness and cease tugging. Practice generosity as a way of life and you will be astonished how much it can change your life and increase your energy supply.

"There is a third level beyond tugging and giving, both of which can be seen to be two expressions of the same process. Rather than looking to another person for your food supply and for confirmation, a third vector approach would be to establish a partnership towards a purpose that is higher than both. I call this process triggering.

"If people continue to tug at each other, then they have only their own energies to draw on, but if they can bring together their joint efforts to connect to something higher and bring into the situation an essence or a presence that enhances both, then they will have triggered a process that can satisfy the needs of both and more. With tugging one partner gets fed, while the other supplies the food. With triggering, not only both are enhanced, but a situation is created within which a third thing can happen. To have a higher purpose is to be collecting a medium within which new energy presences can form up and appear, thus bringing meaning to the lives of those who contribute to this situation.

"If you want to know more about tugging, giving and triggering, observe carefully your conversations and dealings, and try to distinguish between these three scenarios. Decide which situation you would want to promote in your life and find ways to do so. I cannot tell you what to do or how to behave, I can only alert you to the many possibilities that unfold in front of you every moment of every day."

I realized at that moment that I could be much more in control of my own life and yet again decided to take up the challenge of becoming my own support system.

"So to recap," Grandmother concluded, "tugging is a demand for a greater supply of energy; giving is supplying the energy and triggering is a situation within which a person, a couple or a group of people cause a new supply of universal power to be tapped into, thus enhancing all participating parties."

Chapter Twelve

Healing

It was my mother on the phone. I was getting ready for my big date and she was calling me about Grandmother. There seemed to be a pattern in my relationship with my mother. She was always away when I needed her, accompanying her husband on jobs that took him from state to state, from one company to another, consulting here, there and everywhere. But when I was doing fine, she would inevitably call and ask me to do the impossible. It seems that I was her buffer against guilt, so it was always me that was supposed to look after Grandma, or make sure my younger brother was all right. Always her willing servant, I seemed to comply with her wishes and put my own needs to one side to fulfill her demands. This time it was no different.

"Go and see Grandmother," she said in that whining voice of hers. I would give anything just to get her to stop. "I have just spoken to her and she doesn't sound well. I'm worried about her." Then go and see her yourself, I thought and immediately felt uncharitable and selfish. After all, I loved my grandmother, for it was her that had looked after me from my early teens, after my mother remarried and went traveling around the country from one place to another in a never ending cycle of chasing the growing technological needs of expanding companies. My stepfather was some kind of computer expert who knew how to solve all kinds of networking and programming problems and glitches. Good for the family economy;

not so good for us children longing for more quality time with our parents. So I knew right away which way this was going to go. She knew how to play on my guilt and get me to do what she wanted.

"All right," I said, "I'll go over now."

"Good girl. I knew I could count on you. Thanks. Grandmother will be very glad to see you."

"I know," I sighed. "Bye Mum." I put the phone down, wondering how on earth I was going to fit everything in. I looked at my watch. It was already six o'clock and Alice wasn't home yet. Perhaps if I hurried up, I could go and see Grandma and be back for eight. That seemed a reasonable solution. I didn't think I would need more than twenty minutes to get there, another twenty to get back and an hour to spend with her should be enough. That left another twenty minutes to get ready, but to be on the safe side, I should try and be out the door in fifteen minutes. I quickly got the shower going, undressed, got in and washed my hair. I was out in about five minutes (quite a record), drying myself, when I heard the front door key and Alice's voice, calling from the living room.

"Hello, anyone home?" I came out of the bathroom with a towel wrapped around me. She was putting some groceries away into the kitchen cupboards, saying, "I thought I'd do some shopping. That's why I'm late." She turned to face me and looked surprised.

"And where are you going?" she asked.

"Out," I said, not wanting to say anything more about where and with whom, but knowing that the next question would inevitably come. And it did. "With whom? Did you meet someone nice at that photo shoot Friday?" I hesitated, but there was no point in lying because he would be coming to pick me up at the house anyway.

"It's Brian," I sighed. I could feel my shoulders drooping, waiting for the verbal response that I knew was coming.

"But I thought that was all over," she exclaimed. "You said you weren't going to see him again. I thought we agreed that he was just a womanizer looking for his next conquest. So what do you think you are doing getting all dolled up for him?"

"I'm not getting all dolled up," I protested weakly. "I've just washed my hair, that's all."

"Well, you don't wash your hair when we go out to the movies or for a drink."

"That's true," I replied, and turned to go into my bedroom to get dressed.

"Now wait a minute," Alice continued, undeterred by the sight of my back. "Why are you doing this? It will only bring you heartache and disappointment." I turned round to face her. She had taken a few steps in my direction and although she was now closer to me, I noticed that her voice was louder and so was mine when I asked, "What is it to you? What do you care who I see or do not see? If I wasn't living here, you wouldn't even know."

"It's because I care about you. And you are living here. And it's not just anybody you're seeing; it's a man with a reputation. And I got you the job that put you in his way! It will make me feel partly responsible when you get hurt. I warned you before and you ignored my warning. He's no good, Barbara, he's no good!" The more she was getting upset, the more stubborn I felt about defending my freedom to do what I felt was best for me.

"Well, that's just too bad," I said, "because I am going to see him."

"All right," she lifted her hands, as if she was bailing out of the situation, "but don't come crying on my shoulder when he hurts you again!" I noticed she said when, not if. This time I turned around and kept on walking to my room. It was getting late and if I was going to go and see Grandma and get back in time to meet Brian when he came to pick me up, I needed to get going. I started to dress and I was just fastening my skirt, when there was a knock on the bedroom door and Alice opened the door to my room without waiting for my reply. She stood there, illuminated by the light from the corridor, as she rested both arms on either side of the door frame.

"Don't go," she said and she sounded pleading now. I couldn't believe how passionate she was about this whole affair.

"Listen, Alice," I tried to explain. "I am an adult. If it is a mistake, I will soon find out. But let me make my mistakes. You can't keep trying to protect me and mothering me. Let me find out for myself if he is good or not good for me."

"But I feel responsible. You're staying in my house and I don't want to worry about you every time you go out that door."

I was really getting annoyed now.

"Then don't worry, Alice. Get a life! That will give you something to worry about." Well, that did it; she really exploded after that.

"I do have a life!" She was yelling now. "It's you who are behaving like a spoiled brat." I could not understand what was going on. I lost my temper, too.

"You're just saying that because you still want him for yourself!" Well, that was definitely the wrong thing to say. Alice just looked at me and I could almost see the words freezing in her mouth and not able to escape her throat. She stood there for a moment, then finally she whimpered in a very quiet voice, "That's not true." I could tell she was close to tears. "That's not true," she repeated as she turned on her heel and walked away down the corridor. I felt exhausted. I sat on the bed for a moment, wondering what had happened. I then followed her down the corridor and into the living room where she got hold of a tissue and sat down on the sofa. I stood there, barefoot, fastening my skirt as I spoke.

"I am sorry," I said. "I didn't mean that. I'm sorry."

Alice was blowing her nose. "Yes, you did. Yes, you did," I heard in between the sniffles. "You still think that we had an affair and I am a woman scorned." I thought about it for a moment and had to admit to myself that she was right.

"And are you?" I asked.

"Of course not. I think it's more a case of the man being scorned and now he is taking it out on me, through you."

"Oh no, I don't think that's true. I don't think that's true at all." We both fell silent. I think we were both pretty exhausted at that point and there wasn't that much more to say. We had said it all and we would never agree as to what the truth of the situation was. I looked at my watch. It was a quarter to seven. Somehow that scene had taken forty-five minutes. There was no way I would be able to get to Grandmother's house and back and spend time with her and get ready and dry my hair, which was still wet, all within an hour and fifteen minutes.

I went into the bathroom and closed the door behind me. I felt dreadful. I didn't want to argue, I hate antagonizing people and I much prefer people to like me than hate me. But I also was looking forward to tonight's meeting with Brian and didn't want anything to spoil that. I also needed to think what to do to keep my promise to my mother and somehow fit in everything I needed to do. I looked in the mirror. The woman looking back at me looked tired and my wet hair was messy and clinging in strands to my head. I picked up a towel and started drying my hair, looking around at the same time for the dryer.

As I began drying my hair, I made a decision. I would take Brian with me to see Grandmother. It might cheer her up and I also felt that those two would hit it off. They both seemed to have some kind of healing power and I felt that they could benefit from meeting each other. Suddenly I felt relieved and relaxed, no longer rushing to fit everything in a short space of time.

I emerged from the bathroom fifteen minutes later, ready and looking more like myself. I took a deep breath and decided that I would sit with Alice and try to help her work through this emotional trauma she seemed to be experiencing. I was beginning to see this whole situation as her problem, something she was going through, perhaps due to stress or loneliness. Who knows. I always felt that the most difficult thing to understand about life were the intricacies of another person's mind and soul.

As I walked into the living room, I saw that she was still sitting on the sofa, sipping a cup of tea she had obviously made herself and staring into space.

"Are you alright?" I asked. She looked at me briefly and dabbed her eyes with a tissue she was holding in her right hand.

"Sure, I'm OK." She looked away. I walked towards the sofa and sat down next to her.

"I'm sorry I upset you," I said. "I really didn't mean to. I think the whole thing was childish."

"I agree," she replied. "Let's not talk about it any more."

"All right," I agreed. "Are we going to be able to continue sharing?" I needed to know.

"Why not?" She looked at me again. "People argue and we are no different."

"Yes, I guess so, but sometimes there are irreconcilable differences."

She was smiling now. "We're not married, you know. You can leave any time," she said.

"I know, but I need to be able to get on with the person I share with." We sat there for a while, trying to establish a new truce between us, but avoiding the subject that was really bothering both of us; Brian's name never came up in that conversation.

The doorbell rang promptly at eight o'clock and I quickly gathered my coat and bag. "I'll see you later," I said as I walked towards the door.

"All right," she replied feebly, and I could almost feel the tangle of emotions that were playing with the thoughts in her head. I quickly opened the door and just as quickly closed it behind me, before Brian, who was standing on the doorstep, had a chance to say anything or look into the interior of the house.

"That was fast," he commented, before even greeting me. "I guess I'm not welcome here."

"I don't know. And I don't want to find out," I replied diplomatically, not wanting to go into the whole story of what had happened earlier that evening. I smiled at him and changed my expression and tone of voice, trying to sound cheerful and positive.

"Hi. Nice to see you." I stood close to him and he kissed me on the cheek.

"Hi. Let's go somewhere private," he whispered. We started walking down the stairs towards the street.

"Well, I need to see my grandmother. She is not well and I promised my mother I would look in on her tonight. Can you come with me?" I could feel him hesitating, so I hastily added, "It won't take long." Brian stopped at the bottom of the stairs to the house and looked at me. "All right," he replied. "Where does this grandmother of yours live?"

When she opened the door, she looked a bit pale and her movements were slow, but she did not look at all surprised to see Brian.

"Come on in," she said before we had a chance to explain, and started walking towards the living room. We followed her and as she was walking in front of us, she added, "I just put the kettle on for a lovely cup of tea." It made me think that this obsession with tea making and drinking must have been caused by the remnants of her British blood, which still circulated in her veins. We walked through the living room and stood by the stove in her small kitchen, watching as she poured out three cups.

"Grandma, this is Brian," I said, and she replied, "Nice to meet you, Brian," without even turning around, as she continued to go about the business of making tea.

"Nice to meet you, too," Brian replied and we stood there waiting for her to finish the tasking of pouring the tea. Just as she always did, she had made tea in the teapot, the old fashioned way and poured the essence through the strainer, before adding water from the kettle. She then handed us our rose patterned china cups and saucers, and said, "Let's go to the living room. There's milk and sugar on the table there." We walked back into the living room and Grandma sat on the sofa. I settled down beside her and Brian sat in the old armchair that I remembered Grandfather used to love.

"So what brings you here?" she asked and immediately proceeded to answer her own question, "No doubt that busybody mother of yours sent you, so instead of going on a nice date you ended up coming here."

"It's all right, Grandma, I wanted to come," I only half lied. "And I'm sure Brian doesn't mind." Brian sat forward in the armchair. "No, I don't mind at all," he said and smiled.

"Well, as you see, I'm all right. I'm still alive and I'm not planning to check out any time soon."

"That's a relief," I replied, trying to keep my voice light, but watching her carefully, knowing that I would have to report on her health to my mother within the next twenty-four hours. "Brian has healing hands," I changed the subject. I hadn't planned to say that; it just came out of me. Grandma looked at Brian with a long, penetrating gaze.

"Oh, really?" she half said and half asked.

"It would seem so," he said modestly. "I don't know why, but when I lay my hands on someone who is ill, they seem to calm down and get better faster," he added.

"Then you have a gift, son. And with a gift like that comes responsibility. But don't start bragging and telling folks about it, or you won't be able to do anything else with your life. On the other hand, if you don't use your gift to help people, you'll be wasting it." She poured some milk from a small china pitcher, then picked up her cup and sipped the tea.

Brian put his cup back onto the saucer on the coffee table in front of him. "But that's a contradiction," he said. "How can I help people if I don't tell them about it?" he asked. Grandma shrugged her shoulders.

"That's for you to figure out," she said. "You must find your own limitations and look after your gift, as you would look after an expensive jewel. If you exhaust yourself, you will lose both your gift and your health. If you don't use it, you will lose it as well."

"Thank you for the advice." Brian picked up his teacup again.

"There is one other thing you need to know," Grandma said.

"What's that?" Brian asked.

"If you can cure, you can also inflict. If you can heal, you can also cause someone to become ill. So you must be careful what you think and what you wish for. Above all, be careful who you get mad at. They could become your victim. The ability to heal means that there is a power that lives inside you that can affect other people, for better or for worse." She sat back on the sofa and continued, "I know because I've been a healer all my life, but I've kept it very quiet." She paused for a moment and then turned to Brian with a question, "What do you think would happen if it was discovered that you could cure AIDS with the touch of a hand?"

Brian took a deep breath, as no doubt the image unfolded in his head; then he replied, "That would be so amazing. I could help so many people ..."

"Wrong," Grandma interrupted. "They would lock you up in some laboratory to see if they could produce a drug from your blood or tissue or DNA; they would fly you around the world to cure the people they would want you to cure and within a couple of years you would be dead. And if the government and the pharmaceutical industry didn't get you, you would end up being inundated with requests and curing thousands of people, and you would be dead within a year."

Brian shifted uneasily in his chair, and began to say, "I don't think ..." when Grandma interrupted him. "Look at me," she said. "I've been healing all my life. But who is there who can heal me? Nobody. So here I am, wasting away and I know my time is approaching, but there is nothing I can do."

"No, Grandma, I am sure you will be around for a long time yet. You will probably outlive us all." Grandmother turned towards me. Her voice was gentle and persuasive when she said, "No, sweetie. It's no use trying to fight it. When the time comes, it comes and it is coming. I made my choices in life and caused my energies to be depleted and for my immune system to be run down. Now I am paying for that extravagance. But do you know what? I don't regret a thing and if I had my time over, I would do it all again. Because I can look back on my life and there are many people that I have been able to help and restore to good health. Like this one here." She put her hand on my knee. "You might not know it, but I dissolved a cancerous tumor in your breast and you wouldn't be here with us today if you hadn't come to see me about it." I put my hand over hers.

"I know, Grandma, I know. And I am very grateful."

"No need to be grateful to me. Be grateful to that which gave you life and wanted you to be here. Try and find out what that is—that is how you can repay me."

"Sure, Grandma. I'm working on it." We sat for a moment in silence, sipping our tea, until Grandmother broke the silence, "All right, it's time you were out of here. You've seen me, you can tell your mother that I'm all right and she needn't fuss. I'll give you all ample warning when my time draws near. In the meantime, go and enjoy your evening."

"Thanks, Grandma." I leaned over and kissed her on the cheek. She never was one for effusive displays of emotion, so she just patted me on the back in a brief embrace and got up to escort us to the door.

We didn't go far. It was a small Italian restaurant around the corner that I liked and it was getting too late to start adventuring looking for new cuisines. Besides, there was a lot to talk about and I think we both felt urgent about getting started. So we sat down and even the hasty approach of the waiter with his white apron and professionally smooth subservient pose felt like an intrusion, at least to me.

"What can I get you to drink?" he asked and proceeded to entice our appetites with a list of specials. We asked for water and pleaded for some time to think, and as soon as he was gone, we started talking, both at once.

"I just want to apologize for springing that visit on you. It was an unexpected call from my mother ..." I said, while he was saying, "Your grandmother is a very interesting lady ..." We both laughed as we tried to slow down and listen to each other. In the silence our glasses of water arrived and we were left alone again.

"She is a healer. She cured my cancer," I said.

"Really?"

"Yes, she has a gift and she has been helping people all her life. But it hasn't brought her riches or even appreciation, or companionship, or fame. And now it is making her sick."

"I can see that, but with me it will be different."

"What makes you think you are different? There are people out there who want to destroy healers because they are making their drugs and chemotherapies redundant. I had a very hard time convincing my doctor that I no longer needed any of her cures, like chemo or radiation or surgery, despite the fact that the X-rays and scans showed that the cancer was gone. 'Just to be sure it doesn't come back,' the specialist kept saying."

"I am so sorry that you had to go through all that."

"Well, don't be. I am fine now and it was the greatest lesson of my life. I am a different person now, thanks to that ordeal."

"I can imagine that that would be a life changing experience."

"It certainly was."

After those few minutes of conversation, the waiter was back and we needed to make our choices. As I contemplated the specials, I smiled to myself because I could hear my mother's voice in my head, as she had said to me when I was beginning to go out with boys, "When you go out on a date," she had said, "especially a first date, choose something that you can eat elegantly." So, pasta was out and I settled for a salad, especially since I didn't feel hungry any more. There was too much going on inside that I needed to get out for there to be room to put a lot more in. Brian chose the grilled salmon and finally I felt there was the time and space to speak about our unfortunate beginnings and to prod him to find out whether there was any hope for the future in all this.

"About Alice," I began, but Brian interrupted me. He leaned forward and took my hand.

"This is not about Alice. This is about us. You promised to keep a secret and you broke your promise. It doesn't matter what it was about. It could have been anything. But what concerns me is whether you can keep a promise. I am afraid I will always be wondering whether a secret shared is secure with you."

"I am not going to start promising now. I want to be careful about secrets and promises. So perhaps it would be best if you didn't tell me any secrets. At least for a while."

"I can agree to that," Brian said and released my hand to take a drink of water. "There is another aspect to this," he said after a moment of silence.

"What is that?" I asked.

"Well, I don't think you believed me. I think you still think Alice told you the truth."

"No, I don't any more," I replied truthfully.

"Ah, but you did," he said hastily.

"Well, to be honest, for a while I wasn't sure. But judging from her reaction to the fact that I was going out with you tonight, I think you told the truth and I think she still cares about you."

"That could be true."

A moment passed and he said, "I don't want to talk about Alice. I want to talk about you. Do you think it is wise for us to keep seeing each other? I have always been told that you should not date anyone you work with. Alice is a case in point."

"It might not be wise, but I would ask an alternative question: what do you want?"

"I want to but I am still not convinced you can keep a secret."

"I can. I know my saying that doesn't prove anything, but give me the opportunity to prove it to you. And if you want to keep our affair quiet, you will have to meet me in quiet places, like here."

Brian sighed, thought for a moment and finally declared, "All right, I am prepared to give it a try."

I was ecstatic and excited, but I did not want to show my enthusiasm, so all I did was say, "So am I."

At that moment the waiter came back with our dishes and, as we were both hungry, we sat there for a while munching the food with occasional remarks complimenting the chef and the choice of restaurant. It is true, it was a fabulous place to eat, always so fresh and tastefully presented, too, with little extras like fresh bread with an olive oil and herbal dip, and a freshly baked cookie with the coffee.

So I wondered what this meant for our future, both at work and in private, but kept telling myself that it is best to progress one step at a time and that the future did have a way of revealing itself, no matter how our efforts might try to mould and shape it to our own convenience.

"You know, if only I hadn't said anything to Alice," I started, but Brian interrupted me.

"I need to tell you about the two *ifs*," he said. "In Polish there are two separate words for each one." I was intrigued. Brian continued, "One is for the past and there is a different word for the future. The *if* for the past—gdyby—is futile, because it cannot happen; you cannot reverse the past. The *if* for the future, though—jeżeli [pronounced yezheli]—is full of possibilities."

I thought about this for a moment and decided to adopt the futuristic *if* as my friend. We had started our relationship on the wrong foot, or so it seemed to me at the time, but I was hopeful that our affair still had the chance of blossoming into something more substantial.

Chapter Thirteen

Roles

The next day I was standing by the reception desk, having a chat with Alice, trying hard to preserve the vestiges of our tested and uncertain friendship, without telling her too much about Brian or about my growing feelings for him. She was being cordial, but not saying too much and I was saying a lot of totally irrelevant things. Amazing how much there is to say when you are trying deliberately not to say too much.

As we were chatting, a young woman walked through the door and I could immediately tell she was a dancer. I've always been able to recognize a dancer when I saw one, perhaps because I had been to ballet school as a child myself. I read somewhere that a dancer's spine is different to everyone else's spine and they certainly hold themselves in a very erect and elegant way. It above all shows in the head and neck. She was walking tall and she had a certain refinement that, I believe, comes from dedication to one's craft and hard work.

She walked straight up to the reception desk and asked, coming right to the point, "Where can I find Brian Polowski?" We both looked at her with curiosity, wondering what this girl could possibly want with Brian at a furniture delivery warehouse.

"I'll take you to him," I volunteered and Alice smiled in agreement. "Yes, she can show you the way," she said and immediately started typing on her computer keyboard.

As I was walking towards the warehouse and Brian's office, I started talking with the girl. I first introduced myself and then asked her if she was a buyer, knowing that the answer would most certainly be negative.

"No," she laughed nervously, "I'm not a buyer. I've come because my mother is a neighbor of Matt Bendicks. Do you know Matt?" she asked.

"Yes, I do. He works in the warehouse here," I replied.

"Well, Mr. Polowski did some healing on Matt and he made a remarkable recovery," the girl continued. "Now Matt is going around telling everyone about Mr. Polowski's healing hands."

I still did not understand how that would bring the girl to our workplace.

"Well, I am a dancer and I twisted my ankle," she continued and it was at that moment that I noticed a small limp in her step. So, I was right, after all. She was a dancer! "Twisted ankle means no work," she said, "so I wonder if Mr. Polowski can help me."

"I don't know if he will be able to see you," I said, concerned that the girl might be causing trouble for Brian by being there. "He is quite busy and I am not sure this is the best place for a healing." I slowed down my step, hoping that the girl would reconsider her action. But she was undaunted and kept on walking, almost as if she knew where she was going. "It's all right," she said. "I won't take long. I just want to see him for a minute."

I decided that Brian was an adult and could speak for himself. Anyway, it was none of my business to protect him; we were not really a couple yet. We arrived on the warehouse floor and the girl was looking around at the stacks of boxes and the furniture displays. We were walking by the exact spot where Matt had been lying just a few days before and I could still feel the impact of what had occurred there. The girl stopped, as if she had felt it too. She took a moment to look around. Only one truck was being loaded at the time, so there was a lot of empty space around her.

"So where is he?" the girl asked. I pointed to the door of Brian's office. "He usually is in there," I said. "If he's not there, then I don't know where he is. He could be anywhere. He might even be away from the building."

"That's all right, I'll check it out," the girl said and she confidently walked towards Brian's office. I stood and watched her as she boldly knocked on the door. As soon as I heard Brian say, "Come in," I turned around and walked back to my office, not wanting to hang around idly, waiting for my curiosity to be satisfied.

My curiosity was satisfied later when the girl walked through the open plan office where I was consulting with one of our bookkeepers. She walked by and stopped by the bookkeeper's desk. Her face was radiant and she was smiling. "He's amazing," she said in a whisper. He just put his hand on my ankle and the pain went away. Can you believe that?" I looked up from the computer screen where I was checking an order recently sent in by one of my clients in another town.

"Yes, I can believe it," I said, thinking of Matt and how his pain had clearly subsided the moment Brian placed his hand on Matt's chest.

The girl walked by with a light springy step, almost as if she were dancing her way to the exit. I had no idea then what it would lead to.

On Sunday I went to see my grandmother again. I told her the story of the encounter with the dancer and how Brian had healed her by laying his hand on her ankle. My grandmother asked me how I knew that the girl was a dancer and so I explained that dancers tend to carry themselves differently and that they often have a fineness about their features. I also told her that the girl had told me she was a dancer, after I had detected that this was indeed the case. Grandmother then proceeded to explain to me about roles.

"You can learn about roles by studying your surroundings and the behavior of the people you meet," she said. You can also learn from the experience of other people, from their stories, from literature, the movies, from works of art and from observation. According to each person's experience and history, they create for themselves a 'stereotype gallery'—a collection of types representing various professions, attitudes and age groups, displaying a range of behavior and physiognomy patterns. As soon as a word is mentioned, like dancer or butcher or teacher, a picture flashes into our mind and only gets altered if contrary information is received. For example, if a story featuring a butcher is told, then the storehouse of our brain will obligingly flash up a relevant picture—possibly a corpulent, sturdy man in his late forties with a white apron, stained with blood, deep set eyes, a moustache—in the imagination this is a narrow-minded individual who is a tyrant in his domestic life. He is standing in front of his shop with a butcher's knife in his hand—the attribute of his trade. In our perception of him he personifies our feelings for his profession. If the person we meet is quite different to this, how long will it take us to alter an assumed imaginary type? Or will we simply reconcile ourselves to the fact that this must be the exception to the rule?" Grandmother paused for a moment and then asked me, "Is that anything like your image of a butcher?" she asked.

"Mine was very similar, except he didn't have a moustache," I replied. "He was clean shaven."

"I guess my stereotype goes with my experience and the images I have taken into myself. Time moves on and fashion changes," she said with a smile. "Let's take a look at some other stereotypes," Grandmother continued. "The gallery includes such characters as the pale as flour, hard working baker who gets up at four in the morning to bake the bread, and the spinster teacher with her hair drawn back in a knot, wearing glasses, a grey suit and a blouse with a cameo brooch. Did you ever really meet such a person or is she a combination of characters from books and movies and our own memories? And what about the accountant with his pin striped suit and briefcase, or the judge with his stern look, the gay hairdresser or clothes designer, the ballet dancer, the pop singer, the absent-minded professor, the jolly talkative bus conductor or the wild-haired conductor of an orchestra? How many of these would you be able to recognize on the street and how many really comply with your established images?

"As soon as we want to apply a new role to our own lives, we can reach for one of our ready-made stereotypes, like a comfortable pair of gloves and simply act it out. We easily pretend we are being hurt, happy, polite, industrious or confused. We are all actors and pretenders, putting on and taking off roles and masks as we see fit—anything to prevent others from seeing our real selves. Somehow we never think we are good enough, educated enough or attractive enough as we really are. We are always in pursuit of the approval of others and will go to extraordinary lengths to get confirmation and assurances that we are liked, appreciated, valued and loved."

"As you explained in the lesson on tugging last week?" I asked.

"Exactly," Grandmother replied. "But realize that mostly others perceive us according to our roles and do not see beyond the facial expression to appreciate our true essence. Depending on our age, profession, education and social status will they immediately slot us into one of their own ready-made stereotypes and will not feel comfortable with us until they are able to do so. Isn't that why people have their initial standard questionnaire, usually starting with the question, 'So what do you do for a living?' and then moving on to acceptable questions about family, place of origin, interests etc. Some of these questions remain unspoken, like, for example, asking someone about their age, unless they are very young, when it is permissible to ask. But the question is nevertheless there and the answer is usually guessed at. Another unasked question is the status of a person's bank account, but it is often guessed at based on their car, their clothes and their speech. All these assessments are done semi-consciously in order to establish the other person's eligibility for one's pre-set categories, such as, 'worth knowing,' 'interesting,' 'gain can be obtained here,' or 'watch out,' 'threat,' 'potential competition,' or simply 'boring' and 'not interested.' So if you want to make a lasting impression on others or become unique and un-boxed and un-labeled in their thinking, you will first have to break out of the mould they have prepared for you and the next one they will consequently try to squeeze you into—cutting off a bit here and adjusting something else over there. And don't look surprised," my grandmother said. "You do the same when assessing other people, don't you?"

I had to admit that I did. I told Grandmother of a time when I had assumed that a girl I met at a party had come with her father, when to my embarrassment it turned out that the older gentleman she was with was in fact her husband.

"That's right," my grandmother confirmed. "Once someone

escapes one of your stereotypes, you immediately proceed to try and find another from your personal gallery, into which the other person can comfortably fit. For example, once you found out the girl was married to the older man, you probably immediately assumed that she had married him for his money." I smiled but said nothing. She was probably right, but I didn't want to admit it.

"As you can see, this lesson is closely related to the lesson on assumption. In fact all lessons are related." She paused for a moment, then continued, "Have you noticed how uncomfortable a person can become if they cannot slot you into one of their stereotype roles?" Grandmother asked and then added, "This is when they get dislodged from their own role, for people do have roles for dealing with roles. For example, I am sure you have a role for talking to a policeman or a job interview role or the visit to the doctor role and the list goes on. But once a person is dislodged from their role, for example when they enter a new experience for which they do not have a role, you might get a glimpse of the real person inside. This sometimes happens when a person is drunk, very tired or stressed.

"Development is learning to accept the role-less role, because in those moments a person can learn about themselves. Uncomfortable it might be, but with every unsettling experience the range of roles expands because a new one is being built to cover this new situation. Learn to escape your roles by adopting and discarding new ones all the time. To help others do the same, learn to ease them out of the roles they have adopted with you by asking surprise questions and by broaching new subject matters they had never previously discussed or even considered. It means you will be constantly surprising others and yourself by acting out of character and being different today, but it will keep you refreshed and energetically buoyant, open to new possibilities and sensitive to the current needs of the time.

"One way to escape your roles—the ones you have manufactured yourself as well as the ones others have imposed upon you—is to never say the words 'I am' to describe yourself, thus fixing yourself into a role. So rather than saying, 'I am a secretary' or 'I am a furniture dispatcher,' say, 'I currently work as a furniture dispatcher,' thus giving yourself room to maneuver out of a role and become something totally different tomorrow."

Following Grandmother's lesson, I felt I needed to re-examine all my roles and find new ones to superimpose on the old. It reminded me of the sensation of shopping for new clothes, only this time I did not need to spend any money, just change my image and act out a new character, one that I would feel comfortable with, but would be challenging at the same time. It sounded so easy, but altering entrenched behaviors is difficult and every morning for the following week I tried to decide who I wanted to be that day—a warrior, a confidante, or an ingénue. It would usually last for an hour or two and then I would forget, as soon as I became involved in the routine processes of the day. As a result of this experience I decided that I still had a lot to learn.

Chapter Fourteen

The Anti-thesis

I decided to ask Brian if he wanted to go with me to the Halloween party at Sterling Silver Insurance. After all, I didn't know anyone at the company and I thought that if this was a thank you for my work during the photo shoot, then my boss should also be acknowledged for his part in the success of the day, because he had sent me to do the job. Was I confusing personal preferences with professional attitudes? Most certainly yes, but I didn't mind at all.

When I read the small print on the invitation, I noticed that costumes were required. I had no idea what to wear, I had no money to go out and buy something that would look half decent and I definitely did not want to ask Alice if I could borrow anything of hers; anyway, I had no idea if she owned any Halloween costumes and had no intention of asking. Besides, I always thought it was more inventive, original and artsy to invent and make one's own costume, rather than relying on suppliers to the masses, which would put one in danger of meeting someone else in exactly the same costume.

I somehow could not imagine Brian wearing a costume, but nevertheless, I decided to ask. I realized I did not have his home telephone number, so I needed to ask him at work. This felt awkward, but I decided to do it anyway.

The following day I arrived early at the office because I knew that Brian usually started work at seven or eight in the morning, always there before the installers left on their delivery routes. I walked through the busy loading bay and knocked on his door.

"Come in," he said and as I opened the door, I saw him sitting at his computer, no doubt coordinating the next day's deliveries. He looked up from his work and waited without saying a word. I held the invitation in my hand.

"I got this from Sterling Silver Insurance when I was there the other day for the photo shoot. They've invited me to their Halloween party next Saturday. Would you like to go with me?"

He smiled, a bit like you would smile at a child who has asked for the moon. "No, I can't. Much too busy." He turned back to the computer. I stood there for a moment until I realized the conversation was over, then I slowly turned around and left the room. I found him so hard to read; he seemed to run hot and then cold and I really couldn't figure him out.

Later that afternoon I was having lunch in the little canteen room set up for employees, when Brian walked in. I had never seen him there before, because he would always either eat out or work through lunch. This time he wasn't there to eat either. He came up to the table where I was sitting with my sandwich and sat down without asking for permission. He clearly had something to say, so I waited expectantly.

"I don't go to Halloween parties," he said without an introduction, coming straight to the point. "My folks are Polish and they celebrate Halloween in a different way. It is a time to remember your dead and visit the cemetery and the graves of your loved ones. So I will be spending the evening in quiet contemplation, honoring my ancestors and deceased relatives. But I hope you have a good time." He looked at me with intensity and I felt he meant what he was saying. He smiled and added, "And don't forget to do some good PR while you are there. After all, they are one of our biggest customers." He stood up and with one more look he headed for the door. I had not said a word during the entire encounter. I just nodded my head and smiled.

I decided to go on my own, so I needed to figure out what I was going to wear. I was having a bath and pondering this important decision when I hit on an idea. I was looking at a pile of bath towels on the shelf in the bathroom, stacked up in their stripes of color. Both Alice and I liked the luxury of large towels and we each had our favorite color—hers were pink and mine were a deep cherry red. I had the idea that I could sew two towels together—one for the front of my costume and one for the back, leaving slits for arms. Then I would take a length of three-ply toilet paper and wear it like a sash and write upon it "Miss Bathroom." The idea appealed to me and soon I was adding accessories—I would buy some of those little guest soaps that come in many shapes and colors and thread them together into a necklace. Then perhaps I could make earrings of bath pearls, if I found a way not to spill the liquid soap inside. I could wear slippers and use a loofa glove as a purse. I was quite enjoying myself putting this together in my mind, so as soon as I got out of the bath, I dressed and went to work to complete my costume.

On Saturday night I got dressed. I felt a little silly in my two towels, but I remembered my grandmother's advice—put yourself in uncomfortable situations and you will learn about yourself. If you keep within habitual confines and known situations, you will remain within an already established role, but if you find yourself in a new situation, you will be forced to think in new ways, make new decisions and overcome your desire for comfortability and predictable routines. So I decided to go and observe myself, as if standing outside of myself, but nearby—an exercise I had read about somewhere but had never really tried. I thought this was a good opportunity to do so, as I didn't really know anybody at the Sterling company and didn't care very much what anybody thought about me.

When I walked into the Sterling Silver Building, I was amazed at the transformation. The great lobby and reception with its two floor high ceilings had become a ballroom with the orchestra on the second floor, in the hall outside the accounting offices overlooking the dance floor. There were tables all around the walls and on the landing upstairs, next to the orchestra. Between the elevators there were tables with food along one wall and a bar with drinks along the other. There were hundreds of people milling around, all wearing the greatest range of costumes I had ever seen. It was loud and noisy and it was difficult to hear anyone talk above the music. I was greeted at the door by a large man in uniform who asked me for my invitation. He exchanged it for a card entitling me to one free drink at the bar, he then directed me down a corridor to his right where there were a few offices and the restrooms. He said that I should go into the office marked "Cloakroom" to leave my coat. I followed his directions and entered a large office suite which had been turned into a cloakroom with a number of coat rails on wheels, shelves and a cloakroom attendant—a young girl dressed in black with very red lipstick. I handed her my coat and she gave me a plastic number with a safety pin attached. I turned to leave the office when the door opened and in walked Andrew, the man who had graciously posed for the photographs some days before.

"How are you?" he asked and quickly added, "Are you here on your own?"

"Yes," I replied. "And I don't know anyone."

"Well, let's have a drink together and I'll introduce you to some folks," he said and I smiled as he handed his coat to the attendant. He was wearing a black cape with red lining underneath his coat. He was dressed in black and pulled out of his pocket a set of plastic teeth with fangs. He showed them to me, but did not put them in his mouth. He just laughed and put them back in his pocket.

"I don't feel like being a vampire tonight," he said. He guided me to the bar, which we finally got to, pushing our way through the crowd and circumnavigating the dance floor. When we finally got there he ordered two glasses of wine and I handed him my ticket. There was a little bit of room by the bar so we stood there trying to talk, but found that we had to shout at each other and repeat what we were saying for the other one to hear.

"I'll tell you what," he shouted in my ear. "Why don't we get two more glasses of wine and go upstairs to my office so we can chat?"

"All right," I replied.

He ordered two more glasses of wine and when they were placed before us, he handed them to me and said, "Take these and I'll take the other two."

I followed him to the elevator and he pressed the button with his foot, as he was still holding the two wine glasses and did not have a free hand. I thought it was a graceful maneuver, as he was able to lift his leg up to hip height without spilling a drop. As soon as the elevator doors closed I said so. He did the same again, pressing the button to the 11th floor.

"Irish step dancing," he said. "It keeps you incredibly fit." We were leaving the noise behind us, which was quite a relief.

Once we were in his office, we talked for a couple of hours. He wanted to know all about me and Versatile Furniture, about my childhood and family. He told me his story and we talked about movies and politics and food and Irish dancing. It was easy and fun and the conversation helped me forget about Brian and Alice and all the unresolved issues in my life. Finally, when the wine was gone and it was getting late, he asked, "Do you want to dance?" He then led me back downstairs to the lobby/ballroom. There were fewer people now and more room to move around in, so we danced to the rhythm of the samba and the waltz and the rumba and some more traditional renditions of modern tunes. He was a great dancer and although I had not had much experience of ballroom dancing, he guided me so that we were able to glide and move across the wooden floor with ease.

Another hour went by and we carried on our conversation between the dances, sitting at one of the tables or perched on stools by the bar, sipping wine and getting to know each other. It felt as if I had known him for a long time; we had so much in common. The conversation flowed easily and the time passed quickly. It was just about midnight and I decided it was time to go home, when the orchestra played a drum roll and a man stood in front of the musicians leaning against the balustrade on the second floor and addressing all the people below who had stopped what they were doing, waiting to hear what was going to be said.

"That's Hans Gruber, our CEO," Andrew whispered in my ear as we stood in the middle of the dance floor. There was a wide staircase leading up to the second floor as well as an escalator that was not running at the time. Mr. Gruber was holding a piece of paper.

"Thank you for coming," he said, "and helping to make our traditional Halloween party such a memorable occasion. I hope you are enjoying yourselves." He was speaking through a microphone pinned to his lapel so everyone could hear him. He was the only person not wearing a costume. Even the orchestra were wearing Viking head dresses and leather tunics. "I have the results of the competition," Mr. Gruber announced. The room went quiet and everyone faced the orchestra on the second floor landing where Mr. Gruber stood. I looked around, quickly trying to guess who could have won the competition. There was such a variety of costumes in every conceivable category—animals, mythical figures, super heroes, historical people, fictional heroes, film stars, singers, idols ...

"We decided to award a prize for the most original and ingenious costume," Mr. Gruber said and you could feel the expectation rising in the room. "We have unanimously agreed that the prize for the most original costume should go to Barbara Faye."

I couldn't believe it. All heads were turning towards me and all eyes were scrutinizing my home-made costume. I felt myself blushing; I had no idea how they all knew who I was. Andrew put his hand on my shoulder and whispered in my ear. "Congratulations," he said. "You really know how to make something out of nothing." I smiled and was almost wishing I had never come, when Mr. Gruber said, "Please come up and collect your prize." I hesitated, but Andrew delicately pushed me in the direction of the stairs. People parted as I walked toward the flight of stairs and up to where Mr. Gruber was waiting with an expectant smile and an envelope in hand.

"Congratulations," he said and shook my hand. "You have just won a voucher for a holiday for two in Hawaii." He handed me the voucher and I could feel myself blushing again. I thanked him, took the envelope and turned towards the stairs. As I began descending towards the lobby, people started clapping and soon the orchestra picked up their instruments and began playing. Andrew was waiting at the bottom of the stairs and asked me to dance.

"So who will you be going to Hawaii with?" he asked.

"I don't know yet," I replied. "It depends." I don't know why I said that, but he immediately picked up on it. "Depends on what?"

"Depends on what happens in the next two weeks." Again, I wasn't sure why I had said that, but I had a feeling I was telling the truth. Andrew stopped asking and kept dancing. He was a really good dancer.

Andrew walked me home. It was a surprisingly mild evening for this time of year and we were chatting all the way, sharing our opinions about movies, books and travel. Andrew was good looking and clever, well educated and obviously on his way towards a brilliant career, and I was flattered that he was obviously taking an interest in me. I told him that I was sharing a house with a friend and that it was too late for him to see me to my door, so we parted at the stairs to the house and as we said goodnight I held out my hand. He smiled and said that he had really enjoyed our time together and then he asked if he could see me again. I said yes and he kissed me on the cheek, still holding onto my hand. He then walked off and as I watched his diminishing figure walking away from me, he turned towards me once again and waved goodbye. He then waited until I opened the door and walked into the house.

When I walked into the living room, Alice was lying on the sofa, reading.

"Did you have a good time?" she asked.

"I did," I said with enthusiasm. "I had a great time. I danced all night."

"Really, who with?" Alice sat up and closed her book, obviously curious.

"You don't know him; he's a salesman at Sterling Silver Insurance. I met him while we were doing a photo shoot there."

"Well, that sounds interesting. You seem to be popular these days." I couldn't help feeling that there was a touch of jealousy in her intonation.

"I guess it's because I am so damn attractive," I tried to make light of it.

"So what do you think makes you so attractive?" Alice asked.

"I have no idea, but I could make a guess."

"OK, tell me what you think." Alice was following me into the kitchen. I opened the fridge, looking for a cold drink. I did feel good about myself and I wasn't going to dampen down my response to make Alice feel better. I knew that I would be listening to what I was going to say and that what I was going to say would influence how I thought about myself, so I decided to pitch for the best.

"Well, let's see. I think a cheerful disposition is attractive, the fact that I am interested in other people, helpful and pleasant to be with. And, of course, my long legs and thick red hair might have something to do with it as well." I laughed, because I couldn't quite believe I was saying all these things. Also, Alice's expression was getting darker and darker, as she no doubt was comparing herself with my description."

"I don't think you're that cheerful or pleasant," she said with a frown. "I think you are rather selfish. Perhaps you are different when you talk to men."

"Perhaps I am," I said, undaunted. I pretended not to be bothered by her remark, but I did feel myself getting upset. "I think I'll go and take a shower," I said, and left the kitchen with my can of Perrier in hand, heading for the bathroom.

"What are you so pleased about?" my grandmother asked the moment I walked through the door that Sunday. I knew I would not be able to keep anything from her; she knew my moods even better than my mother knew them or than I was able to recognize them myself.

"I had a great time yesterday," I said as I followed her into the kitchen. As was her custom, she took the kettle from the stove and poured us both a cup of tea. Her back was turned towards me as she asked, "So what were you doing last night?"

"I was invited to a Halloween party at an office where I had done some work, and I won a prize for the most ingenious costume."

"Really? And what did you wear?" she asked as she handed me a cup of steaming hot tea, and we began to walk towards her living room, cups and saucers in hand.

"I was Miss Bathroom and I wore two towels sewn together, adorned with various bathroom paraphernalia."

She laughed so hard I was afraid she was going to spill her tea. She made it to the sofa and sat down, placing the cup on the coffee table in front of her. I felt a little bit disconcerted—the more she laughed, the less I felt like laughing.

"Why is that funny?" I asked.

She wiped away a tear. "I'm sorry," she said. "I just find it really funny—imagining you in some swanky downtown office wearing a couple of towels."

"Well, they thought I looked good." I became defensive. "In fact they awarded me with a trip to Hawaii."

Grandmother stopped laughing, but she had a big smile on her face when she asked, "So when are you going?"

"I don't know yet and I don't know who I will be going with either."

"So the trip is for two?"

"Yes, but I don't have any vacation time for the first six months, so I can't go until December at the earliest."

"Isn't winter a great time to travel to Hawaii?"

"Yes, but I don't want to go alone." I listened to my voice and I must admit, I sounded like a spoilt child. Grandmother took a sip of her tea and placed the cup back onto the saucer. "You have lots of time to think about this," she said. "What's the problem?"

"The problem is that I am confused," I confessed. "I met someone at the party."

"And?"

"And nothing."

"Well, my dear," she said, "it all comes back to that first question— what do you want?"

"That's the problem. I don't seem to know what I want. I thought I did—I said I wanted a job and I got a job. I said I wanted a relationship and I started going out with Brian. But now I no longer seem to know what I want."

"That's exactly it. You have caught yourself up. You thought as far as having a job and going out with a guy, but now you have achieved that, you no longer know what you want. That is why you need to have short-term, medium-term and long-term goals, otherwise you will keep catching yourself up and being at a loss as to where to turn to next. It didn't take you long, did it? Within a few months, here you are, not knowing what to do or what to want, simply because you have achieved all the desires that were on your list from a few months ago. That should teach you to think big and wish for more.

"It's not good enough to decide what you want and expect the universe to deliver it up to you on a platter. You need to fulfill your part as well. You took the first step in your decision-making and something responded—you have had a success. But now you need to double your efforts and keep asking the same question—what do I want? That first burst of energy helped you get a job and the beginnings of a relationship, but now you are being tested. Every action has an opposite and equal reaction; it is a law. Everything you do will bring about its opposite in the form of an anti-thesis. I recognize your mood—you have achieved a small success, but make sure you do not jeopardize your own achievements by not knowing where to go next. So I must ask you once again, what do you want?"

I looked at her and it suddenly became clear. "I want to be like you," I said. "I want to be wise and serene and have that inner stillness that allows you to make the most of each moment."

Grandmother looked me in the eyes and responded after a moment. "In that case you are facing a lifetime of study and dedication," she said. "You will need to work hard to discover why you are here." She hesitated for a moment and then asked, "You do believe you are here for a reason, don't you?"

I hesitated briefly because in all honesty, although I believed there was indeed a mission for me to fulfill, I had never really seriously considered what it might be. But I was not going to say so in case she thought me to be shallow and not worthy of our precious meetings. "Yes, I do," I replied and my voice sounded somewhat feeble, even to me.

"Good," she said. "That is one admission I hope you will remember. After all, millions of sperm set out on a long and arduous journey to reach that one egg that your mother's ovary discharged the month you were conceived. That's a lot of effort to produce one unique human being with a unique and original set of skills and DNA. It is then up to you to find out what those skills are for and how you can best put them to use."

I started thinking about what she had said, but she continued without giving me a chance to pause or respond. "You have a special gift," she said, "the gift of clairvoyance. People with special gifts like that have a responsibility to use them to help others. I cannot tell you what to do, but it is important that you do not utilize your gift for self gain, otherwise you will lose it."

It was very quiet in the room for a moment and I could only hear the ticking of her old-fashioned mantelpiece clock.

"You see, the anti-thesis is always there and you must be ready to deal with it," she said after a brief pause. "You came in this morning very pleased with yourself—you won a competition and had a good time. So just be careful, because now you are vulnerable. You have heard the saying, Pride comes before a fall?" I nodded. "It's true. It's when you relax and feel you are invincible that you are in the greatest danger. So remember to always keep one step ahead of the anti-thesis, because the moment you stop in your tracks because you are self-satisfied and ready to rest on your laurels, it will catch up with you and cause you to regress."

That Sunday evening I stayed home, still feeling tired after a night of dancing, drinking and conversation. This time Alice was going out on a date so I had the house to myself. I decided to watch a movie and was just about to settle down on the sofa in the living room, when the phone rang. It was Andrew and he was calling to thank me for a lovely evening and to ask whether I would like to come out for a drink. I told him I was busy but that perhaps another time we could get together for a chat.

When Alice returned, I made sure to tell her about the call. I wanted to divert her attention from Brian and to make her think that Andrew and I were heading towards a new relationship. She listened to me and I could tell that her date was not very successful; she seemed depressed and easily annoyed.

"Life is so easy for you," she said. "You seem to get what you want with almost no effort at all."

"That's not true," I protested. "It might seem to be like that, but I have had to work hard for everything I have. In fact, I own almost nothing—no place to live, no savings, no prospects. In fact, all that I own is in that bedroom down the hall," I pointed in the direction of the room I was currently occupying.

"Yes, but men like you," Alice said, in a tone that sounded like she was complaining. "So you will never be lonely."

"Come on, Alice," I replied, realizing that this conversation was really all about her. "You are a very attractive girl. Perhaps if you smiled more often and tried to be interested in the men you go out with, then perhaps your relationships would last longer." Alice was sitting on the sofa next to me. She now turned towards me and pulled her legs up onto the cushion that was located between us. "I was out with Jimmy from Marketing," she confessed. "And there was absolutely nothing—no spark, no interest whatsoever. How can I be interested if I am bored out of my mind?" she asked, rather pathetically.

"I guess you can't," I admitted. "I am talking about those occasions when you would want something to happen. There are many subtle ways in which you can show that you care."

"Like what?" she demanded.

"Ask questions," I replied and at that moment I realized that a question is a quest for ions—for energy that flows from one person to another. "Become interested in their lives, their interests, their work, their dreams, their family and their history. It will make a big difference, you'll see," I reassured her.

"Oh, I know all about that," she said. "But somehow I think there's more to it. I think men are above all interested in sex. Conversation is important, but only afterwards."

"But sex wears off," I said. "Or at least that initial attraction does. And if there isn't something deeper to replace it, then the relationship won't last."

"Oh Barbara, you are such an idealist!" Alice said. She then yawned and added, "I'm going to bed. I'm tired." She swung round, lowering her legs onto the floor and marched off towards her bedroom.

Chapter Fifteen

What Others Think Matters

On Monday I spent the day away from the office—I had been sent on a training course to learn about the new computer software that had recently been installed in the office. It finished early that afternoon, so I phoned up my grandmother and asked if I could come over.

"You might say that you don't care what people think about you, and a lot of people say that, even though mostly they don't mean it," she said when I started complaining about Alice and how she thought I was selfish and childish. "But let me tell you why it does matter, in the sense that it becomes matter, or manifests eventually in your behavior and character formation.

"So firstly—" I pulled out my notebook and started writing because it felt important to record her words of wisdom— "it matters what you think about you because you are people too. How you perceive yourself is what you will inevitably become. As you think, so you are programming your many parts. So, for example, if you think you are poor, you will remain poor; if you think you are attractive, others will respond by being attracted to you; if you think you are happy, you will radiate happiness, and so on.

"The next reason why it is important how people think of you is because as they think, so do they radiate that image, and the more people think of you in a certain way, the more that image becomes compounded and the harder it is for you to break out of it and change people's minds. Say you tend to be taciturn and people who know you have registered that fact. Well, they will soon stop asking you to speak up at meetings or other gatherings and it would take a colossal effort on your behalf to break through that image and to become talkative and expressive to the point where others would acknowledge the new you. Sometimes a person changes their job not because they are fed up or bored, but simply because they need to change their image with new people who don't yet have preconceived ideas about them.

"Therefore it is wise to set out building character descriptions in people's minds according to what kind of image you wish to portray. So, for example, if you want people to respect your time, make an effort to always be punctual and reliable by arriving early to appointments, meetings or business gatherings. A person who rushes in late, always full of excuses, will never be perceived as a serious business partner or joint venture candidate. People in business like to work with those that they can rely on to deliver on time, keep their word and be where they said they would be at the appointed hour. Trust is the foundation of an effective partnership. I know we have already spoken about punctuality, but I want to bring it up again in the context of this lesson, which could be titled, 'It matters what other people think of you.'

"You would be surprised how quickly thoughts become reality if repeated long enough and forcefully enough. If, for example, you are able to convince people that they are younger than they are, then as soon as they believe it, their aging process will reverse. There was an experiment conducted in the seventies by Dr. Langer, a professor of psychology at Harvard University, in which two groups of older men over 70 were recruited: an experimental group and a control group. Both groups spent five days at an isolated retreat center surrounded with paraphernalia, magazines and props from the fifties. The experimental group spoke about the fifties in the present tense and were not allowed to speak of anything that had happened in the ensuing 20 years; the control group were also talking about the fifties, but in the past tense and they were permitted to speak about more recent events. Both groups did remarkably well and their signs of aging diminished and even reversed; however, the experimental group did better than the control group.

"These days there are so many books written about the power of the mind and the effectiveness of affirmations. You really need to take control of your thinking process if you want to harness the strength of your imagination to work for you and to help you achieve your goals. It is such a powerful gift and tool, yet very few people know how to use it correctly.

"The real power of what you want comes from the reason why you want it. The greater the reason, the more the chance that it will come true. Try to have desires that reach beyond your own aura and make sure that you want them for the good of others or the community or the district or in fact all of humankind. That way you will be connecting into a powerful grid that can supply you with enough energy to overcome most obstacles or anti-theses. Think what motivates you in what you wish for and what you do and you will have a roadmap of the energy supplies that are feeding your desires."

I wrote this last instruction down but I wasn't sure how to approach this new tasking. However, I decided not to ask just yet but to try to understand better what she was saying when I had more time to contemplate the matter. A moment later my grandmother gave me more specific instructions. "Take the list of what you want that you wrote down when we first started to meet," she said. "Add to the list descriptions of what you want to be as well as do or have. So now you have three categories—be, do and have. So, for example, 'I want to be a teacher or writer,' or 'I want to be rich, or successful.' Then there is the do list—'I want to write a book, travel, make money.' There is a difference, of course, between being rich and making money," she added after a brief moment.

"One is active and one is passive," I said. "I see that. One is being, one is doing."

"Precisely," she confirmed. "The third category is having—for example, 'I want to have a house, a job, a boyfriend,' or, 'I want to have money.' It doesn't say how you are going to get it."

"The doing list might explain it," I suggested.

"Yes, it might," Grandmother agreed. "I want you to go back to your list and look at it from the standpoint of these three categories. Then concentrate on the list to do with being and think of the qualities you would want to embody, such as courage or patience or honesty. I assure you that these qualities are quite real and tangible and when you live them, they become part of you, expressed in your behavior, posture and even in the lines of your face."

I looked at my grandmother's face, as if I was seeing it for the first time, trying to detect the qualities that were etched upon it. I could clearly see her compassion, care, sensitivity and generosity— expressed in the eyes, the smile and the intensity of the line of her mouth.

"I think I understand," I said.

"That is when what is inside becomes visible outside," she said. "It becomes matter for all to see. And we are all experts at reading other people's faces and posture, though perhaps not always consciously. So once you know what you want to have, to do and to be, you can set about becoming the very thing you want."

I wrote that sentence down in my book, because I thought it summed up the whole concept of making what you want become part of your life.

When I arrived back at the house, Alice was watching a game show on television. I went into the kitchen, made myself a sandwich and poured out a couple of glasses of juice. I decided I wanted to be friendly and generous to start this exercise of creating my own portrait. I took the glasses into the living room and handed one of them to Alice.

"Here you are, a glass of apple juice," I said. She held out her hand and I could see the surprise on her face as she said, "Thank you." I could tell I was already beginning to rewrite her impression of me. Perhaps not so selfish, after all. Funny, how small acts of kindness can make a difference. I set down my own glass on the coffee table and went back to the kitchen to fetch my sandwich.

"How was your course?" Alice asked when I returned and sat down beside her on the sofa.

"Oh, the course was fine," I said. "I just got back from

Grandmother's place. That was far more interesting."

Alice turned off the television and we ended up spending a couple of hours talking about what we wanted and the various aspects of our life we would like to change. We considered the difference between having, being and doing and we discussed the many qualities and attributes we would like to have, be and do.

Chapter Sixteen

Give and Take

On the following Tuesday I passed Brian in the hallway. We were walking in opposite directions and he was obviously in a hurry and preoccupied with something, but he stopped and asked me, "How was the party?"

"It was great," I replied. I didn't think he had any time for details, but he had already heard about it.

"I heard you won a prize for your costume," he said.

"Yes, a week's trip to Hawaii for two," I said.

"Nice. Congratulations. How about dinner tonight and you can tell me all about it?"

"That will be fine," I said.

"Come over to my place. I'll cook. Seventy-four Westchester Terrace. Dinner at eight."

"All right, I'll be there."

And with that he was gone. I could see his silhouette receding down the corridor. I was stunned. This seemed like a whole new departure in our relationship and I wasn't sure I was ready. At the same time I felt an excitement and a sense of anticipation, as if my whole life was going to change.

It was hard to concentrate on my work that day. People were coming up to me and congratulating me—-the news about the prize had already spread around the office. They also kept asking me who I was going to take to Hawaii with me and every time I would say that I didn't know yet, which would then precipitate a whole number of suggestions and requests. "Well, if you don't know who to take, I have some vacation time left and I would love to go to Hawaii. I've never been to Hawaii," they would say, or, "How about selling that other ticket? I know someone who would pay good money for such an opportunity." I would smile or laugh, but make no commitment. After all, I had no idea what I was going to do and as Grandmother had pointed out, there was a lot of time to decide.

It was around midday when Andrew phoned. I was surprised to hear his voice so soon again, but it felt like talking to an old friend.

"I really enjoyed our time together," he said. "How about dinner tonight?"

"No, I can't," I replied. "I am busy tonight."

"Well, how about tomorrow then?"

"Tomorrow would be fine."

My head was in a spin. Two dates in two days! I had not had a serious relationship for at least a year and here I was contemplating who was more attractive, Brian or Andrew. I decided to let events unfold at their own pace and to get back to my work. I needed to organize an important delivery for the next day: display furniture for a toy shop in a large mall. I was just assembling a list for the warehouse guys to put together, when Alice came into my office.

"Do you want to go out for lunch?" she asked.

"Sure," I replied, quite relieved to take a break and get some fresh air. It was cold out as a brisk wind was blowing and the last dry leaves were floating around in the chilly air. "Where do you want to go?" she asked as we got in the car.

"Let's go to the coffee shop around the corner. I have to be back by one," I replied. Alice didn't say anything but she silently drove past the little coffee shop and before I knew it she was parking in a side street in front of an Italian restaurant that looked vaguely familiar.

"Where are we?" I asked.

"It's good," she replied. "You'll like it."

We went in and as we were being seated I realized it was the restaurant Brian had taken me to on our second dinner date, some months earlier. We ordered water and began to look at the menu. As soon as we were left alone, Alice asked, "Did he bring you here?"

"Who?" I asked, pretending not to have a clue who she was talking about.

"You know very well, who—Brian," she replied and I am sure I could detect a strange venom in her voice. There was something snake-like about her that day.

"As a matter of fact, he did," I said and added with expectancy, "So?"

"So nothing," she replied. "It's just that this is his usual pattern. Next he'll invite you home for a meal." I must have blushed, but I said nothing. I was sure she could see it.

"Well, did he?" she asked.

"Did he what?" I acted ignorant.

"Invite you home for a meal of course," she replied. I was getting annoyed.

"Alice, this has to stop. Stop prying into my affairs."

"Aha!" she exclaimed. "I knew it! He did!"

"What is the matter with you?" I decided to go on the offensive. "Can't you leave us alone?" This was a big mistake because she immediately caught on to the phrase I had used.

"Us? Us! Since when are you an us?" she was raising her voice and I began to feel embarrassed. The waitress came up and asked in a sweet voice, "Are you ladies ready to order?"

"I am," said Alice and her voice sounded harsh. "I'll have the pasta Alfredo."

"Very well," said the waitress and turned to me, "And you?"

"I'm out of here," I replied, got up, grabbed my coat and walked out the door. I was fuming. She had no right. How could she? These were the only phrases that kept running through my head as I bundled up into my coat and started walking towards the main street. I had no idea how to get back to the office, but I spotted a couple getting out of a taxi and hailed it. It did a u-turn and stopped at the curb. I went back to the office and threw myself into work. I successfully avoided walking past the receptionist's desk all afternoon and stayed late at work so as to escape riding back home with her.

By the time I finally got home, Alice was not there. It bothered me that we needed to talk this through, but for the time being there was nothing I could do. So I quickly took a shower and got dressed. I wore black pants and a striped blouse, with boots and a black jacket. I looked in the mirror and felt quite satisfied with the result.

Brian lived in an apartment building and I had to ring his apartment number before he could buzz me in. The buzzer came before I even managed to announce myself and as I walked up the stairs to the third floor, he was standing in the doorway waiting for me. A delicious smell wafted into the corridor from inside the apartment.

"Come on in," he said. "Let me take your jacket."

"What are you cooking?" I asked. It smelt delicious.

"It's a surprise," he said. He hung up my jacket in the hall closet and led me into the kitchen. There was a bottle of German Riesling open on the kitchen counter and two large wine glasses. He poured out the wine and handed me a glass. "Let's drink to the pleasures of the palate," he said.

"To the pleasures of the palate," I repeated and we clinked our glasses together.

"Very nice wine," I said and although I am no connoisseur of vintage wines, I could tell it was smooth and quite fragrant. I looked around the kitchen and was impressed how clean and ordered it looked; not at all what I would have expected from a bachelor living alone. It was quite small but compact, with everything within easy reach. I could feel a little buzz as the wine went to my head.

"Are you ready to eat?" Brian asked.

"Yes, I'm ravenous," I said. "I didn't have any lunch today."

"Oh, why's that?"

I wasn't going to tell him the truth, not in a million years. "There just wasn't the time," I said. "I had to prepare the delivery to the Toys Forever shop," I lied.

"Well then, let's eat." He opened the oven and took out what looked like a delicious fish casserole, holding it with a tea towel in one hand and an oven glove on the other, so as not to get burnt.

"I'm a good cook," he explained, "but I only know how to make a few dishes. This is my salmon with onion, sage and raisins. Works every time," he said, holding the steaming hot dish. "You bring the wine and glasses," he added and I picked up the bottle with one hand and the glasses with the other. I followed him into the living room which was bright and airy, with a glass top table that was laid for two—it had a colorful salad and a hot plate in the middle. The china dishes were white and large and the place mats were made of thin strips of bamboo. There was also a white couch in the room and a comfortable armchair. One whole wall was lined with bookshelves full of books and CDs.

"Take a seat," he said as he placed the dish on the hot plate and took off the oven glove he was wearing on his right hand. He picked up a serving spoon from the table and started serving.

"Eat while it's hot," he said and then he served himself. He sat down opposite me and passed me the salad.

"This looks delicious," I said as I helped myself to some salad. "And indeed it is," I added as soon as I took the first mouthful. It was a curious taste, but very good. I thought he could run a good restaurant. "How long have you lived here?" I asked.

"About six months," he replied between mouthfuls. "Do you like it?"

"It's very nice," I said. "And you keep it so clean," I added.

"Oh, that's not me," he replied. "I have a cleaning lady who comes twice a month."

"Lucky you." I picked up my glass. "Here's to your cleaning lady," I said and he repeated after me, "To my cleaning lady." We emptied our glasses.

About twenty minutes later we finished eating and I got up to collect the dishes and take them into the kitchen. Brian got up as well and picked up the casserole dish with some of the salmon still in it and followed me to the kitchen. I was placing the dishes in the sink when I could feel him walking up behind me. He reached his arms around me and put the casserole dish in the sink on top of the two plates I had already placed there. I could feel his body behind me and felt tingles of excitement all over. He wrapped his arms around me, pulled me towards him and was kissing my neck. I turned around and put my arms around his neck. We kissed and it just felt so right and warm and exciting to be in his arms. I could feel his hand lifting to my breast and I knew that tonight we were going to be intimate, when the telephone rang. He pulled himself away and said, "I'm sorry, I have to get that," and he walked back into the living room. I followed him after a moment and as I walked back into the room, I heard him say, "All right, I'll be there. Just wait." He put the phone down and I looked at him expectantly. "It's all right," he said. "Someone I know is ill and I must go." He hesitated for a moment and then added, "Why don't you wait here?" he asked.

Now it was my turn to hesitate. I thought of going home, but then I thought of Alice and I decided to stay. "All right, I'll wait," I said.

It was after midnight when I heard the key in the lock. I was sitting on the couch, reading one of Brian's books and dozing off in between paragraphs. So when I heard the door open I was a little bit sleepy and a little bit disorientated, and it took me a moment to remember where I was and why I was there. As I looked at the figure coming through the door and as consciousness slowly returned, I realized it wasn't Brian.

"Who are you?" I asked the man as he closed the door behind him.

"I could ask you the same question. Who are you?" the stranger said and his speech was slightly slurred. He stood there for a moment blinking rapidly, and then he raised his hand. "No, don't tell me," he said. "You must be one of Brian's girlfriends."

I didn't expect that and it hit me like a bolt. However, I was more alarmed about who this intruder was than by his words.

"And who are you?" I repeated. He took a couple of steps forward and started to take his coat off. I stood up from the couch. "I'm Brian's brother," he said. "He lets me crash on his sofa when I'm too far gone to drive home." He threw his coat over the back of the sofa. "And I'm too far gone," he said as he sat down on the couch. As he did so he grabbed my hand, so that I was forced to sit down next to him. I could smell the liquor on his breath.

"Come and keep me company," he said and still holding me by my right hand he put his left arm around my shoulders. Even though intoxicated, I could feel that he was strong.

"Brian will be back any moment," I said.

"That's all right, he can join in the fun." I started to pull myself away, but he held on tight.

"Let me go," I said. I was getting angry and upset.

"Just a little bit of fun," he said. "Come on, you'll love it." He lowered his face towards mine. The smell was disgusting. I managed to lift my left hand towards his face and pushed him back. He grabbed my left hand with his right and leaned towards me. I fell backwards onto the sofa. He fell on top of me.

"Leave me alone," I yelled. I managed to lift my left leg and kick him in his right hip. The pain took him by surprise and he let go of my hand. I then managed to free myself from under him and roll onto the floor. He fell face first onto the sofa.

"That wasn't nice," he said into the sofa. I grabbed my bag and darted towards the door. He sat up and was calling after me, "Come back. Let's have some fun!" I could hear him get up from the sofa, but I was by the door. I opened the door and escaped onto the corridor. The cold hit me and I realized I had left my jacket inside, but I wasn't going back there. I ran down the stairs, rather than waiting for the elevator, and out into the cold November air.

Back at the house Alice was waiting for me. I was absolutely freezing and no doubt she could tell immediately that something was wrong.

"What happened?" she asked and I believe she was genuinely concerned. "Where is your jacket?" she asked again in rapid succession. I walked into the kitchen and put the kettle on. "I don't want to talk about it," I said.

"It's Brian, isn't it?" she asked.

"Don't start," I turned towards her. "Just leave me alone."

"But I am your friend," she protested. "I needed to warn you. And you see, I was right all along. Just look at you."

"It wasn't like that," I said, but gave up trying to convince her.

"I know what it's like. You're going out with the wrong man and that is all there is to it. Why don't you go and sit down and I'll make you a cup of tea?" I didn't know what was worse—Alice prying into my affairs or Alice trying to mother me, but I was so emotionally drained that I was glad to take her up on her offer.

"All right," I said, "but just don't ask me any more questions."

I was too exhausted to move, so I just lay down on the sofa and pulled a blanket that was folded over the back of the couch over me and slowly began to warm up. A few minutes later Alice brought in a cup of tea and sat next to me.

"How are you feeling?" she asked.

"I'm all right," I said as I was trying to think of a plausible story that would explain why I had returned without my jacket. And then something very strange happened. Perhaps it was the proximity of another human being, perhaps it was the care she was showing me, perhaps it was the exhaustion and excitement of the evening and what I had been through, but I suddenly burst into tears and let Alice comfort me, as she put her arm around my shoulders. When I had calmed down somewhat, she asked again, "It was Brian, wasn't it? Did he hurt you?"

"No," I sobbed and as I did so I realized I shouldn't be saying anything. I pulled a tissue out of the box that Alice kept on the table next to the sofa and blew my nose. "No, it wasn't Brian, it was someone else."

Alice looked at me with surprise. "Who?" she asked, and then repeated, "Who?"

"It doesn't matter," I said. I was determined not to say anything more. "Just leave me be," I pleaded. I pulled away from her and sat up on the sofa. "I need a bath," I said. "It will help me get warm."

"You're right," Alice replied. "The water is already running," she added.

"Thank you, Alice. Thanks for being so understanding."

The next day at the office the phone rang first thing in the morning. An early phone call at 8:30am usually signified trouble from a concerned customer, but this time it was Andrew.

"I'm phoning to remind you about tonight," he said.

"I remember," I replied.

"Do you want me to pick you up?" he asked. I wondered if that would be wise. If Alice saw him, she might assume he was the man I was with the previous night. Or she might say something in front of him that would embarrass me. I thought for a moment and then replied, "Let's meet at the coffee shop on the corner of Main and 17th Street," I said, thinking that I would only have a five minute walk to the café.

"All right; how about eight o'clock?"

"That will be fine," I said.

That morning I sat in my office and worked on the computer. I realized I was avoiding Brian and I could feel his presence, wondering why he was not getting in touch. I decided I would not make the first move. I felt it was up to him to make amends. After lunch I was scheduled to travel with our driver to an installation in the industrial district of town. I was due to meet new clients who were setting up a flower import business and were furnishing their offices located above a warehouse. I stayed at my desk throughout the lunch hour, but nobody phoned and there was no sign of Brian. So promptly at two o'clock I went back to the warehouse and met up with Ahmed, the driver, who was ready with a fully loaded truck.

"We'll need to do this in two trips," he said as soon as he saw me. I looked towards Brian's office and with the corner of my eye I saw that it was dark.

"That's all right," I said. "We can reload tomorrow."

We got into the cab and we pulled out. Just as the truck was leaving the parking lot, I spotted Brian pulling in in his grey Toyota. I realized I would probably not be speaking with him today.

At the Flowers for Business warehouse there were a couple of hired hands waiting for us. Ahmed backed the truck up to the loading bay entrance of the building and while the men started unloading, I walked around the building to the office entrance. As I walked in, I could see a Flowers for Business display in the lobby; I realized that Flowers for Business imported and sold artificial plants and flowers in all colors and sizes. It made me smile to see such an array of color and foliage. I walked up the stairs to the second floor and I introduced myself to the receptionist.

"We're from Versatile Furniture," I said, "and we are delivering your furniture. Is there any particular order in which you want it set up?" I asked.

"Just a moment," the young receptionist said. "I'll call the office manager."

A moment later, a smart looking woman in her forties, with short black hair and wearing a well-fitted cream color dress came into the reception area.

"How do you do?" she said with a slight Jamaican accent. "I'm Amanda. Are you the young lady from Versatile Furniture?"

"Yes, pleased to meet you," I replied, shaking her hand.

"Let me take you to our offices," she said and she walked me through a door into an open plan office. The place was almost entirely empty, except for some screens that were already set up and a couple of desks in the corner. "This is where the salesmen will sit," said Amanda. As she said that, the door to the back stairs leading to the warehouse opened and the three men—Ahmed and the hired hands— came in carrying a couple of chairs and a small cabinet. Amanda pointed to a plan that was pinned to a screen near where she was standing. "This is your design," she said, "that Brian Polowski put together. Please make sure that the furniture is distributed correctly. If you need anything, please ask the receptionist." And with that she turned away and walked out of the office. I looked at the plan.

"Ahmed, do you understand this diagram?" I asked. Ahmed smoothed his beard as he contemplated the blueprint.

"I am not sure," he said and then he added, "Let's just bring the furniture in and when Mr. Polowski arrives, he can tell us where to distribute it." I was surprised, because I had no idea Brian was due to come to the site. I quickly adjusted my thinking and at the same time I registered that my heart was beating faster.

"All right, bring it in," I said. Ahmed and the two men went towards the back door and as they approached it, the door opened and in walked Brian.

"How are you getting on?" I heard him ask the three men and Ahmed replied, "We're delivering the furniture, Mr. Polowski, but we don't know where to assemble it."

"That's all right," Brian said, "just bring it in and I'll tell you where to place it. I have the floor plan right here." He opened the file he was holding in his hand and pulled out a diagram of the furniture layout.

"All right, Mr. Polowski," Ahmed said and he proceeded through the back door with the two helpers to get another load.

Brian was walking towards me. He came right up close and whispered, "What happened to you last night? Did James scare you off?"

"He certainly did!" I replied. "He tried to rape me!"

Brian laughed. "James would never do a thing like that," he said. "He was probably just trying to be friendly."

"Is that what he said? Well, he's lying!"

"Look, I don't know what went on between you two," Brian said and he was very serious. "But I know my brother and I know that he would never harm you or anyone else for that matter."

"So where did you go last night?" I asked after a moment's silence.

"I was asked to come and help someone in distress. It was a healing."

"So how did it go?" I asked.

"It was remarkable," he replied. "I was there most of the night. It was the mother of someone I knew and she needed help. By morning the woman was asking for breakfast and sitting up in bed."

"That's amazing," I said. "What was wrong with her?" I asked.

Brian did not reply because the men came back into the office, carrying another chair and a desk. Brian turned towards them. "That goes right here," he said. He then turned towards me and said, "Perhaps you would like to help by bringing in some of the smaller packages?"

"Certainly," I said as I made my way towards the warehouse and the truck.

It was well after five when we had finished for the day. Everyone had gone and Amanda had left us keys to lock the place up. We were going to come back the next day to finish the job. Ahmed drove off in an empty truck and the two men wandered off, having been paid for the day's work.

"I'll drive you home," said Brian.

"All right," I replied. As I got into the car I noticed that my jacket was lying on the back seat. I had gone to work in my old anorak and was glad to see my jacket again.

"Thank you for bringing my jacket," I said.

"You must have left in a hurry," Brian said as he started up the car and pulled out of the parking lot.

"As I told you, I was escaping your brother's clutches," I said. He just smiled and shrugged his shoulders.

"Well, how about dinner tonight?" Brian asked.

"I can't," I replied. "I'm busy."

"All right, how about tomorrow night?" he asked.

"Sure, that will be fine," I said with a sigh. I realized that going out with two men could be an exhausting affair with all these dinner dates night after night. Clearly, it couldn't go on like this for long.

It was half past six when Brian stopped the car in front of the house. The car was still running when he leaned over and kissed me. He put his arms around me and his kiss sent shivers up and down my spine. I didn't feel like getting out of the car, but I managed to pull myself away.

"I'll see you tomorrow at eight," he said.

"OK, tomorrow night at eight," I repeated. My head was swimming as I got out of the car. I opened the back door of the sedan and retrieved my jacket. "Thanks for the ride," I said and Brian drove away.

That night Andrew and I met at the coffee shop on the corner. He was already there when I arrived, fashionably five minutes late. He had ordered two coffees, so when I sat down at the table there was a hot drink in front of me.

"So, Barbara," he said, "where do you want to go to eat?" I quickly thought of places I did not want to go to, in case I met someone I knew.

"I don't know; how about Chinese?" I asked.

"I know just the place. But before we go, there is something I want to say."

"I'm listening."

"I want you to know that I am serious; I am not playing the field. I've been in a serious, long-term relationship for two years, which unfortunately ended about six months ago. I feel I am ready to start dating again and my intentions are honorable." I smiled at this old-fashioned phrase. How strange to hear it mentioned in these modern times when commitment seems to have gone out of vogue. I looked Andrew in the eyes and said, "I believe you, though I am not sure I am ready for such a commitment."

"Well, as long as you are not sure you are not ready, I am ready to proceed."

"All right then, let's go and eat," I said. "I don't know about you, but I am starving."

"OK, let's go," Andrew said. He stood up and picked up my coat from the back of my chair and held it up for me, so all I had to do is slide my arms into the sleeves, and then he lifted the coat onto my back. Another gesture that I had not seen or experienced for a long time. It was flattering and a touch scary to receive such attention so early in a relationship.

During dinner we talked about our past, our families, our studies and our favorite movies. The time passed quickly and pleasantly and when he dropped me off at Alice's house, he kissed my hand and said goodnight.

When I entered the house Alice asked me about my evening and I told her that I had a good time. I told her about our Chinese meal and how Andrew had said that his intentions were serious. She laughed and asked, "You didn't believe him, did you?"

"Of course I did," I replied.

"But you know you cannot trust men," she said. "After the way Brian treated you, you should know better!"

"What do you mean, 'after the way Brian treated me'?" I asked.

"Well last night something went wrong between you and Brian, that was clear."

"Alice, it wasn't Brian. How many times do I have to tell you?"

"Oh, you are stubborn," she said. "I know him and I've been

hearing stories about him for years. He doesn't treat women well."

I decided not to say anything, because anything I said seemed to turn against me.

On Thursday night I went out with Brian. He said his brother was still staying with him in his apartment, so we went back to the little Italian restaurant that Alice seemed to know about. I didn't tell him that I had been there with her.

We ordered a bottle of Chianti and spaghetti and Brian started to explain to me what had happened on Tuesday night.

"A few days ago someone came to see me at the office," he said. "The girl was a dancer and she had twisted her ankle. She asked me if I could do anything for her because she couldn't dance and she had no way to make a living. She lives next door to Matt and Matt had told her about me, and she thought I could help her."

"And did you?" I asked, knowing of course that he had already been successful.

"I just put my hand on her ankle for a few mintes and she immediately said that the pain had gone away. Then she started to walk around the room and she wasn't limping any more. I think I was even more surprised than she was."

"I saw her," I admitted. She told me that you had cured her."

"Did she?" Brian looked surprised.

"So what has that got to do with Tuesday?" I asked.

"Well, after that I took a vow that I would help anyone who asked me to. You see, I think it is my duty to share my gift," Brian said. "So when she called on Tuesday night and told me that her mother had had an accident, I felt obliged to go and see her."

"And what happened?" I asked.

"Her mother was in terrible pain. She had fallen down the stairs and her back was hurting. They had not gone to see a doctor and her back clearly was not broken, but the pain was excruciating. So again, I just laid on my hands and the pain went away."

"So what happened after that?" I asked, realizing that two hours after he had left the apartment, Brian still had not returned.

"I sat with the woman for a few hours until she fell asleep and I was satisfied that indeed she was better. Nancy was so impressed, she said she would get a group of people together and I could demonstrate my healing powers and teach them to become healers."

"And what did you say?" I asked.

"I said I would think about it, but I think it is a good way to fulfill my destiny by getting healing out into the world."

Brian continued to talk about his vision and about healing the world and helping people. He had big plans and I wasn't sure there was room in his vision for me.

During the dessert he told me about his plans for the weekend. "How about I take you out of town for an adventure?" he asked. "We'll be back Sunday afternoon." I wasn't sure it was a good idea, but I answered before I had time to think it through, "All right," I said, "I'll be ready."

"I'll pick you up on Sunday at ten," he said.

When he walked me home, he kissed me goodnight and again I felt the shivers of excitement running through my entire body. It seemed that every time we parted, I would have my doubts whether we would ever get together again. At some instinctive level I felt afraid for his safety.

Friday night I went to see my grandmother.

"I am so confused," I told her. "I wanted a job and I got a job. I wanted something exciting to happen in my life and I won the costume competition. I wanted a relationship and now I am dating two guys and I don't know what to do. I love being with Brian but he seems unpredictable. Andrew is reliable and I feel secure with him, but it is not as exciting when I am with him."

Grandmother sighed. "Have you ever heard the saying 'give and take'?" she asked.

This was frustrating. I didn't come here to define known adages, but I decided to humor her. No doubt she was going to come up with another lesson. "It is something that is said to children and adults during arguments, to explain that one cannot always have one's own way and that other people might have interests that conflict with our own," I said.

"Exactly. It also expresses the idea that there should be a balance in any particular life between these two directions and that for humans to get on, one needs to consider the needs of another and not insist on one's own requirements and preferences as a priority, at least not all of the time. So far all I am hearing is what you want, but other people have their needs and desires too, which might not always coincide with yours. So let's look at this idea of give and take.

"Early on in our dealings we learn to give a little and as we grow up, we are expected to become partners and team players and to accommodate the wishes of others. But sometimes we give less, while presenting to others the adopted face of generosity, as in asking someone 'What do you want to do?' and hoping they will want what we already know we want to do. Mostly people try to give as little as possible, especially if it will cost them, with the exception perhaps of when they are dealing with those close to them (though it must be said that sometimes people will more readily give to strangers than to their own kin). By majority the world is ruled by the game take and take, rather than give and take, or give and give, which is very rare indeed.

"The moment you are born, you become a taker—you take your food from the planet, either through your mother if she is breast feeding or via a prepared formula. The planet supplies us with four kinds of food: solid, liquid, air and energy (which can also be defined as earth, water, air and fire—the four elements). As far as energy is concerned, the full will always run to the empty. So in any exchange between two people, it is always the weaker that will take from the stronger. Therefore anyone who sets their feet upon the path of becoming developed and stronger will eventually energetically become a giver, whether they like it or not. But if they are able to establish a higher connection to universal energies, they won't mind the giving because they will know how to replenish their stock of energy. In fact the more they give, the more they will receive and the stronger they will become. Mostly in the world people look at any situation and ask 'What is in this for me?' whereas a developed person will look around to see where they can best give away their energies and knowledge, knowing full well that every time they empty out, they are making room for more.

"A person with high energies running through them has a lot to give. If they don't, they are in danger of becoming stagnant. This is the difference between the person who has always something new going on with them and the person who keeps repeating the same actions, ideas and thoughts over and over again. To continue on this journey with me you will have to become more impersonal and think more in terms of what you might call abstract ideas and propositions. So as a principle, become more generous, more compassionate, more giving and don't worry about the rewards; I assure you, they will come of their own account. Were you not given at birth everything you needed to grow and journey through life? Now is the time to begin to give back.

"Yes, you will need to continue to in-take the four foods and these are readily supplied by the planet. Your higher foods are likewise supplied by the universe and there is no price attached to them. Providing you are on the frequency of these higher energies, they will freely flow into you so that you can partake of these higher realms. The word 'par-take' is much more fitting here than the word 'take,' as it implies a partnership, a sense of participation, agreement and earning what you receive. It is at this point in their development that a person has the energy to give and it is very much like in the biblical saying, 'my cup runneth over.' It allows a person to give without counting the cost and to become a beacon of light to others.

"As a person develops there comes a point when there is no one for them to take energy from, as all their energy comes from the planet and the universe. It is then that all their dealings with other people will be on a giving basis. But if they are connected to energies, presences and essences that are higher than planetary level, they will be happy to do so because their stocks of energy are always being replenished and they know that the more they give, the more they get. They will give to receive. Of course such a person is a rare occurrence in the planet's history and usually is given the name saint, savior or avatar.

"One way to become a giver, rather than a taker, is to deliberately have in oneself a mental stance that says, 'What can I give in this situation?' rather than 'What can I get from this situation?' which can apply to any dealing in your life. In reality, of course, we are always giving and receiving, because that is what we humans do—we process energy all the days of our life. The question is, how conscious are you of the energies you process and what stance do you want to take, as part of this great energy feeding chain, this giving and taking feast that life is, this receiving and transmitting station that this planet is designed to be? What part do you want to play? If you think of the expression 'to take part,' it says that it is up to us to choose where we want to place ourselves in the scheme of things—we take our position. But in taking a part, will you also give a part? In the end, if we are takers by majority, we will set ourselves *apart* from the great gift that creation is, rather than being *a part* of it. By taking more than we give we can only become energetically constipated!

"When you were born, you received a gift—a body, a soul, a spirit and all your faculties—everything you need to have a productive, rewarding and universally connected life. It is important to pay back for these gifts because only from the position of payback and appreciation and value can you build something that is everlasting that will survive your physical death. The gift you have received is a platform and a beginning and a way of receiving further gifts that can survive this life. It is only in the way of giving to receive that these further gifts can be bestowed upon us.

"So don't expect too much of yourself or others and have within you the idea that one always has to earn what one gets. Work first and don't think about the rewards, because they will come on their own account. Anyway, your view of what these rewards may be is so limited that if you try to project what you are next supposed to get, you will limit yourself to stay within the realms of what you already know and what you already have. Therefore I suggest you adopt the saying 'Give to live.'

"You have heard the saying, 'What goes round comes around,' and this is very true, for energy cannot be destroyed. So if you give as a way of life, you will also get in return. To use an analogy, if you have money in the bank, this is the money that you have managed to stop from circulating (though the bank will continue to circulate it for you, earning profit for themselves and perhaps a little bit for you). It is money you have taken, whether earned or received as a gift. In the electrical realms, energy that is not circulating can go stale. You cannot accumulate force or electrical wealth, but by giving it away, you can only get more. In other words, you bank your energy by giving it away; you earn interest by being interested in everyone and everything else." I smiled at this analogy because it seemed so appropriate and easy to understand.

"Think how you respond when you are given a present," she continued. "Don't you want to pay back and reciprocate, whether by note or kind word or by deed, perhaps some time in the future? Don't you always remember those who have given when you needed it most? Well, creation is like that too and creation will remember its givers. So a giver, rather than a taker be."

Chapter Seventeen

Giving Thanks

On Sunday Brian picked me up and we traveled out of town to a farm, where Nancy, the dancer lived with her husband and two children. They had horses and cows and a large barn with stables and a paddock. The farm was in a secluded area and they had obviously put a lot of care and work into their domain. Nancy's husband was away and she had invited a number of friends and acquaintances to come together and meet Brian, the healer. They all seemed to have some ailment or condition that needed urgent attention; I also felt that they had come out of curiosity. There were about a dozen people in the room and after we all settled, you could feel the expectation and excitement mounting in the atmosphere. There were people sitting on the two sofas and the four dining room chairs that were brought in from the adjoining room, as well as a couple of people sitting on the floor. All eyes were on Brian, who sat in an armchair and started by explaining that healing was a gift and that it was accessible to anyone who believed in it and was prepared to work for it.

"The healing energy is free," Brian said. "I do not pay for it and I will not charge you for it. It comes from the universe and it will return to the universe when I stop practicing healing. It has its own intelligence and sometimes it comes, but not always. I do not command it; it chooses when it wishes to manifest." He paused for a moment and then spoke in a dramatic whisper, as we all felt something special and magical in the room's atmosphere. "It is here now," he said and as I looked around I could see that everyone felt it—their faces were glowing and all eyes were shining. Even the colors of the furniture and objects in the room looked brighter, shinier and more attractive, as if someone had come in and peformed a really thorough spring cleaning. It felt like being transported into a different world where miracles are possible. It made me wonder about the work of saints and special people who throughout history have performed extraordinary deeds, bringing healing, hope and humanity to desperate people.

It was quiet for a moment and then a girl who was sitting on the floor, spoke up. "I have cancer," she said and she took the scarf she was wearing off her head and we could all see that she was bald. Nevertheless, there was something very attractive in her face, like a glimmer of hope. "Can you heal me?" she asked in a matter-of-fact way.

Brian looked at her for a moment and then said, "I don't know." After a further moment of deep silence, he added, "Bring a chair out here," and he pointed to the space in front of him, in the middle of the circle.

A man got up and offered his chair, then proceeded to sit on the floor in the space vacated by the girl who got up and walked towards the empty chair.

"What is your name?" asked Brian.

"Jenny," she replied.

"Sit down in the chair," Brian said. Jenny sat down facing him. Her knees were almost touching Brian's. He waited for a moment, then he said, "Hold my hands." He extended both hands towards her and she took hold of them, while she continued looking into his eyes.

"Imagine the cancer gone," he said. Jenny nodded and closed her eyes. At that moment a strange thing happened. Nancy's young son ran into the room crying, "Mommy," but as soon as he passed the threshold, he stopped and quieted, not wishing to disturb. Nancy got up from the sofa and walked towards him, but she didn't need to say anything, because he was already turning around to leave. Nancy led him out of the room and soon she was back. "He felt something," she said softly as she sat back in her place on the sofa. In the meantime

Jenny had kept her eyes closed and looked as if she were in a trance with a faint smile on her face. Some of the other people had closed their eyes as well and seemed to be meditating or praying. I don't know how long the moment lasted, but it felt like a long time. Finally Brian addressed Jenny. "What did you feel?" he asked.

"At first I felt tingling and some heat," she replied. "And then, as you held my hands, I could feel the energy passing from you to me. It was almost like holding on to a live wire," she added with a smile.

"That is the healing energy," said Brian. "It doesn't belong to me; it just passes through me. I wish you a full recovery," he said as he disengaged his hands from her grip.

"Thank you," said Jenny.

After that there were a few more demonstrations, in which Brian showed those gathered how to feel and see an aura and the energy fields around people. It was an amazing demonstration, because although we had all heard the word before, we didn't really know what an aura was. When Brian stood in the middle of the circle with arms outstretched over his head, there were audible gasps as several people could clearly see colored lights around his arms and body.

"You need to learn to unfocus your eyes," Brian explained. "Look long distance over my head and just relax your eyes." A few more people could see a glimmer of light radiating over Brian's head.

"You all have an aura," he explained. It surrounds the body and is made up of very fine electrical and magnetic charges. It might be easier to see around a healer—it simply depends on who you are and what you think about."

"That was a fascinating meeting," I told Brian later in the car, as he was driving me home. "There definitely was something in that room. A distinct atmosphere or energy," I added.

"Yes, and it is growing in strength daily," Brian said. "As long as I am its custodian, I feel the responsibility to pass it on and to offer healings to people who need it."

"It seems like a very demanding mission," I said.

"It is," he confirmed. "But I wouldn't want to do anything else. I work because I need to earn a living, but this is my real vocation.

When that healing energy is present, I feel alive and I know it is what I need to be doing. But it will only come when there is a need."

It was quiet for a moment, then he added, changing the subject, "I am not sure I should commit to a relationship at the moment. My time is spoken for and every moment needs to be dedicated to helping others." I wasn't sure how to respond. I felt like this was the end of the beginning and the beginning of the end both at the same time. There was nothing between us and yet it was ending; or perhaps there was something that was not being given a chance to blossom into a relationship. Either way, I felt a loss and a grief.

"I felt today that I could be of help to you," I said. "Perhaps we could establish a different kind of relationship." As I was speaking I was curious what was coming out of my mouth. "I know things about people and sometimes I can tell what is wrong with them," I said. "I could help you."

Brian looked at me as he was pulling up in front of Alice's house.

"Don't get me wrong," he said. "I find you attractive. I want to make love to you. But I also need to consider the consequences and how that would affect my work, your work and the healing work that I need to do."

"Well, I think it is not by chance that we went together to that gathering today. I know what kind of cancer Jenny has. Do you?" I asked, trying to prove my point.

"No, I don't" he said. "She didn't say."

"No, she didn't, but I know. She had ovarian cancer, but you cured it."

"Really?" He looked surprised.

"Yes, and you will soon find out." I kissed Brian on the cheek and got out of the car. He still looked stunned as I closed the door on the passenger's side and bent over to wave goodbye.

I spent Thanksgiving Thursday at my parents' house where three generations of women contributed to the feast. My mother baked the turkey, some potatoes and cooked the asparagus, Grandmother brought the salad and provided the cranberry sauce and I made my delicious Ambrosia—a pineapple cream dessert. It was a rare opportunity for my grandmother to talk about the old days and the importance of the giving of thanks.

"Every day I say thank you," she said as we were seated at my mother's dining room table with the food laid out in front of us. "There is so much to be thankful for. If you are not thankful for what you have, how do you expect to achieve more? How would you feel if you gave someone a precious present and all they did was gripe and complain?"

I wasn't sure whether these comments were directed at my mother, me, or no one in particular. My grandmother continued, "The universe is no different; it will give to those who appreciate its gifts. We were given the precious gift of life and there is nothing more precious than that. So today, let us be thankful for our life, our health and the opportunities that lie before us. We are here for a reason and every day we can try again to fulfill our unique mission. Whether you are old or young, life is an adventure, an allowance and a gift, so treat it well." Following this short lesson, Grandmother nodded at my stepfather who picked up the carving knife and fork and proceeded to carve the turkey for our Thanksgiving dinner.

I went to work on Friday, because there was a delivery that needed to be organized, but many employees were away visiting their families or friends in many parts of the country. Alice had gone to see her parents in North Carolina and I was looking forward to having the house all to myself. I was working on the computer, making a list of items that needed to be loaded onto the truck that afternoon, when the phone rang. It was Andrew and he wanted me to know that he was stranded at an airport in Colorado, waiting for the weather to clear, so that he could catch his next flight out west. He told me that he would not be around for ten days and that he would be in touch as soon as he got back. I was still talking to him on the phone when Brian walked into my office.

"You were right," he said and I had no idea what he was talking about.

"About what?" I asked and I quickly said to Andrew, "Got to go," and put the receiver down.

"About that girl, Jenny," he replied. "She's cured. No more cancer, though they are still giving her radiation treatment to make sure, but they've suspended the chemotherapy. And she did tell me it was ovarian cancer. So you were right on both counts."

"That's great," I said. Although I had made that prediction, I was just as surprised as he was. I knew I had the gift of clairvoyance, but I still had not learned how to know when it was working and how to trust my own visions, as they always appeared unexpectedly, without warning.

"Yes, it is great," he confirmed. "But what does it mean for me? What are the consequences of such a state of affairs?"

"Well, you've always wanted to be a healer," I said. "It looks like your wish is coming true."

"Yes, but Barbara, I'm scared," he said and indeed he looked vulnerable in a way that I had never seen before. "I better get back to work," he added and turned away. His vulnerability made me feel protective and even sorry for him. I waited a few minutes to make sure that he had time to get back to his office and I phoned him up.

"Do you want to come round for dinner tonight?" I asked when he picked up the phone.

"I'd love to," he replied and after a moment's thought, he added, "What about Alice, won't she mind?" he asked.

"She's away," I said, "visiting her parents."

"That's right," he confirmed. "What about eight? I'll bring the wine."

"That will be great," I said. As I put the phone down, I had a frightening vision—I could see Brian's body lying on a slab in a morgue. I quickly dismissed the vision because I had no way of knowing what time frame the vision pertained to, if it was real at all. Perhaps it just was a manifestation of my innermost fears. Still influenced by the atmosphere of Thanksgiving, I decided to concentrate on the fact of his life and our growing friendship instead.

Chapter Eighteen

Jealousy

Brian was on time and I was ready when he arrived, as promised, with a bottle of wine in a paper bag in hand. I had even surprised myself, that I had managed to clean up the house, boil some rice and cut up all the vegetables for a stir-fry—one of the few dishes that I was really good at making. I had also made a colorful salad with lettuce, carrots, spring onions, tomatoes and yellow peppers. There was even an apple pie in the oven, though I had not baked it myself, but nobody needed to know. As soon as he walked through the door, I took the bottle from him and set it down on the small table that was near the entrance. I took his coat and hung it up in the closet. Then I was about to pick up the bottle and carry it into the kitchen, and there was this awkward moment when we just looked at each other. Something sparked between us and I took a step towards him and he embraced me and kissed me. It was a long, exciting, delicious kiss and it was difficult to tear myself away. In fact, I didn't want to and I was quite prepared to let the dinner wait and let the pie burn, but Brian finally pulled himself away and asked, "So what have you got cooking? I can smell something good!"

"Well, that's for dessert, but we do have a stir-fry with shrimp, rice and vegetables and a salad. I should have asked you if there is anything you don't eat."

"I don't eat red meat, so this sounds great." I walked towards the kitchen and Brian picked up the wine and followed me. "Where is your corkscrew?" he asked. I opened a drawer and handed the implement to him. I then reached into another cabinet and pulled out two of Alice's best crystal wine glasses. Brian popped the cork and poured the wine. It was white, cold and dry. "To your health," I said.

"To the future," Brian replied and we touched glasses. We both knew that tonight was the night and we were prolonging the introductory moments, putting off the grand finale.

I lit a ring on the stove, placed the wok over the heat and started adding the vegetables to the oil.

"This should be ready in a few moments," I said.

"That's fine, no need to hurry." He was standing next to me. "Can I do anything?" he asked.

"No, I think I can manage," I replied as I put the peppers and carrots into the wok. Soon I was adding the final touches of tamari sauce to the stir-fry and then dishing it out into a bowl, ready for the table.

"Well, let's eat, the food is ready." I said. I picked up the wine glasses and Brian helped me carry the bowl with the stir-fry to the table.

As we sat down and helped ourselves to the food, I asked another question that had been bothering me ever since he had suggested dinner. "I thought you didn't want a relationship," I said. "So why are you here?"

"I am not sure," Brian replied. "I can't make a commitment, but I think there is a reason why we are together tonight. When you said that Jenny had ovarian cancer, and it turned out to be right, I thought that perhaps we could work together after all."

"Working together does not mean having a relationship."

"No, it doesn't, but I think this is meant to be." Brian reached for my hand across the table. "When I touch you," he said, "something happens. I can feel a transfer of energy, like I have never felt before." I could feel it too. "I think you are powering my gift of healing."

"That sounds like a selfish reason to me," I stated, somewhat hurt that he was contemplating a relationship with me in order to gain power.

I withdrew my hand.

"I didn't mean it like that," he said. "I would hope that my power is adding to your power as well and that we can both gain more power from each other."

"I understand that that is possible," I said, remembering my grandmother's words about people who give energy, those who take it away and those with whom a person is able to manufacture more, by tapping into a third source.

"I don't know where this is leading," Brian said. "And I don't want to make any commitments, but I want you." He put down his fork, leaving the unfinished food on his plate and walked towards me.

"Come here," he said and pulled me up from my seat and drew me towards him. I could feel his body and I knew that the moment had come. We started kissing and his hands were soon unzipping my sweat suit top. He then started guiding me towards the bedroom, and I soon realized that he was leading me towards Alice's room. I didn't want to pull away from his advances, so I let him lead me towards Alice's king size bed. As soon as we reached the bed, we fell onto it and continued to embrace and help each other undress. My top and pants were soon on the floor, his pants and shirt were thrown on the other side of the bed and he was in the process of undoing the clasp on my bra when in the distance I could hear a key turn in the lock of the front door. I pulled away and gasped in shock, "Alice's back!" Brian looked stunned and bewildered and quite immobilized. He didn't say anything.

"Quick, get dressed!" I said as I scrambled off the bed, doing up my bra and reaching for my top. But it was too late and I could see Alice standing in the doorway, with her mouth open and eyes looking as if they would jump out of their sockets. She was silent for a moment, but soon she regained her voice and screamed, "What are you doing in my bedroom?"

I reached for my pants as Brian was scrambling for his clothes, hastily putting on his pants as well. "I'm sorry," I said.

"It's all my fault," Brian admitted. "We were having dinner and I carried her in here. I didn't know whose bedroom it was."

"Well, get out," she was still screaming. Brian got hold of his shirt and went for the door. Alice stood aside to let him pass. I picked up my top and followed him into the living room. I could hear Alice closing the door behind us. From the living room I could see her suitcase by the door.

"I'm sorry," Brian said.

"Don't be," I replied. "It's not your fault."

"I should have known that was her bedroom," he confessed. "I've been in it enough times."

"It's all right. You better go," I said.

"Are you sure? Don't you want to leave with me? We could go somewhere and have a coffee."

"No thank you, I better stay." I said. Brian walked towards the door and I followed him.

"I'll call you," he said. He was still buttoning his shirt. He took his coat from the closet, kissed me on the cheek and left. As I closed the door behind him, I could hear Alice coming out of her bedroom. I could tell she had been crying. She was calmer now, but very angry.

"How dare you bring him in here and then make love to him on my bed?" she demanded through clenched teeth. She was holding a tissue and dabbing at her eyes.

"Alice, I'm sorry. I don't know what came over us."

"I knew it. I knew it would come to no good, your sneaking around with him."

"I'm not sneaking!" I protested.

"Yes, you are! You think I don't know what is going on? I see everything. I want you out of here!" she added. My head was swimming. Where could I go at this hour?

"But Alice, I have nowhere to go."

"Yes you do, go to that grandmother of yours. She always gives you good advice. See what she tells you this time."

I couldn't believe this was happening, but I decided to do what she said. So I went into my room without a word, packed a couple of bags and started to walk towards the door. I could see that Alice was in the kitchen, washing up the dishes we had used during dinner. I dropped my bags and walked to the door of the kitchen and said, "I'll pick up the rest tomorrow. I can't carry everything in one go." Alice didn't reply, so I just headed towards the door, picked up my bags and left into the night. As I reached the street with my two bags, I wondered whether Alice would find the apple pie in the oven and enjoy a helping or two. I smiled at the thought and wondered whether it would be over-baked by now.

I did go to my grandmother's house and it took me a while to wake her up. Finally she came downstairs in her dressing gown.

"Is that you, Barbara?" she asked.

"Yes, Grandmother, it's me. Something happened."

My grandmother opened the door and let me in.

"Oh dear," she said, "look at you." It was raining and my hair was wet and no doubt my mascara was smudged and I must have looked a mess.

She led me to her guest room and said that we would talk the following morning.

Next day was Saturday and we had breakfast together. I told her all about Brian and Alice and what had happened the previous night. Her first response was to reprimand me for letting myself be led into Alice's bedroom. She told me I had no right being there and that Alice had every reason to be angry. She then considered the history of our relationship and became thoughtful.

"Alice is jealous," my grandmother said. "It's as simple as that. It is very strange that people are jealous of each other, when there is plenty of everything on this planet to satisfy everyone's needs. And yet jealousy prevails, especially when two women are attracted to the same man or when two men are attracted to the same woman. So what do you think jealousy is?"

"I don't know, but now that I am thinking about it, I get the sense that it is a desire to possess something that cannot be possessed."

"That's very good," Grandmother confirmed. "It is true that possession lies at the root of jealousy. Because if we were totally selfless and impersonal, we would want for another person what they would want for themselves. But somehow there often seems to be a clash of interests between people. In a workplace or in a team, people will often be jealous of each other, rather than be glad that someone is doing well. In any discipline there will always be someone who is better than you, unless you happen to be the best in the world. So why be jealous? If there is someone who is more advanced, more experienced, more talented, then there is someone to learn from. If you are the absolute best at what you do, who are you going to learn from? Who are you going to look up to?

"Decide, if you can, never to be jealous. Jealousy can eat away your energy and even cause illness; it makes everyone lose—the person who is jealous, as well as the person who is the object of their jealousy. Imagine a situation in which there is a team who have worked together on a project. The boss comes in and is pleased with the result. He turns to one of the members of the team and praises him or her, without acknowledging the rest of the team who are also present. How will the others feel? Will they be pleased that their co-worker receives all the praise or will they be jealous that they have not been singled out and praised like their team-mate? Will the one who has been praised have a hard time in the future because the others will be jealous of his success and want to hold him back? Also, will he acknowledge the work of the team and make sure they are appreciated as well? What if he is more talented or more hardworking than the others and the praise was deserved? Will the others be fair and admit that he had earned such recognition or will they still be jealous? And what if the praise is not deserved? Will they make sure the boss finds out who had really done the work?

"You see, there is a subtle difference between jealousy and envy. Jealousy is destructive and it would cause a person to prefer no one had a success rather than if it were to be somebody else. Iago in Othello personifies jealousy, destroying both himself and Othello, as well as causing the killing of Desdemona. Jealousy is indeed the green-eyed monster as it is an emotion that causes a dark green color to appear in the aura and virtually eat away at the energy of the person. Envy, on the other hand, is much less harmful. It will cause you to wish you had what another person has achieved, but it is not destructive in that you do not begrudge them their success; you only wish you were equally successful. Envy can turn positive if, inspired by the achievements of another person, you decide to follow their example and become determined to achieve a similar success.

"But in the case of a relationship, if a person is set on being with a certain man or woman who are already in a different relationship, if they are unable to control their desires, this can lead to jealousy. I am afraid that is what Alice is experiencing. As I said, it is a very destructive and difficult emotion. It never leads to any good, and it usually involves self-deception, lying and all kinds of pretences."

"So what should I do?"

"I would advise you to think of Alice as a sick individual who needs help. Be gentle with her but don't give in to her demands. Try and understand that the girl is in pain. She probably genuinely believes she is protecting you from a fate similar to her own. So be diplomatic, but you also need to get on with your own life. And by the way, you can stay here as long as you need to."

Chapter Nineteen

Security

I couldn't sleep that night. I kept tossing and turning on Grandmother's sofa bed that she had made up for me the night before in the spare room. It was so strange that every time Brian and I tried to come together, something would happen to keep us apart. I was also thinking about Brian's healing powers and where that endeavor was leading him. What would happen if the drug companies found out he could heal cancer or even AIDS with a wave of the hand? What would the authorities say? Was it even legal for him to continue doing what he was doing? Did I want to get involved? I could see a life of uncertainty, late night calls and unexpected travel to distant destinations where some poor soul would be lying in pain, begging for help, because the medical profession had given up on him or her. And then, on the other hand, there was so much good that could be done and perhaps we could work together, perhaps I could help see what was wrong or what needed to be done. Perhaps together we could form a team and help alleviate some of the misery that was plaguing this world.

Then there was Andrew, who was serious, reliable and ready for a commitment. Although he did not excite me, I believed that he would offer me a stable relationship, a good life with a roof over my head and food on the table, perhaps even a couple of kids and holidays in the sun. I smiled to myself when I thought about such a possibility. I had been a wanderer for too long and I felt the attraction and pull of a secure suburban life. But then, how long would it last?

I didn't see Brian that weekend. I called his house twice, but once I got his answering machine and the second time I recognized his brother's voice on the phone. The first time I left him a message, telling him where I was and leaving him my grandmother's phone number, and the second time I simply hung up. As soon as I put the receiver down, the phone rang. It was James.

"Did you just call?" he asked. No doubt he had caller ID, so there was no point in lying.

"I did," I said.

"Is that Barbara?" he asked. I was surprised to hear my name.

"Yes," I replied.

"Sorry about the other night," he said. "I think I had a little too much to drink."

"A lot too much," I corrected him.

"Well, I'd like to make it up to you. How about coming out for a drink tonight?"

"No, thank you, I'm busy," I said.

"But you called Brian, didn't you? Brian is out of town on some mission of his. So how about I take his place?"

"No thank you," I made it sound as firm as I could muster.

"Well, let me know if you get lonely. You know where to find me." I couldn't help thinking that he was the biggest creep I had ever met.

Sunday evening I sat with my grandmother and we had a light supper together.

"So what do you want from a relationship?" Grandmother asked after I had explained my predicament, and how I felt about Brian and Andrew. I thought for a moment and then replied, "I used to think that I want excitement and passion, but now I am beginning to think that I want security." It was quiet for a moment and then I added, as an afterthought, "Perhaps I am getting older."

"Well, let's look at what you mean when you say security," Grandmother said. Then she asked, "What do you mean by the word security?"

I hesitated for a moment, but I didn't feel the question was difficult, because I had given it a lot of thought during the last few days. "Security is stability," I said. "It means being able to rely on the status quo continuing; it means not having to worry about the basics, knowing that they are taken care of on a regular basis. It means being financially free to get on with my life without worrying where the next rent payment is going to come from. It means having a stable relationship in which my partner would be reliable and comforting, always there for me at the end of the day. That's what security means to me."

"All right, let's look at what you have said so far," Grandmother said and yet again, I knew I was in for a lesson. "So far, you have spoken a lot about your needs and what security means to you," she continued. "But let's look at it impersonally. Everything you have said could be understood to come under the umbrella of what is already known and established. Take home, for example. Most people do feel secure at home, or at least they try to make home as secure as possible. What does that mean? It means no unexpected intrusions, it means a place where a person can relax, unwind, enjoy the basic pleasures and necessities of life, like a meal, a sleep, ablutions, sex, some TV, a hobby and a stable relationship. All these things are either to do with maintenance to allow continuance or facilitate the getting rid of the expendable—as in cleaning, both in the physical sense and also as far as the worlds of energy are concerned. These processes are necessary to survive and to live to see another day, but we humans have another need as well, which is to do with how we intend to progress and what we would want to promote into the future. Every human has their wishes, their desires, their urges, ambitions, missions, visions or mere fantasies, but we all have them. These are the energy spurs, cogs and wheels that keep us going, that push and prod us on to do something useful, to do better, to improve. Mostly people leave the home to find their next platform, to follow their dream and realize their potential. We all try to make the journey from Kansas to Oz, from security to the whirlwind of new opportunity. Home is what we know, what we have already accomplished and established and what makes us feel secure. Good or bad, it gives us our daily refuge, a roof over our heads, a meal, a human exchange. If things go wrong, if you get sick, you run for home, where the rules are understood and mostly obeyed, where every move, corner, path, custom are practiced, well trodden, made safe, where there are no surprises, no sudden changes, no unexpected demands.

"So what prevents us from exploration into new territories? Fear—it causes a person to back off, into a situation or relationship that is like a well-worn garment; it makes our every move predictable and our weaknesses acceptable. Imagine that your experience up to this moment is a box, then the limitless possibility of what you may become is everything outside that box and it is virtually unlimited. Anything new, any new situation, every undiscovered piece of ground, all un-thought thoughts, unheard sounds, unseen sights, un-smelt scents, untouched objects—all these represent your future, as long as you are prepared to come out of the box into what is new. The proportions of the box would be more like a dot within a huge blank expanse because, taking, for example, the number of places we know as opposed to those we do not know—on the planet, in history and in the universe—it is hard to even imagine what that would be. To take an easy to count example of homes, how many have you lived in and how many have you visited?"

"I don't know," I replied. "I have lived in four homes and probably I visited about a hundred," I estimated.

"Let's say the average for the world is five people per dwelling, then there are more than twelve hundred million homes you haven't been in. And that only represents the current times. What about the past and the future? What about other buildings, like community halls, churches, theaters, hotels, monuments? What about elsewhere in the universe? What could that figure be like?" She paused and the room was quiet for a moment, as I contemplated these figures.

Grandmother continued. She was on a roll. "This new adventure and discovery of what we may become requires a person to change their thinking, instead of thinking that the box of what has been done is already established and adequate and that it represents security. You need to see that the way of progress, development and evolution is change, appearing under the guise of something new and original. To get in touch with these aspects of one's opportunity, one must come out of one's box of established patterns into the wide-open space of onsetting new times. To do this one must see and think of change as representing a new kind of security, because the old ways have not brought about human evolution, have they? And if we are to think in universal terms, we need to see that the universe is a safe place. If the word security could come to represent everything outside of the box, then thinking about the future would become so much more accessible, tangible and realistic. For where else would our security lie, if not in the chance of change? If this planet were to continue as it has done for millions of years, with the human as it has evolved to this point, then there would be no future for us, the planet or the universe within which we live. So think of security as outside of that box."

I could feel my mind stretching to accept this notion, but I also felt that if I truly adopted it into my thinking patterns, my life would change. So I decided to give it a try.

On Monday Brian re-entered my life. I went into work early, so that I could avoid seeing Alice at the reception desk. Indeed, there were very few people around in the office, though the accounting department was already busy and the loading bay was humming with activity in preparation for the day's deliveries. As I walked up to my desk, I saw a note and I immediately knew it was from Brian. I picked it up even before I had time to take my coat off and it said simply, "Meet me for lunch. I'll wait for you in the car park at one o'clock." So I got on with my work, staying close to my desk and punctually at one I grabbed my coat and went outside. He was sitting in his car at the far end of the parking lot, so no one would see him. I got in and we drove off. As soon as we were away from the building, Brian asked, "So what happened? Did she calm down? Was it all right?"

"Didn't you get my message?" I asked.

"No, what message?"

"I spoke to that brother of yours and I also left a message on your answering machine, explaining that I was staying with my grandmother. She kicked me out."

"Your grandmother kicked you out?"

"No, of course not. Alice did."

"Oh, I'm sorry to hear that. That was my fault."

"No, it wasn't. I should have said something when you were leading me into her bedroom. But I let you do it."

He smiled at the memory of that night. "So what are you going to do?" he asked.

"I don't know. I need time to think."

We stopped in front of the same Italian restaurant where Alice had quizzed me about Brian, but I still didn't want to mention that instance. I felt we needed to talk about the present and the future, not the past. Already Alice was receding into my history.

As soon as we sat down, the same waiter that seemed to know Brian acknowledged him with a smile and came up to our table. "What can I get you?" he asked.

We ordered the specials and continued to talk.

"So where were you this weekend?" I asked.

"I was out of town, meeting some friends of Nancy. After that healing I did when you were there, there were several more requests. So I went out to Nancy's farm and spent the weekend doing healings." He paused and then continued, and I had a feeling that he was delivering a well-prepared speech. "I don't know if you want to be with someone like me." Brian looked at my quizzical expression and continued to explain. "You see, my life is missioned; it is not my own. I have made a decision. I have the gift of healing and therefore it is my responsibility to use it to the benefit of others. I don't know where it will lead me, but I do know that I must follow its calling. I cannot change that and turn aside and have what might be considered a 'normal life.' My life is an adventure into the unknown and if you want to join me in it, then welcome to my world. But if you want a suburban house, two kids and the kind of stability that a well-paid job would contribute to the household, then forget it. I am as unpredictable as next year's weather." He paused for a moment and smiled, obviously pleased at the analogy. We fell quiet as the waiter delivered our food.

"I don't know what I want," I said, "but I am trying hard to figure it out. It seems that whenever we get together, something comes between us to stop us or separate us. It's either your healings or your brother or Alice. Your life indeed seems very unpredictable."

"That's exactly right," he confirmed. "It has always been like that." There was silence for a moment and then he said, unexpectedly, "Let's go away for the weekend. No cell phones, no computers, no phone calls, just a quiet time together." He reached for my hand across the table and squeezed it. This was a big surprise; just as I had decided that this was the parting speech, here he was starting it all up again. It was almost like dealing with two different people—one was attracted to me and couldn't keep his hands off me, while the other was dedicated to the idea of being a healer and wanted to be free and unattached. I had no idea how I was going to cope with these two—Brian One and Brian Two, as I nicknamed them in my mind.

"Sure, let's do it," I said to Brian One, hoping that Brian Two was not going to sabotage our time together this time.

Chapter Twenty

Value

The weekend was the most extraordinary experience of my life, but not in the way I would have imagined. Brian picked me up from my grandmother's house at seven in the evening. I had packed in the morning and had bought a few clothes for the trip; it always makes me feel better if I have something new to wear. I was excited and a little bit scared at the same time. It was already dark and as we drove out of town, the houses we passed were already illuminated with multi-colored Christmas lights and the front gardens were decorated with reindeers and Santas aglow with light. The atmosphere was festive and there was a chill in the air; it felt like it was going to snow. We didn't talk much during the drive and Brian played some background music as we drove on for what seemed to be a long time. I did ask him where we were going, but he said it was a surprise.

When we did arrive, we pulled up in front of an average looking suburban house; not quite the splendid surroundings I had been imagining.

"Where are we?" I asked.

"I want you to meet an old friend of mine," Brian said.

"Who's that?" I asked.

"He was in the army and got shot in the leg by mistake during practice. He can hardly walk since the bullet has damaged the nerve. He is in constant pain and I think I can help him."

"But I thought we were going to have a weekend without healing, without phones and without other people," I protested.

"If we can help someone, I think we should try. That is a motto I would wish to live by and I would hope that you could agree. I thought it would be a good way to test our compatibility as partners. You see, I think our entire future is at stake here," he added.

"All right," I said, "so are we supposed to be staying with this friend of yours?"

"Yes, he will put us up for the weekend. I grew up in this area," he added. We got out of the car and Brian walked around it, opening the trunk with his key. I joined him, ready to help with our bags. At that moment a light came on in a downstairs window and the door opened. A man in jeans, a sweatshirt and slippers stood smiling in the doorway.

"Brian," he called out and I could see his breath in the cold air. "So good to see you."

"Hi Antony," Brian stepped forward holding my elbow and walked up to the house. The two men shook hands. "This is my assistant, Barbara," he said and I smiled as I shook hands with Antony. He had a soft, pleasant face and a warm smile. "Nice to meet you," I said as I wondered whether Brian meant I was his assistant at work or in healing.

"It's a pleasure," Antony said. "Please come in." He guided us into the living room.

"Do you want something to eat?" Antony asked.

"No, let's get to work," Brian replied.

"I think I need a shower," I interjected. "It's been a long drive."

"OK, I'll bring the bags in from the car," said Brian. I remembered the car trunk was still open.

"I'll help you," I said.

"And I'll make some coffee," volunteered Antony.

Forty minutes later we had all gathered back in the living room. Antony was sitting on the sofa with his pant leg rolled up, revealing a nasty scar and dent in his leg, just below the knee. Brian asked him a few questions about the pain. I had noticed that Antony had a bad limp and was in fact dragging his right leg, as if he had very little feeling in it at all.

"It hurts all the time," Antony said. "Some days are worse than others and I always know when it is going to rain." He smiled but immediately having said that, he winced with pain. "Can you help me?" he asked.

"I'll try," Brian replied. He walked up to the sofa where Antony was sitting and placed his hand over the wound, kneeling on one leg beside the sofa.

"Can you feel that?" he asked.

"I can feel warmth, which does feel soothing," Antony replied.

I watched for a moment and then I stepped forward. I put my hand over Brian's and guided it towards Antony's knee. The nerve damage is in the knee," I said. "That's where you need to do the healing." Brian looked at me surprised and then looked questioningly at Antony.

"She might be right," Antony said. "There was a second wound in the knee, but the scar is almost gone. I banged my knee really badly when I fell on the concrete."

Brian didn't say anything but let me guide his hand towards Antony's knee and held it there for what felt like a long time. I didn't take my hand away because I could feel the energy passing from me to Brian and into Antony's leg. I felt that the healing was accelerating and instinctively it felt like the right thing to do.

"I can certainly feel that," Antony said. So could I. The atmosphere in the room changed. It was very quiet and the smallest sound, like the ticking of the clock on a small table nearby and the sound of the fridge that occasionally kicked in and came in from the kitchen next door, a cat outside, perhaps on a neighbor's lawn—all these sounds seemed loud and almost intrusive. Antony leaned back and every muscle in his body seemed to relax. He closed his eyes and sighed. In the meantime my hand was burning hot and I could feel that Brian's was too. Still, we held our hands there for what seemed like a very long time, but probably amounted to only minutes. Finally I took my hand away, because it was hot, throbbing and began to hurt. I straightened my back, while Brian kept his hand over Antony's knee for a while longer. Antony looked completely relaxed, for the first time since I had met him. Brian eventually stood up and asked, "Are you all right?"

Antony opened his eyes, smiled and replied, "Never better. The pain has gone," he said. Brian held out his hand.

"Why don't you try to stand up," he said to Antony. Antony took his hand and pulled himself up from the sofa. He stood there for a moment, as he put his weight on both legs. He waited for a couple of moments while he shifted his weight from leg to leg. He then said, "I feel no pain." Brian moved aside and Antony took a couple of steps away from the sofa. He stopped and looked back at us with an incredulous expression on his face. "No pain," he said. "I can't even remember when I felt no pain," he added. He took another couple of steps and then started pacing around the room, increasing his speed. He obviously felt bolder now, as he placed one foot in front of the other. The limp was gone.

"I'm walking like I used to," he said and shook his head as if he still couldn't quite believe it. He then did something obviously daring: he hopped on one foot, then on the other.

"I can't believe it," he said. "Still no pain." He was now hopping from foot to foot; it looked like he was doing a jog. Then he stopped, and looked at Brian. He had tears in his eyes.

"You cured me!" he said. He walked up to Brian and held out his hand. The two men shook hands and then embraced. "Thank you," Antony whispered.

"It wasn't me," said Brian. "It's the healing force. It comes through me, but it isn't mine. I cannot command it."

"Well, in that case I thank the healing force," Antony said.

"Can I have a glass of water?" Brian asked.

"Sure," Antony replied and he went to the kitchen to fulfill Brian's request.

"That was remarkable," I said to Brian with genuine admiration.

"This is just the beginning," Brian replied.

"What do you mean?" I asked.

"The world needs healing and I feel it is my destiny to bring it to the world. I have big visions and I can see a whole series of clinics, schools and hospitals."

Antony came back into the room with three glasses of water on a tray. He placed the tray on the coffee table.

"I still can't quite believe it. Still no pain" he said.

Brian reached for a glass and handed another one to me.

"Miracles do happen," he said.

"They certainly do," confirmed Antony. We stood around for a moment and then Antony said, "My daughter is sleeping upstairs. She has had ear infections on and off for the last eight years; she is now twelve. She gets a high temperature and they give her antibiotics and she suffers a great deal of pain. Can you help her?"

"I can try," Brian replied. "Maybe tomorrow."

"All right. Perhaps I should let you two get some sleep. I'll be upstairs, first door on the right, if you need anything." Antony walked out of the room and I noticed that he was still walking without a limp. As soon as he left, I turned to Brian.

"I had no idea this would be a healing trip," I said.

"Well, I thought it would give us time to be together, to get to know each other."

"Here in this house? We're surrounded by other people. We can't make love here." There, I said it. I let him know about my expectations. I think he understood for he stood there quiet for a moment.

"All right, let's go for a drive," he said. He took me by the hand and led me towards the front door.

"We're going out for a while," he shouted up the stairs so Antony could hear.

"All right, I'll leave the door open," Antony called back.

Brian picked up the keys to the car, which he had left on a table next to the door and we both put on our coats.

"Come on," Brian said.

We walked into the quiet suburban night and got into the car.

"Where are we going?" I asked.

"We're going to a quiet spot," Brian replied as he drove away.

He was soon driving down a dark road with no road signs or lights.

"Do you know where you are going?" I asked, somewhat concerned. It had been a long day and I was tired. I was beginning to regret that I had reminded him that we were supposed to be spending some time together without intrusion.

"Don't worry," Brian said as he patted my knee and allowed his hand to wander up my thigh. I felt shivers go through my body. "I know this area well. I grew up near here." He soon turned off the road onto a gravel path and in a couple of minutes a view opened up—we were driving towards a lake and the moon had just risen over the horizon illuminating a silver pathway along the surface of the water. It was a beautiful clear night with a million stars shining brightly.

"I used to come swimming here at night and sometimes I would take a boat out and just sit and meditate in the middle of the lake."

"How beautiful," I said. Brian parked the car and reclined his seat. "The reclining knob is on the other side of the seat," he said. I found the knob and turned it, so that the seat reclined. "Take your coat off," Brian commanded as he struggled out of his and threw it onto the back seat. I followed his example and struggled out of my coat. Brian took his glasses off and leaned towards me. Not the most comfortable place to have a first sexual encounter and we had to find a position that would work, with my head resting against the side window and one leg propped up over the steering wheel, but it was nevertheless a thrilling experience, though physically uncomfortable. I felt closer to Brian than ever before—I couldn't believe it was finally going to happen and I felt excited, thrilled and aroused as I could feel his body on top of me and as his hands wandered and explored underneath my sweater, searching for my breasts. He kissed me and it was the most erotic experience that had ever happened to me. I returned the kiss with everything I could muster and just at that moment we were illuminated by a light and we could hear the engine of a car as it pulled up behind us. We quickly sat up, adjusting our clothes. The car was facing the lake and we were at a dead end, with the car behind us blocking our retreat. So all we were able to do was sit there and wait. Someone got out of the car behind us and we could tell he or she had a flashlight because we could see a beam of light moving in our direction. A moment later a police officer was knocking on the driver's window. Brian rolled the window down.

"Can I see your driver's license?" the officer asked as he shone his beam of light in my direction. I winced and covered my eyes. Brian pulled out his wallet and showed his license. The officer examined it and said, "Can you step out of the car, Sir?" I felt the fear creeping up my legs and taking place of sexual desire I had experienced just a moment before. Brian obediently stepped out of the car. He seemed to be standing there by the lake, talking to the officer for a long time, but it was probably only minutes. In the end he opened the car door, came back into the car and started the engine. I could see the beam of light retreating in the side mirror and I heard the engine of the police car starting up. The car behind us reversed and the policeman was soon gone. It was quiet and peaceful again.

"What happened?" I asked.

"He wanted to see if I was sober," Brian said. "When he saw that I was, he said he would let me go, but that I should be on my way." He started to reverse the car. I just sighed, as yet another adventure had come to an abrupt halt. Brian drove back to the house in silence; we were both quiet. There were a number of times when I wanted to tell him how much I enjoyed being with him and that I hoped one day we could consummate our relationship, but somehow that word sounded too much like consume, so I just kept quiet. I felt that anything I could think of saying would sound somehow banal and meaningless, and that the whole incident was just so very unfortunate, but funny as well. I felt a smile glued to my face and I looked in the mirror on the other side of the visor to straighten my hair. I looked flushed and my eyes were shining. Brian looked at me from time to time and smiled, but said nothing. A couple of times his hand reached out towards my face or thigh and my hand covered his to acknowledge the sentiment and the warmth we seemed to be sharing.

As we reached the house, it was shrouded in darkness; clearly both Antony and his daughter were fast asleep. Antony had lost his wife to cancer and lived alone, though Brian had told me that he was currently seeing someone. We opened the front door and tiptoed to the back of the house where the guest rooms were located. Brian accompanied me to the door of my room and kissed me goodnight on the check, and we both went our separate ways.

In the morning I was awoken by voices and I realized that Antony was already up and that he and his daughter were having breakfast. I got up and knocked on Brian's door.

"Are you awake?" I asked.

"Now I am," came the reply and I could tell he had just woken up. I opened the door and peered into the darkened room.

"Antony is up and is making breakfast," I said. Brian reached for his glasses. "I'll be up shortly," he said as he looked at the alarm clock on the bedside table.

"I'll have a quick shower," I said "and then you can use the bathroom."

"All right," Brian said as he sat up in bed. I so wanted to enter the room and kiss him, but I decided it wasn't the right time or place. I closed the door and walked down the corridor towards the bathroom.

Twenty minutes later I was dressed and ready for the day. I walked into the kitchen and greeted Antony and his daughter who were sitting at the breakfast table. Two other places were set with plates, cutlery and glasses of orange juice. I sat down and took a sip of juice.

"This is my daughter Janet," Antony said.

"Hello," I nodded in her direction. "Nice to meet you, Janet."

"Hello," the girl answered. She was at that awkward stage—no longer a girl and not yet a woman and clearly struggling with her self-image. She lowered her head and concentrated on her plate which was covered with scrambled eggs on toast, smothered with ketchup sauce.

"What would you like?" asked Antony.

"I'm not sure. What have you got to offer?" I asked.

"We have eggs, toast, or oatmeal. What do you usually eat for breakfast?"

"I usually don't," I said. "Maybe I'll just have a drink and then wait and see."

"Suit yourself," Antony said and then he added, "I can still walk without a limp. Janet noticed as soon as she saw me walking" he said, and he turned to the girl. "Didn't you, honey?"

"Uh huh," she replied.

"It's a miracle and I think someone should write an article about it."

"Am I going to have a healing today?" Janet asked.

"Yes, as soon as we've had breakfast," I said. "If that's alright with you," I addressed Antony.

"Oh yes, I think that would be great. If we can save Janet from having ear infections, I think she would be very grateful. Wouldn't you, honey?"

"Yes, I would," said Janet as she delivered a large piece of toast with eggs and ketchup into her mouth. As she opened her mouth, I could see she was wearing braces. Brian walked into the kitchen and I could feel my heart beating faster. I tried to act calm and took another sip of my orange juice. He walked up to the table and looked at Janet.

"Hi Janet, I'm Brian. Do you remember me? I think I saw you last year."

"I remember you," Janet said. "You're a friend of my dad's."

"That's right. Did he tell you about the healing?" he asked. His hair was still dripping wet.

"Uh huh," she replied.

"Well, as soon as you've had breakfast, we can get to work."

"Don't you want to eat anything first?" Antony asked.

"No, I'll just have a cup of coffee."

"Coming right up," Antony said as he got up from the table and walked over to the coffee machine that had been percolating away. He poured a cup and brought it back to the table. Brian took the cup from him and thanked him. "I'll just go into the living room and see where is the best place for the healing," he said. I got up as well and followed him into the living room.

"How are you?" I asked as we were both looking around.

"I'm fine," he replied. "How about you?"

"Very well," I said. "So how about the sofa?" I asked.

"It's a bit low," Brian said, "but I guess it will have to do. I wish I had a healing table."

He was obviously concentrating on what he needed to do next and I felt that now was not the right time for a chat about personal matters. He propped some pillows up at one end of the sofa and then moved a chair closer to it. He sat down on the chair and held his hands over the spot where the child's head would be.

"This will do," he said. I stood quietly a few paces away, waiting for the session to begin.

A few minutes later Antony walked into the room with Janet. Brian gestured for her to lie down on the sofa.

"Go on, honey," Antony said as he gently pushed her in that direction. Janet obediently complied and sat down on the sofa, her knees almost touching Brian's chair. She looked up at him and asked, with obvious fear in her voice, "Is it going to hurt?"

"No, it shouldn't hurt at all," Brian said and then he added, reassuringly, "If it does hurt, let me know straight away."

"All right," Janet said as she lay down on the sofa.

"Which ear is it?" Brian asked.

"The right ear," Antony said as he sat down on another chair at a distance but at an angle from which he could observe what was going on. At the same moment Janet pointed to her right ear.

"Just relax," Brian said and Janet closed her eyes and sighed. "I am not even going to touch you," he added. "I'm just going to place my hand over your ear and I will tell you if I move it, and I'll explain what I am doing."

"All right," the girl said and her voice sounded quieter and more relaxed.

I took a chair and sat close by. "I can feel warmth," Brian said, as he placed his hand over the girl's ear.

"Ow, that hurt," Janet exclaimed as she brought her right hand up to her ear. Brian removed his hand.

"It's all right," he assured her and he gently removed her hand with his. "Let me try," I said and I don't even know why I said it. I didn't wait for him to respond; I just walked up to the sofa and placed my right hand over Janet's ear.

"That's better," Janet said and she smiled with her eyes closed. "That feels very cool and nice."

I instinctively reached for Brian's hand. "I'll place my hand on top of yours," I whispered. "Just like yesterday." Brian nodded.

We placed our hands next to Janet's ear and held them there. A few minutes went by and as I could feel Brian's hand heating up beneath mine, so I noticed at the same time that Janet was relaxing and that her breathing was becoming slower and deeper. A few minutes after that she was sound asleep, but still we held our hands over her ear.

"I think that's enough," I whispered to Brian when my hand got so hot and sweaty I felt it could no longer be doing any good, holding onto Brian's hand like that. Again he nodded and we took our hands away. Antony tiptoed closer to the sofa and picked up a blanket from the armchair nearby.

"I'll just leave her here so she can rest," he said as he covered her sleeping body. The three of us tiptoed out of the living room into the kitchen. We sat down at the kitchen table where the breakfast dishes were still as we had left them. We looked at each other but no one said anything for a minute or two. Suddenly I could hear a key being turned in the lock of the front door.

"That's Stacey," Antony said. "My girlfriend. She's a doctor." A few minutes later Stacy walked into the kitchen.

"Hi," she said and Antony stood up to greet her. They embraced briefly. "I didn't know you had company," she said as she started to take her coat off.

"These are my friends, Brian and Barbara," Antony said. "They have just performed a healing on Janet."

"Oh really?" Stacey said and I could immediately tell that she was being suspicious. "Let me see the child," Stacey added, adopting the confident air of a doctor in charge of a patient.

"She's in the living room, but she's asleep. She fell asleep during the healing." These last words were said as Antony followed Stacey who was already on her way into the living room, having left her coat draped over a chair in the kitchen.

Brian and I looked at each other and we quickly got up and followed the other two into the living room. Stacey walked straight up to the sofa where Janet was sleeping peacefully. She put a hand on the girl's forehead and exclaimed, "The child is burning up. She has a fever! She needs to go to bed immediately. Antony, why don't you carry her upstairs and I'll examine her?"

Janet opened her eyes and looked at Stacey. Her expression indicated that she did not recognize the woman sitting in front of her, on the chair that Brian had vacated just some minutes ago.

"She has just had a healing," Antony protested.

"The girl is sick," Stacey insisted. "You're her father—do something. Now!"

"These are my friends," Antony tried again. "They are healers." Stacey waved her hand and did not even look in our direction—we were standing behind her, a few paces away.

"That's nonsense. Janet needs help now." Stacey said.

"Look," Antony exclaimed. "Just look at me!" He started walking around the room. "Haven't you noticed anything?"

This time Stacey looked around and was following Antony's walk as he started pacing in circles. It was clear that she was humoring him while her mind was on Janet and the fact that she was certain the girl needed medical attention.

"I see you," she said. "So what?"

"So what?" Antony cried out as he completed a circle and stood in front of her. "Stacey, please think again. Haven't you noticed anything? Was I able to walk like that yesterday?" Stacey opened her mouth to say something, but she stopped herself. Her eyes grew large with surprise. She hesitated as she replied, "No, you couldn't walk like that," she said, enunciating every word. "What happened?" Her attention was finally diverted from Janet who had sat up on the sofa and was watching the scene that was unfolding in front of her.

"My ear hurts," she said softly, but Stacey was scrutinizing Antony and no longer paying attention to her.

"I had a healing from my two friends here. The results were immediate and unmistakable. They are healers, can't you see?"

Stacey swiveled on her chair and looked at both of us. We were still standing close to the kitchen door, observing the scene as it was being played out. Stacey then looked back at Antony.

"That's nonsense," she said. "There's no medical explanation for such a cure."

"I know," Antony said with enthusiasm, as he walked up closer to her. "But it did happen, whether there is an explanation or not!"

"We'll talk about that later." Stacey turned back to face Janet. "Let's go upstairs and get you to bed. I'll take a closer look at you upstairs. Can you walk upstairs?" she asked the girl.

"I think so," Janet replied as she swung her legs around and slowly got up. Her cheeks were flushed and she seemed to wobble when she stood up. Stacey got off the chair and held her, while Antony rushed to her other side.

"I'll help you get her to bed," he said and the three of them walked towards the door leading into the hallway. We could hear them going up the stairs.

"What happened?" I asked Brian.

"I don't know. She should be better, not worse. She was fine when we started and now it seems that the healing has brought on another ear infection. I don't understand it."

A few minutes later Antony came downstairs and the three of us went back into the kitchen.

"Stacey is checking up on Janet," he said. "It seems she has a fever and there is a discharge coming out of her ear. Stacey wants to put her on antibiotics."

At that moment we could hear Stacey coming down the stairs and a minute later she walked into the kitchen. She was holding her cell phone in one hand and a piece of paper in the other. "I must go back to the hospital," she said. "One of my patients is in a critical condition." She walked up to the table where the three of us were sitting and handed Antony the piece of paper.

"Here," she said. "I've written out a prescription for Janet; she needs some antibiotics to deal with this infection. You can get them at your local drugstore. The sooner you start giving them to her, the better. I'll look in on her tomorrow." She picked up her coat and bag from the chair. Antony stood up.

"I'll walk you to your car," he said.

As soon as Antony and Stacey left, Brian said, "We can't let Janet take those antibiotics. The worst is over." He then added, "She will recover, I know it."

A few minutes later, Antony returned. He sat down with us at the table.

"I apologize for Stacey's behavior," he said. "She's a scientist and a doctor. She doesn't believe in anything alternative, and she certainly does not believe in alternative medicine. She thinks it's akin to witchcraft and superstition."

"Yes, that was pretty obvious," said Brian.

"I just popped up to see Janet before I came in here and she's sleeping like a baby. I think she's on the mend," Antony said.

"I know you're right," confirmed Brian.

As Brian was saying these words, Antony placed a small red bead on the table. "This came out of her ear together with some puss," he said. Brian picked up the bead and rolled it around between his fingers, looking at it intently, as if he was searching for a clue.

"That's it," he finally said and then he repeated, "That's it!"

I was confused. "What do you mean, 'that's it'?" I asked.

"That's it—this bead has been causing all the problems over the years. She probably stuffed this bead into her ear when she was two or three, or whenever the ear aches began, and her body has been trying to eliminate this foreign substance ever since, but has been unable to do so.

"Until now," said Antony.

"Until now," confirmed Brian.

"Well, that would mean that she is cured," I ventured.

"That's right," confirmed Brian. "I believe she is cured."

"Amazing," Antony said shaking his head in disbelief.

"You must not allow Stacey to give her any antibiotics," Brian turned to Antony. "She needs the chance to heal naturally and I will help her."

"I will do whatever you think is right. Do you think Janet needs another healing?"

"I think it would be best to complete the treatment and help her get over her fever," Brian said.

"In that case, that's what we shall do. I trust your judgment," said Antony.

"All right, but on one condition."

"What's that?"

"No antibiotics."

Antony was still holding the prescription in his hand. He didn't say a word but simply tore up the piece of paper.

"No antibiotics," he repeated.

"Let Janet rest," Brian said. "We'll do another healing later. In the meantime Barbara and I will go for a walk."

"All right," Antony said. "I'll stay here in case Janet wakes up. So let me give you a key to the house." He got up and walked up to a row of hooks by the kitchen door, which led to the garden. He took a key off the hook and handed it to Brian. "Take it," he said. "Consider this to be your house; you can come and go as you please. I'll have some lunch ready in a couple of hours."

"Thanks," said Brian. He took the key and put it in his pocket. "Let's go," he said to me, as he got up and walked towards the front entrance. We put our coats on and walked out of the house, leaving Antony still sitting at the kitchen table.

The house was located near a park and it didn't take us long to walk up a path leading to an artificial lake. There were ducks on the water and a gravel path wound its way around it. The trees were already bare and the air was cold. I put my hands in my pockets to keep warm. We stood by the pond and I watched a toddler nearby with his mother feeding the ducks. The birds were making a lot of noise as they gathered close to the shore and were vying for position to receive the food. The child was laughing as he attempted to throw the crumbs as far into the water as he could. The mother was also taking part in the feeding exercise, creating a secondary gathering of ducks and a couple of swans several feet away.

The sun came out from behind a cloud and it became slightly warmer. Brian put his arm around my shoulder.

"I can't imagine any woman wanting to share the kind of life that I am destined for," he said.

"What do you mean?" I asked. "What kind of life?"

"A life of service," he said.

"But what does that mean?" Brian put his other hand on my shoulder and turned me to face him. He stood very close to me and I could feel his breath on my forehead as he spoke.

"It means that my life is not my own. It means that I have

been sent to this world to heal and teach. It means that I must do everything in my power to help others. It means that my mission or my ministry, or whatever you want to call it, will occupy my time, my every free moment. It means that any relationship I might have with a woman must take second place. It means traveling to places all over the country, wherever there are people who need and want my help. It means …" He hesitated for a moment as I waited. "It means that I can't get married and have children, at least not for now."

"I'm in no position to think of marriage or even a serious relationship," I said. "I don't even have a place to live at the moment. But I do feel I could help you in your mission."

"I don't know," Brian said. "It's not much of a life, traveling from place to place, meeting groups of people who need help. I don't think it is right for a woman."

"But you saw what happened with Antony," I protested. "It was both of us that healed him. I don't think it would have worked if I wasn't there. I don't know if Janet's bead would have come out of her ear either." I put my arms around his neck. "I want to help," I said. "I think women are just as resilient as men, perhaps even more so." I stood up on my toes, bringing my face closer to his. "I want to be part of your life," I whispered and he kissed me, as I had hoped he would.

When we returned to Antony's house, we found our host upstairs in Janet's room. The girl was sitting up in bed and she looked vibrant and happy. Antony was sitting on her bed while Janet was eating some soup. She no longer looked feverish and she smiled at us as we walked through the door.

"I'm fine now," she said and she took a spoonful of soup. "Dad told me that there was a bead in my ear and it got flushed out. Funny, I don't remember putting it in my ear."

"You were probably too small to remember," Antony said.

"I'm glad you're better," Brian said.

"I don't think you'll be getting any more nasty earaches," I added. "In fact, I am sure that's over."

"Thank you so much," Janet said.

"We're going to start packing," Brian said.

"OK, I'll be down in a minute," said Antony.

As we were walking downstairs, Brian said, "I think we should leave soon. I don't think Stacey will be pleased to see us when she comes back."

"I think you need to spend a few more minutes with Janet," I said as we walked into the living room and sat down side by side on the sofa. "She needs one more healing session to make the recovery complete."

"It's true, I did say I would do that."

A few minutes later Antony came downstairs, holding the empty soup bowl and spoon in his hands.

"I'll go and check on Janet one last time before we go," Brian said.

"That would be great," Antony said. "Thanks for everything."

"It's all right, I do what I can." Brian stood up and headed for the door. Antony sat down in the armchair opposite the sofa. Brian left the room, closing the door behind him.

"The world needs to know about your unique gifts," Antony said. "I have a friend at the local newspaper. I'll get him to write an article," he added.

"I'm not sure that's a good idea," I protested.

"Oh yes, it is. You can do so much good in this world. Think of all the illnesses—AIDS, cancer, heart disease … there is so much misery out there. And you come in and within a few hours my limp has gone and Janet is cured of her ear infections. It's a miracle."

"Yes, but we still need to work and earn a living and carry on with our healing work, without being mobbed by hundreds, if not thousands of people …" I noticed I was saying "we" as if we were already a team. At that moment I could hear a key turn in the front door and soon Stacey walked into the living room. She had taken off her boots and was standing in the middle of the living room carpeted floor in her stockinged feet.

"Hi," she nodded at both of us and then demanded, "How is Janet?"

"She's fine," Antony replied. "I just gave her some soup."

"Good. I'll go up and see her."

"No, please don't. Brian is up there giving her a healing."

"Oh, what nonsense!" Stacey exclaimed. "Have you given her the antibiotics?"

"Well … no," Antony hesitated for a moment.

"Why not?" Stacey demanded.

"There was no need. She's much better now."

"Oh, so you're the doctor now and you know what is needed?" she said with sarcasm in her voice. "Just because she is momentarily feeling better doesn't mean she doesn't need the antibiotics to prevent the return of the inflammation and the fever."

"Please, let Brian do what he came here to do," I pleaded. "His healing is working and Janet won't be needing any medication."

Stacey turned her head in my direction and glared at me.

"And who are you to know what is needed?" she asked.

"I'm a clairvoyant and a healer," I responded. Stacey just laughed.

"And I'm the Prime Minister of China," she said and she turned back to Antony. "I'm going back up there. If I have any say in this house, that girl needs proper care and I intend to give it to her." Antony stood up.

"No, you're not," he said and I could tell he was getting angry. "These good people have healed me and you have seen the results of their work—I no longer limp. And if you care for me you will let them help Janet as well. Over the years no antibiotic has done for Janet what they have done today. The bead that came out of her ear has clearly been there for years."

"What bead?" Stacey asked.

Antony walked over to the mantelpiece where he had placed the red bead.

"This one," he said. Stacey walked over to the mantelpiece and took the bead from Antony. As she was examining it, she asked, "This came out of Janet's ear?"

"It most certainly did," Antony replied.

"But how could that be?" she asked again.

"I don't know," Antony said. Stacey took another look at me and shrugged her shoulders. "I don't get it," she said. "But I still need to look at her."

"That's fine," Antony said. "Just take your coat off, sit down and relax. Let's wait until Brian comes down." This time Stacey listened and she sat down in the other armchair, still wearing her coat and all the time examining the bead, rolling it around in the palm of her hand.

"Science can't explain it," she said to no one in particular, shaking her head in disbelief.

A few minutes later Brian walked into the room together with Janet who looked healthy and happy, smiling a great big smile that exposed her upper teeth and her braces.

"She's fine," Brian announced. He then noticed Stacey. "Hello Stacey," he said, and I noticed a slight hesitation in his step.

"Hi," Stacey replied but she didn't move from the chair. It seemed like she had abandoned the idea of examining Janet.

"We should be on our way," Brian said and I got up from the sofa, ready for the trip back to the city. There seemed to be a taciturn agreement among the three of us—Brian, Antony and me—that lunch could wait for another occasion.

I woke up the next morning with a remarkably clear head and my mind was made up. Grandmother was right—if my life was to amount to anything at all, I needed to follow my instinct and enter the larger domain of universal security, rather than hide within the protective shell of my local imagined security. My head was filled with images of Brian. Some things I found quite comical about him and sometimes I felt like I couldn't understand him at all, but I was attracted to him and his mission and I felt there was a place for me within his world. I believed that destiny had brought us together and that we were meant to do something important in this life. If we could help people lead healthier and happier lives, that would be a special gift indeed. I romanticized about traveling around the country and performing mass healings, like I had seen in the movies and I wondered what it would be like to beat the odds against all medical prognoses.

In the meantime, I felt I needed to find a new job; I wanted to be as far away from Alice as possible and I also didn't think it was a good idea to continue a relationship with Brian while working for the same company. I needed a place to live because I knew my grandmother was used to her own space. She did say I could stay as long as I wished, but I needed my independence as well. So over the next few days I bought the newspaper every morning and checked the 'Wanted' section, looking for a job. But I also felt a reluctance to leave the place where I would have the daily opportunity of seeing Brian and where I felt comfortable with the work and most of my co-workers. Alice and I were not speaking with each other, so I would just walk by her desk and ignore her and she would do likewise, averting her eyes every time I walked by.

After we returned from our weekend Brian seemed to disappear. I knew he was at work and I even heard his voice a couple of times when I walked by his office, but I didn't get to see him for a few days and he never phoned. I felt that he was avoiding me, or perhaps he was just busy and had other things on his mind. Then on the Thursday I bumped into him while I was overseeing a delivery that was being made that afternoon to Sterling Silver Insurance. He stopped for a moment as I was standing by the truck within the loading bay. Before he had a chance to speak I asked him, so that no one could hear, "Are you free this weekend?" I don't know why I said that because I didn't have any plans in mind; it just came out of my mouth.

"I've been invited to a healing gathering," he said. "There are several healers coming and we are going to demonstrate our abilities and techniques to a bunch of interested doctors. I really think this could be a breakthrough for alternative healing in this country."

Two of the warehouse workers walked up to the truck with a big heavy oak desk and placed it on the platform. Brian and I separated and he started walking back to his office.

"Good luck," I said to his retreating back, feeling disappointed.

As I left the office building that afternoon, a man approached me and soon I realized it was Andrew Johnson.

"I need to talk you," he said.

"Alright, let's go to the Starbucks around the corner," I said. "We can walk, it's not far."

It was warm enough to sit outside, so we bought our lattes and took the table as far away from the traffic as possible.

"I've been trying to phone you, but you haven't returned my calls," he said.

"That's true," I replied. "I've been very busy lately. There have been so many extra deliveries, I've been working evenings and weekends."

"I understand work," Andrew said. "I've been busy myself. But if you care about someone, you can at least speak to them on the phone or return their calls. I took a deep breath. He was right, of course. It was time to come clean and tell the truth.

"The truth is, I am seeing someone," I said.

"Well why didn't you say so when I first asked you out?" Andrew asked.

"I don't know," I hesitated. "I wasn't sure. It was all so new and I really like you. But I have become very fond of this other man, so I ..."

Andrew interrupted. "So you started avoiding me," he said.

"I'm sorry. I didn't mean to hurt you. I wanted to be sure of my feelings before making a decision. I'm sorry," I repeated.

"It's alright," Andrew said, but I could tell it wasn't. "I'm glad I know the score now. Let me know if anything changes." He stood up and picked up his coat and briefcase, which had been deposited on an empty chair nearby.

"I wish you well," he said and walked off.

"Bye," I said, but he was already walking back to his car, which he had left at the Versatile Furniture parking lot.

That evening, my grandmother served a dish she had made for dinner. It was a casserole and it made me think of the dinner Brian had made when I visited him for the first time. The aroma wafting from the dish, as she brought it to the table, smelt delicious and full of promise of culinary delights to come, exciting the taste buds in anticipation of their forthcoming experience.

"Grandma," I asked as she placed the dish on a mat on the table and started serving, "how come your food always looks and tastes so appetizing and delicious?"

She carried on serving as she replied, "There are two reasons: one is because I value my food. I am grateful for every meal I eat and every time I am able to put food on my table. It is a gift."

"And the second?" I asked.

"The second is the care that I put into my food. Have you ever heard the expression that mama's cooking tastes best?" she asked.

"Yes, though I couldn't say that it is true in my case. As you know, my mother and your daughter hates to cook."

"But what a mother puts into her cooking is love and care, and this is what I put into my cooking. It is better than the most expensive spices."

As we started to eat, the lamb casserole did indeed taste delicious. Smothered with onions, potatoes and carrots in a delicious creamy sauce, it could have been served at the best restaurant.

"I think this is a good time to talk about value," Grandmother said. "What do you think makes something valuable or value able?" she asked. I thought about it for a moment, recalling all the things that hold their value in the world—gold, platinum, diamonds, emeralds, rubies … Three reasons came to mind.

"I can think of three things that make something valuable," I said.

"What are they?" she asked.

"One is perceived beauty. If something is considered beautiful, it becomes precious, like gold and gemstones, or a piece of art, even though it might not be of use, except for adornment. Clearly we humans like to surround ourselves with beauty."

"That's one," said my grandmother. "What are the other two?"

"Something can also be valued because it is useful, like a car or a tool," I ventured. "If a person's livelihood depends on an axe or a gun or a computer, they will value it and look after it," I said.

"All right, that's number two. What else?" Grandmother was relentless.

"Also rarity makes something valuable," I said. If it is hard to get, it might be considered valuable, or attractive or tasty, like caviar or a Modigliani painting. If there is a scarcity of something, it becomes all the more valuable, like an original edition of an old book that is out of print, or a stamp that was issued with a mistake in the printing process, or an unusual plant."

"So something that is in abundance is less valuable," said my grandmother. "Take, for example, pebbles. Clearly they are less valuable than sapphires."

"As far as human perception is concerned, that's right," I said, being careful to try to have an objective view of the subject.

"What about air?" asked my grandmother. "There is an abundance of air on planet Earth; it doesn't seem to run out. Do you think it is less valuable because there is so much of it?"

I thought for a moment, then replied, "I think we humans value it less because it is everywhere and we don't have to pay for it."

"Ah, then perhaps it's the price tag that makes the difference," she said. "Do you value expensive items more?" I had not thought of this aspect, so I considered it for a moment.

"Not necessarily," I replied. "I value what I appreciate and what I like."

"What about the gift of language?" she asked. "You don't have to pay for the words you use. People over centuries have developed this tool so that you and I may be able to communicate in a clear and precise manner."

"I have never thought of that," I admitted. "It really is a gift," I agreed. "It would be very different if we had to pay for our words, or go to the store and buy them, like we do with food." I smiled at this idea, it seemed so strange and comical. I imagined myself bringing home a bag of words for future use. No doubt I would be very watchful about what came out of my mouth, and probably everyone would speak less, but put more meaning into each utterance. I smiled at the thought.

"There are more ways of paying for something than with money," Grandmother said, as if reading my thoughts.

"What do you mean?" I asked. "How else do you pay for something?"

"You can pay for it with money, with your energy or with your time. Also, have you ever heard the expression, 'to pay attention'?" Grandmother asked. I nodded and she continued. "Sometimes it takes all four payments to acquire something and some things are free, like the air you breathe. Do you value the air you breathe?" she asked again.

"I certainly value it when I choke on my food," I said. "So I guess I value what I cannot live without, but only when there is a threat that it might be taken away from me."

"So do you only value your life when you are in danger?" Grandmother asked.

"I think that's true, though I wish I valued it more."

"Yes, I wish you valued it more, too," Grandmother said. "Think how you value your health when you are ill," she added. "Multiply that a thousand times and perhaps you will get an inkling of how you will feel about your life when your time comes to leave this planet." She smiled and I just sat there, stunned at the thought. I reflected for a moment about all the people, objects and places I valued in my life and it made me realize how much I took for granted. My grandmother had taken me in with no questions asked; she had fed me and taught me and been a leader and a mentor to me throughout these transitional times. There were so many people who had contributed to my education and experience and yet I don't think I had ever thanked them or expressed my gratitude in any other way.

"Grandma," I said, feeling sheepish and somewhat humbled.

"Yes child?" she asked in a soft voice and I realized she probably could already tell that I had been overcome with emotions.

"I want to thank you for all you have done for me ...," I stated, but she waved her hand and I became silent.

"Don't thank me," she said. "It is natural for the older generation to pass on their wisdom and possessions to their children and grandchildren. The way you can repay me and your parents is to be the best you can be, to listen to our advice and be sure to pass on your own experiences, wisdoms and stories to the next generation."

"I will try," I said, meaning every word.

The following Friday evening Brian phoned. He sounded urgent. It was quite late and I was reading a book, sprawled out on Grandmother's sofa. "I need to see you," he said.

"All right," I replied. "Where are you?"

"I'm at the Dog and Bone," he said. "Come and join me." I knew the bar, because it was only a couple of streets away from the office.

"Give me half an hour," I said.

The Irish-style pub was crowded and noisy. As soon as I entered, I spotted him sitting at the bar. He was sitting on a bar stool between two men and there was a glass of whisky in front of him.

"How are you?" I asked, wondering why he had asked me to come.

"This is Barbara," Brian addressed the man on his right. The man turned around and held out his hand.

"Pleased to meet you," he said. I looked questioningly at Brian who started to explain.

"Philip is a doctor," he said. I noticed Philip was drinking water. "He is the chairman of the state Medical Association. He wants me to demonstrate my healing abilities to a group of hundreds of doctors and medical professionals." I could see he was excited. "Philip saw me healing a bad case of rheumatism last weekend."

Philip added, "It was amazing, unbelievable."

Brian continued. "The woman could hardly walk; her foot was full of calcium deposits and very painful. She had needed a cane or a crutch for the last three years to be able to get around, but after I finished the healing, she got up and walked, throwing her cane away."

"We examined her before and after the healing," Philip added. "Four doctors—two general practitioners and two specialists, who were all dumbfounded."

"I told Philip that you are my assistant and that if I am to demonstrate to an auditorium of hundreds of doctors, I need a helper. Will you do it?" I hesitated. I was not sure I wanted to become so deeply involved so quickly. But yet again my heart started beating faster and I replied, without giving it much further thought, "Yes, of course. Have you decided when this demonstration is to take place?"

"There is a national gathering of the Medical Association in Atlanta this weekend," Philip replied, "and we are expecting around a thousand members to attend. I know it is short notice, but this is a great opportunity to convince the medical professions that spiritual healing really works. I feel time is of the essence."

"He has convinced me," Brian added, before downing the rest of his whisky.

"All right, I'll go," I said.

"That's great," Philip said. "I'll arrange a ticket and a car to pick you up tomorrow morning."

I arrived in Atlanta on the Saturday and went straight to the meeting place. The auditorium was enormous and totally filled with people of all ages—there were students and teachers and doctors and hundreds of other representatives of the healing professions. There must have been over a thousand people gathered and every seat seemed to be taken.

In front there was a raised stage with a healing table on it and behind it there were two enormous blackboards with a white movie screen on a stand in front of them. Projected onto the screen were a series of X-rays—from what I could tell they were pictures of a very crooked spine, with a curvature worsening over time—each X-ray had a date beneath it.

I found a seat at the back. I had agreed with Brian that I would sit in the audience and support him mentally from there. There was no time to meet with him before the demonstration; he had arrived earlier and was probably meeting with some of the doctors and other medical professionals.

The auditorium was slanted upwards so that I was looking down towards the stage, as if it was at the bottom of a bowl. More people kept coming and some were beginning to sit on the three sets of steps that led from the three entrances down towards the front rows.

Suddenly all went quiet and a man walked onto the stage and up to the microphone that had been placed in the middle of the proscenium, on top of a wooden lectern.

"Good afternoon," he said. "We have gathered today to witness the miracle of faith healing.

"My name is Doctor Palevi and I come from a long line of fakirs and faith healers. However, as a doctor of medicine and a scientist,

I have broken with my family traditions and have embraced western medicine, prescribing drugs that have been proven to change the balance of the chemical structure of the body and promote a cure. I have worked with surgeons, radiologists and pharmaceutical companies, always trying to discover and promote the latest potion, pill or series of injections. However, today I stand before you in another capacity altogether. I am here to introduce to you today the notion of what the world would call faith healing, but I would refer to as natural healing with human energy."

He paused for a moment and picked up a small device from the lectern. He clicked it and the picture displayed on the screen changed—we could now see the figure of a human with an egg-shape of colored lights around him.

"This is what the human aura looks like," Doctor Palevi continued. "It is an electro-magnetic oval shape that surrounds each and every one of us. I have seen it and it is a most beautiful sight to behold. The colors are constantly changing and no two auras are the same—the colors depend on the person, their health, their mood, their history, their beliefs. It is like looking into a person's most private and personal thoughts and desires—it is all there, if we could only interpret and translate what we see."

He paused for a moment, looking around at the audience and then continued. "I realize that many of you might not believe me but I have seen remarkable results when certain healers, using just the energy coming out of their hands, are able to change and manipulate the energy inside the aura of another person, resulting in a remarkable recovery, that using our so-called scientific methods we are unable to explain or understand. So today we have invited one such healer—Brian Polowski—to demonstrate his skill, or gift, or intuitive ability—whatever you might want to call it."

At this point Brian walked onto the stage. He came up to the microphone and shook hands with Doctor Palevi. "I am not a doctor," he started to speak into the microphone. "But over the past few years I have discovered this unusual ability to heal people's energy fields and to be able to diagnose what is wrong with them. You would probably call me a medical intuitive, but furthermore I am able to change a person's energy pattern simply using these." He lifted his hands and held them up for all to see. "I believe we are all healers," he said. "It is something that can be learned. Dr. Palevi here has been training with me and already he can not only see an aura, but he can feel its perimeters with his hands and he can conduct simple healings, by taking away a headache or a muscle pain with his hand."

Doctor Palevi smiled and spoke into the microphone. "It is true. However, I do not expect anyone to believe me. Brian will demonstrate a healing here today and I believe you will all witness what a hundred, or even ten years ago would be called a miracle, but I believe is the most natural service one human can perform for another. Over to you, Brian," he said and handed him the remote that was connected to the display on the screen.

Brian took it and the picture reverted to the series of X-rays. Doctor Palevi left the stage and Brian started to explain. "I will attempt to demonstrate the power of healing," he said. "Every human can become a conduit for the healing force and I cannot tell you why these hands seem to be connected to some healing energy." He held up his hands again for all to see. "These are the most precious tools you could ever have," he continued. "I never leave home without them." There was a wave of laughter as his audience recognized the well-known slogan from the American Express TV adverts. "The healing power comes when it wants to, not when I command it. It has a mind of its own and nothing is guaranteed. However, everything is possible." There was a moment of silence, and Brian continued. "Before I begin today I would like to say a prayer to that great, divine power that allows us to heal, physically, mentally and spiritually. It does not belong to any particular religion; it is universal." He paused and uttered the prayer in a hushed tone. Several people in the audience bowed their heads. "May we witness today the power of healing. May we remember all those who are in need of solace and health. May their wishes come true and may they be restored to health. Thank you for the gift of healing and may we always be mindful to value its manifestation. Amen."

As he was finishing the last sentence, a man walked onto the stage. He was supported by two crutches and one could easily see that his spine was twisted and that his legs could hardly support any weight at all. As he walked up to the healing table, he said "Amen." Some people in the audience repeated, "Amen."

"This is John March," Brian said. "He has volunteered to take part in today's experiment." Brian walked up to John and helped him take his last steps towards the healing table. He took one of the crutches from the man and held his arm as John came to a stop. "As you can see from the X-rays, John has a degenerative bone disease. Somehow I have had some success in healing bones, perhaps because bones are very responsive to energy frequencies and the power of the healing force." Brian now took the other crutch from John, as the patient turned his back to the audience. Brian then helped John lift his weight onto the bed. John sat there for a moment and we could clearly see that his spine was crooked. He then lifted his legs onto the bed and lay down with his head on the pillow that was placed there for his convenience. He lay on his side, facing the audience, with his knees bent and his arms resting in front of him.

Brian started speaking as he raised his arms and held his hands over John's body. "Before I start the healing, I am simply going to run my hands over the edge of John's aura," he said. "This will relax him and it will introduce me to his frequency and he will start to feel the energy coming out of my hands. In a way, I am simply searching for unusual symptoms in the bio-energetic sphere of this man, otherwise called the aura." Brian started running his hands over John's body, several inches away. "When someone is ill," Brian continued, "you can often detect an unusual heat in and around certain parts of the body. This will tell you where the trouble is located." Brian was no doubt addressing the doctors in the audience. "I know that you have seen the X-rays, and so have I. So I cannot demonstrate to you today the diagnostic power that is lodged in your hands. Nevertheless, I do feel heat above John's spine as far away as this." Brian was holding his left hand about three feet above John's body.

A woman in the front row put her hand up. "Yes?" Brian encouraged her.

"Can I feel John's aura too?" she asked. Brian looked at John and John nodded.

"Yes, that's fine," Brian said. "But let's limit it to one person. Otherwise there will be such a mix of frequencies here that it might impair the possibility of a successful healing." The woman walked onto the stage, entering by the stairs on the left side. As she walked up to the healing table, Brian said, "Place your hand here, where my hand is right now." He took his hand away and the woman placed her hand in the exact spot where Brian had been holding his.

"Yes, I can feel it. I feel extreme heat." She was obviously surprised.

"That's right," Brian said. "Extreme heat. It could be an inflammation or simply the agitated activity of the immune system concentrated in one place."

"Thank you," the woman said as she took her hand away. "I can't believe how easy it was to feel the difference in temperature," she marveled. She then walked off the stage and back to her seat.

Brian continued. "I will try and take some of that heat away." He started pulling at an invisible substance in John's aura and then shaking his hand, as if he was trying to shake off something gooey. He did this several times. Then John spoke up. I noticed he had a microphone attached to the collar of his shirt. "I feel a cool breeze," he said as Brian was yet again manipulating something within his aura. He could not see what Brian was doing, yet he clearly could feel something.

"That's right," Brian said. "I am now going to concentrate on the part of the spine that the heat is coming from." At that very moment the whole atmosphere in the room changed and you could hear a fly buzzing around one of the stage lights. It was very quiet and it reminded me of that day at Nancy's farm when her son ran into the room and felt a presence so powerful that it caused him to retreat. It was like that and I knew the healing force was now present. Even Brian's voice changed as he continued with obvious reverence.

"I am now entering the healing phase of this experiment," he said. "I can feel something in John's aura that feels hot, sticky and alien." He was working hard, I could tell. There were droplets of sweat on his forehead and his face turned pale. He kept swiping something away from the middle of John's back and as he continued to do so, I could see that John's expression relaxed, as if the pain he had previously felt was easing. There was even a faint smile appearing on his face.

"I can feel that," he said. "It's like pins and needles. First it's cold, then it's hot." He slightly stretched his chest, as if he was trying to feel something more and he exclaimed, "It doesn't hurt to do that!" He hunched his shoulders and then straightened them out again. "This is amazing," he said. "Absolutely no pain. It's gone!"

I was looking at Brian. He was concentrating on the work and I could see that he was beginning to wobble on his feet, swaying backward and forward, as he tried to retain his composure.

"Barbara," he suddenly shouted, "I need your help!" I sprang out of my seat, disrupting the people who sat between me and the aisle and ran down the stairs and up onto the stage. I was by his side in less than a minute. Standing next to him I could immediately tell that he was holding onto consciousness with difficulty.

"Place your right hand over mine," he commanded. I followed his instruction and right away I could feel immense heat transferring from his hand into mine.

"I feel it," I whispered. "I'm here. It's going to be all right." I could feel the heat spreading throughout my entire body. It made me feel weak, but I held on and so did Brian. It felt like we were a double human vacuum cleaner, taking into ourselves whatever it was that ailed John. Brian then moved his hand along John's spine, but about six inches above it, swiping his hand towards his legs and down to the feet. I followed his movement with my hand. He repeated the action several times, then he released his hand from mine and stood there for a moment, looking intensely at John.

"Try to straighten your legs," Brian said. John obliged and slowly, very slowly he was able to straighten both legs. At the same time he puffed out his chest and brought both arms over his head. We could see how tall he really was, with both arms and legs stretching beyond the healing table. There were audible gasps, murmurs and exclamations from the audience. We could hear words like, "amazing," "awesome" and "brilliant."

At that moment Dr. Palevi returned to the stage. He walked up to the healing table and said, "Thank you so much. Let's help John get down from the table."

Brian and Dr. Palevi stood on both sides and John slowly sat up. I stood back and watched. John held onto the two men as he slowly brought his legs off the table and placed his feet on the floor. His spine was erect and he was moving his neck from side to side, as if disbelieving that he could really do so.

"I feel great," he said as he shifted his weight to his feet and stood up, supported by the two men. The crutches were on the floor nearby. "I don't think I'll be needing those," he said. He turned around to face the audience, removing his hands from Brian and Dr. Palevi's shoulders, and holding onto the healing bed as he did so. He was gaining confidence in his newfound abilities.

"I think I am going to walk off this stage on my own two feet," he said. He lifted his hands off the healing bed in a dramatic gesture and took a couple of steps on his own. Brian and Dr. Palevi followed him close by, ready to grab hold of him if he would teeter and if it looked like he might fall. But on the contrary, with each step he seemed more sure of himself. He took two or three more steps and turned to the audience. "It's a miracle," he said. "I can walk again!" The audience who had been holding its breath as John was taking his first steps, now burst into applause. A few people stood up and the rest soon followed suit.

"Bravo," they were shouting. "Show us some more," a few people were exclaiming above the crowd. Brian turned to Dr. Palevi.

"I can't do any more today," he said. "I'm exhausted."

"That's all right." Dr. Palevi said. "You've done enough." He turned to the crowd. "That's it for today. Perhaps another time we will show you more. You have witnessed a miracle today. Thank you to Brian Polowski." He clapped his hands together and the audience copied his gesture.

Brian raised his hands and all fell quiet. They took their seats, ready to listen.

"This is not a miracle," Brian said. "It is a very natural healing power. You all have it. But to make it active there are a few requirements. First, you need to believe that it is possible, both for yourself and on behalf of your patient. Second, you need to sensitize your hands rather than relying on the instruments and tools you normally use in medical examinations. Your hands can tell the difference between hot and cold, and they can identify pain and disease. They are the best diagnostic tools you have, but like with every discipline, you need to practice." John stood on the side of the stage, listening as carefully as all those seated in the audience.

"Thank you, Brian," he said. "I need to sit down now." He walked off the stage to more applause.

Brian continued. "I need to leave you now," he said. "I want to thank Barbara here for her help. In fact we both performed the healing today." I walked up to him and smiled. I certainly was not used to standing in front of such an enthusiastic group of people. Brian held out his hand. "Let's go," he said. I took his hand and followed him off the stage. As we climbed down the steps in the wings, I could hear Dr. Palevi's voice explaining to the audience more about what they had witnessed earlier on that stage. We walked down a corridor and into a room where there were a couple of people attending to John who was sitting in a chair, looking pale.

"I feel so tired," he said.

"So do I," said Brian as he sat down in another chair. "Healing can be so draining."

"With so many people watching, you were probably processing their energy as well as your own," I suggested.

"Perhaps you're right," Brian confirmed. A few minutes later Dr. Palevi entered the room carrying John's crutches.

"That was extraordinary," he said. "We now have hundreds of petitions for you to continue the healings," he said to Brian.

"I don't know," Brian said. "Maybe tomorrow ..."

"Of course, you must rest now," Dr. Palevi confirmed.

"I think I'll go back to the hotel," Brian said. I had no idea where he was staying, but I decided to accompany him to his room.

"I'll go with you," I said.

"All right," Brian responded. "That would be nice."

Back at the hotel, I helped Brian undress and get into bed. He was so tired, he could hardly speak. I decided to leave him because I knew

Philip and a couple of other doctors were due to pick him up the next morning so that he could tell them some more about healing the aura. I had a flight back the same night so I thought it would be best to go straight to the airport. Just as I was about to leave his room, Brian opened his eyes and said, "Thank you. You were very helpful today. Perhaps we should form a team after all." He grabbed hold of my hand and added, after a brief moment, during which he was clearly gathering his thoughts, "We Poles are incurable romantics. I can't seem to reconcile duty with desire or mission with love. But I do think you are a very special girl, Barbara Faye." He kissed my hand and then let go of it. He closed his eyes and sighed. Those were the last words he ever spoke to me.

Chapter Twenty-One

Grief

O n Monday morning Mrs. Franks called me into her office. On my way down the corridor I was wondering what she could possibly want to speak about and I found that I worried whether relationships between employees were perhaps against company policy. On the other hand, I wondered whether Alice had said something about me and perhaps I was about to be fired. As I was walking past the reception, I noticed that Alice was there, but I looked straight ahead and pretended not to see her; she also seemed to slump in her chair as she studiously started examining something on her computer screen.

When I got to the door of Mrs. Franks' office, I knocked and entered as soon as I heard her voice inviting me in. There were two men in the room besides Mrs. Franks and they all had serious looks on their faces. They were sitting at a round table that was often used for interviews.

"These gentlemen are from the police," Mrs. Franks said. "This is Barbara Faye, one of Brian Polowski's employees. Perhaps she can help you."

The taller of the two men pointed to an empty chair and I sat down. "We are investigating a murder," he said. "Brian Polowski, your boss, was shot early this morning."

He paused for a moment to let the information sink in. The shock was so great that I was unable to speak for a moment. I felt myself gasping for breath. No, this could not be true! There must be some mistake!

"Do you know if he had any enemies?" the younger of the two men asked. He was of Asian descent, with slight build and jet-black hair. "We are interviewing all his employees," he added.

I brought my hand to my chest in an effort to catch my breath. I could feel the blood draining from my face. I felt nausea and faint both at the same time. I still could not believe this was really happening. I was sure I would soon awaken from this bad dream.

"No, not that I know of," I replied feebly. "We all liked him."

"Any disgruntled employees? Someone who did not get a raise but thought they deserved it? A rival?" the man persisted.

"I haven't been here long," I replied. I urgently wanted to get away and think about what had happened and why.

"That's right," Mrs. Franks confirmed. "Barbara has only been with us for six months, so she probably doesn't even know the other employees that well."

"That's right," I said, hoping I could leave.

The other, older man spoke up. "What was he like?" he asked. "Do you know who he hung out with?"

"No," I replied. "I only know that he has a brother. He was a very private person," I added and I couldn't bear the fact that I was speaking about Brian in the past tense. The policeman handed me his card. "If you think of anything, please contact us immediately," he said.

"All right," I replied. I took the card and stood up to leave. The second policeman added, "And please don't mention this conversation to anyone," he said, "or you will impede our investigation."

"No, I won't," I said and headed for the door. As soon as I turned away from the three figures sitting at the table, I could feel the tears welling up.

On the way back to my desk I had to pass by reception again. Alice was there and she looked up just as I was walking by. I could swear she had been waiting for the right moment.

"What's the matter?" she asked. These were the first words she had spoken to me since we had our falling out and she had thrown me out of her house.

"I can't say," I replied, but I could feel the tears trickling down my cheeks as I quickly turned away from her and headed towards the stairs and my office, where I thought I could safely hide.

That evening when I got back to Grandmother's place, she immediately could tell something was wrong. She did not say anything at first. She just looked at me in that concerned way of hers and took me by the hand. Next thing I knew, she led me into the living room and sat me down on the sofa. She sat down in the old winged armchair and finally she spoke. "I can tell this is serious," she said. And then she asked, "Is it Brian?"

I could not contain the tears any longer; I had held them back all day. Grandmother handed me a tissue from the box that she kept on the shelf underneath the coffee table.

"He's dead," I said, and then repeated, shaking my head in shock and disbelief, "He's dead."

"Who? Brian?" Grandmother asked. Obviously, she too, had trouble believing it.

"Yes, Brian," I responded. "He's dead. Someone shot him."

There was a moment of silence while Grandmother was taking in this latest information.

"Someone shot him?" she repeated. "Who? Why?" she asked.

"I don't know. The police were at the office today asking questions, but they didn't say."

"Do you know where it happened or when?" she kept asking.

"No, I don't." Now I started sobbing, when I thought of our relationship that would never happen.

"I'll make you a hot drink." Grandmother got up and went into the kitchen. I could hear the gas being turned on. A few minutes later she returned with a special Grandmother treat—a cup of hot comforting chocolate.

"Here you are, child," she said. "Now I understand why you are so upset." I felt drained as the sobbing ceased and was replaced by a profound feeling of grief.

"Grief will pass," she said, correctly reading my state. "You are losing your connection to Brian," she started to explain. "When you have dealings with someone, and especially if the relationship is emotionally charged, there is an exchange that goes on between two people. After a while it strengthens and becomes more solid, like a thread or a rope—the channel through which emotions, thoughts, wishes and desires can travel. The longer this goes on, the more of the other person gets lodged in you and the more of you gets lodged in the other person. People who spend a lot of time together often end up looking alike, and if you see them out together, they will often image each other's body posture, perhaps without even realizing what they are doing. This is something you can observe wherever people gather—in cafés, restaurants or doctors' waiting rooms.

"The more emotion accompanies this exchange between people, the more powerful and the quicker the build-up of the frequency of the other person. Then, when the other person dies, the part of you that came from them is no longer fed and maintained. In fact, it is reclaimed by the deceased so it can accompany them on their next journey. That is why you feel grief. Whatever lives in you that is Brian's, belongs to Brian. So rather than holding on to it, let it go; he now needs it, to power him into his next life. You will still have the memories of what had happened between you, but do not possess what is not yours."

I looked at her through my tears. "I so wanted this relationship to work," I said. "It has never had a chance." Grandmother smiled. "Sometimes it's like that," she said. "Sometimes a child dies before it has even had the chance to have a life. Sometimes we meet someone who becomes dear to us and then we have to say goodbye, for whatever reason. Perhaps they go to war or are posted overseas, or become terminally ill. We need to be grateful for what we do have—cherish it while it lasts."

She paused for a moment and I felt her mind wander. She then looked at me and I understood she was passing on an important message, when she said, "Remember this lesson well. You will need it again soon. It is strange how losses do have the tendency to be accompanied by other losses. But remember, it is not to do with you or anything you did or did not do; it is to do with other people's timings and exits. As long as you live, there is a reason for you to be here. As you witness other people leave, perhaps their duty here is complete and finished." I nodded agreement but it was too early for me to really appreciate what she was saying. It felt so unfair that Brian had to leave this world just when his healing career was being acknowledged by some respectable members of the medical profession.

The next day I phoned Brian's apartment, partly because I still could not believe that he had really gone and partly because I wanted to be in touch with his family, to pass on my expressions of sympathy and to find out when and where the funeral would be taking place. I was also hoping to find out more about what had happened and how it happened.

I dialed the number and James answered the phone.

"Hi, it's Barbara here," I said as soon as I heard his voice.

"Oh yes, the girl who ran into the night," he said.

"I heard about Brian," I continued, disregarding his remark. I could feel the tears welling up again.

"Yes, a tragic event." James said, his tone changed.

"What happened" I asked.

"Come on over and I'll tell you all about it," he said.

"I can't," I lied. "When is the funeral?"

"We are waiting for the police to release the body," James said.

"So when will you know?"

"Probably after the weekend. I'll call you."

"Thanks," I said and put the receiver down.

For the following two days I felt like a robot, mechanically fulfilling my duties at work and then coming home to Grandmother's house and either staring at the ceiling, remembering all the times Brian and I had shared together or staring at the television screen, trying to forget my pain.

On the Thursday morning I was sitting at my desk when the telephone rang. It was one of the policemen who had interviewed me and he wanted me to come down to the station.

"You lied to us," he said once I was sitting at his desk and he had fetched me a cup of coffee. I looked at him in surprise. "You told us you didn't know Brian Polowski very well, but we have been told that you went out with him and were in fact a good friend of his."

I blushed. "That's true," I said, as I could see there was no point in pretending any further. "I did know him. Who told you?" I asked. He did not answer my question, but asked me instead, "Why didn't you say so?"

"I didn't want it known at the office and besides, I didn't think it was anybody's business."

"Oh, but it is our business," he said "This is a murder investigation. And do you know what happens to those who obstruct justice?"

"I don't know. Jail time?" I asked.

"It could be," he said. "It all depends on you."

"What do I need to do?" I asked. I was getting scared even though I realized that was what he had intended.

"Just tell us all you know." He put a piece of paper and a pen in front of me. "Who were his friends, what did he do in his spare time, where did he go? That would be a good start."

I picked up the pen and hesitated. I knew I could no longer hurt Brian, and perhaps I could help police in their investigation. I started writing down Alice's name. After all, she knew him well, I was sure of that. Then there was his brother, James Polowski, though no doubt they already knew all about him. Then there was Nancy, the dancer, Jenny and, finally, Antony, Janet and Stacey. The last people I had met through Brian were Dr. Philip, Dr. Palevi and John March. I wrote their names down as well. I couldn't think of anyone else. I handed the piece of paper back to the policeman. He looked it over and seemed satisfied with the result.

But that was not the end of it. The policeman kept me at the station for three more hours, asking every conceivable question about my relationship with Brian. I told him about all our dinner dates and healing meetings and escapades, but I insisted we worked together and were just friends.

Finally the policeman said I was free to go. "We'll be in touch," he added. As I was getting up, he said, "If you think of anyone else, please phone me," again handing me his card. I took it from his hand, turned away and left the police station. I went back to work and tried hard not to think too much about what had happened and what I could have done to prevent it. I remembered my vision in which I saw Brian's body lying in a morgue and I wondered what it meant. Perhaps I could have warned him and saved his life. It was so difficult to know what to think.

A couple of hours later Mrs. Franks came into my office. I was staring at the computer screen, but found it impossible to concentrate. I kept thinking of Brian and wondering what had happened.

She walked up to my desk and said, "I think you should take a couple of days off. It will give you a chance to get over the shock." I looked at her in surprise.

"I know you cared for Brian very much," she added. "Things are pretty chaotic here at the moment, so deliveries will be delayed over the next few days anyway."

I couldn't help asking her. "How do you know I cared for him?" I asked.

"It is my business to know," she replied and smiled enigmatically. "I really do know what goes on around the office."

"Thank you," I replied. "I appreciate your concern. And yes, I think I will take some time off."

"Good. I won't expect you back until Monday," she said and turned to face the door.

I walked outside the Versatile Furniture office building and was about to turn the corner to catch a bus to my grandmother's house, when I saw a Lexus parked in front of the building. The engine was running and I noticed the window on the driver's side was open and Andrew was waving, inviting me to approach.

"What are you doing here?" I asked.

"I came to pick you up and give you a lift," he said, as if it was the most natural thing in the world for him to do.

"That's nice of you," I said. "But how did you know that I would be leaving the office early?"

"I phoned the lady in the Human Resources department because I was trying to get hold of you and you weren't in your office," he said. "She's the one who told me you were leaving early. So rather than phone, I decided to come over and give you a lift."

"Well, that's very nice of you," I repeated and proceeded to walk around the car to the passenger's side. As soon as I closed the door and fastened my seat belt, Andrew started driving.

"Where to?" he asked. I gave him my grandmother's address. We drove around the corner and were cruising down Sycamore Avenue. Andrew said, "I don't think the police are going to bother you any more."

I looked at him in astonishment. "How do you know?" I asked.

"The chief of police is an old friend of mine," he said and smiled. "You're not a suspect. They have many witnesses they are questioning. It will take time."

I wanted to know more. A series of questions escaped me in rapid succession, "Do they have any idea who killed Brian? Do they know why?"

"There were security cameras at the hotel and they are checking out all the guests."

"But why, why did he do it?" I noticed I had said he and that I was therefore assuming that Brian was killed by a man.

"They don't know but they think it could be a professional who did it."

"Oh my God, who would do such a thing?"

"We might never know the answer to that question. But I promise you that if I find anything out, I will let you know."

The funeral took place on the following Saturday and when I arrived at the funeral home, I could see that the parking lot was full and there were many people milling about. There were several people from work—drivers, installers and dispatchers, including Matt, Ahmed, Sacha and people whose faces I recognized but whose names I could not remember. Then there were a number of people whom Brian had healed, including Nancy, Janet, and Antony. Of course his family were also there but I only knew James. His mother and father were both dressed in black and were sitting at the front of the large viewing room. People were walking up to them to pay their respects. I could see that his father spoke to them, while his mother sat in her chair staring at the coffin that was displayed on a raised dias with white flowers all around it. She was dabbing her eyes with her handkerchief and it was clear that she preferred not to speak with anyone.

I decided not to go up to them, but wrote my name in the book that was displayed on a table by the door, for those who wanted to write a message and sign their name. I knew his parents would probably read every entry in the book after the funeral, so I wrote the following words for them to see:

"Brian was a very special man—a great boss and gifted healer, who helped many people become healthy again. He will be missed by many." I signed the note, "Love, Barbara."

It was at that point that I finally felt a new sense of reality and some closure. I sensed Brian's presence next to me, as if he were looking over my shoulder and reading the message I had just written. At the same time I could hear his voice in my head saying, "I am glad we have had this time together. I learned a lot from you. Perhaps we would indeed have made a wonderful healing team, but this time round our destinies are separate—my work in this life has been cut short and yours has just begun."

Then he was gone. I felt that this was the message I had come to the funeral home to receive, so I decided to leave. As I was walking out the door, I came face to face with Philip, the doctor from the Medical Association who had organized Brian's trip to Atlanta.

"Hello Barbara," he said. "I have been trying to get hold of you. I have a message for you from Brian." I was speechless and just looked at him in surprise. "Shall we step outside?" he asked.

"Certainly," I replied and we both walked out onto the parking lot. We walked around the back of the building where there was a well-kept lawn with a few benches on it. It was late fall but the sun was shining and it was unusually warm for the time of year.

"I was there with Brian when he died," he said. "The day after you left, Brian met with a group of doctors at the local hospital. They wanted him to visit a number of their patients to see if he could help them. Brian was only too glad to oblige. So myself and Dr. Palevi, who have been meeting privately with Brian for the past few months, accompanied him on his rounds. What he did that Sunday morning was remarkable. He went around a number of wards, visiting patients with all kinds of illnesses and disabilities. Applying his hands to the sick people's energy fields he was able to bring about some instant results—fevers subsided, pain disappeared and a couple of people woke up from a coma. Every single person felt better after his visit and I believe at least half of them were cured, or definitely on their way to becoming healthy again. By the end of the day Brian was exhausted, but very satisfied with the results. We went back to his hotel where we sat in the lobby and talked late into the night, wondering what this might mean and what he should be doing next.

"The next morning I arrived at the hotel to pick him up and take him to the airport, but he was not in the lobby, so I went upstairs to his room and the door was slightly open. I walked in and there he was, lying on the floor—he had been shot, but he was still alive. Of course I called 911 and they sent an ambulance immediately, but it was too late; he died on the way to hospital. However, he did speak to me before he died. I asked him who had done this to him, but he did not know. He said he was getting ready to come downstairs when someone knocked on the door. He thought it was the bellboy, so he opened the door and a man forced his way into the room, pulled out a gun and shot him. He did not recognize the man, who was wearing a mask; he did not look familiar.

"And then, just as he was clearly weakening from the loss of blood, he said, 'please tell Barbara that I care for her very much. I think she has great powers and can do a lot of good for many people. Tell her to carry on the good work that we both had started.'"

We were sitting on the bench, and I tried hard not to cry, but I could feel the tears rolling down my cheeks. I brushed them away.

"Thank you for telling me," I said.

"There was one other thing," Philip said. "Brian said he had moved too fast, that he was doing too much too soon. He said the world wasn't ready for shamans or healers but that there would soon come a time when it would be. Those were his prophetic last words."

A few days later the policeman phoned again and I was invited back to the police station. This time I sat in front of a desk in an interview room, with no other police officers milling around, and no cups of coffee.

"We interviewed all the people on your list," he said and I felt relief, knowing that the list was truthful and according to my best memory.

"We spoke to Antony Ides," he said, "and he told us you were staying at his house the first weekend in December."

"That's right," I replied, wondering where this was leading.

"Then it must have been you who was out with Mr. Polowski on the night of the ...." He took out a small pad and flicked through its pages, "December third," he said.

"I guess I was," I replied, no longer sure of the date.

"You were in a car with Mr. Polowski when a policeman stopped you and interviewed Mr. Polowski."

My mind raced back to that night by the lake. "That's right," I replied. "The car had already stopped. We were having a conversation," I said. The policeman waved his hand impatiently, indicating that he did not believe me and that it no longer mattered. "Were you having an affair with Mr. Polowski?" he asked bluntly.

"No," I replied quickly.

"Are you sure?" he asked.

"Of course I am," I replied. I was beginning to feel indignant, but tried to retain my composure as best as I possibly could.

Then the inevitable question, "Where were you on the morning of December twelfth at 6am?"

I tried to remember—it had to be the Monday after I had returned from Atlanta. "I was at my grandmother's house," I said and then I added, "I am staying with her at the moment." I thought for a minute. "That was the Monday after I attended a meeting in Atlanta where Mr. Polowski demonstrated his healing abilities, but I did not stay overnight. I came back late Saturday night"

I admitted to kissing Brian on the night of December third and to "other bodily contact," but insisted that we were not having an affair. I was sure this nightmare of interviews by the police would continue, but then something strange happened. The days went by and they did not get in touch with me—either at home or at work. I was quite prepared to be called in for a polygraph test or further questioning, but it simply never happened.

Chapter Twenty-Two

Language

I invited Andrew to come and spend Christmas Day with us, so he joined our three generations of women (my stepfather had gone to visit his ailing father who lived in Seattle). Andrew arrived early for lunch. We had been cooking throughout Christmas Eve, while listening to carols on the radio. We had made a mushroom soup, the turkey was out of the oven and ready and my mother had baked her delicious upside-down cake. When Andrew knocked and I opened the door, he was standing there with an armful of presents and a great big smile displaying a row of white teeth. It had begun to snow for the first time in the season. There was an oversized red scarf wrapped around his neck; the large flakes were falling onto it as well as his hair and collar; they were melting as soon as they came to rest.

"Come on in," I said. "Why don't you put those presents under the tree?" I led him into the living room where we had decorated a small Christmas tree with silver and gold glass balls, tinsel and a silver fairy at the top.

After Andrew had left that evening, I found an envelope under the tree that had somehow gone unnoticed earlier in the day. Inside there was a letter, in which Andrew explained that he had found out from his friend in the police department that Brian's killer had not been identified yet, but that there had been a similar homicide on the west coast. Another successful healer was killed in a similar manner just as his popularity was growing in leaps and bounds. The police suspected that the crime was committed by a professional and that there had been some serious money backing the killer. They did not have enough evidence to prove anything but they thought that perhaps the killer had been hired by one of the companies that would lose a lot of money due to Brian's healing work. This information was strictly confidential and Andrew asked me not to repeat it to anyone. Andrew also wrote that his policeman acquaintance was convinced that they would never be able to find out who had hired the killer.

I decided to phone Andrew to thank him for his gift and thoughfulness. Sometimes information is better than the most expensive piece of jewelry; it can bring closure and settlement and peace of mind. It allows a thought about a situation to be reformed and re-evaluated. It can be a foundation for more effective decision making and for new ideas to be born. Somehow I felt relief that now I knew what had happened and it made so much sense. Brian had been healing people on a much larger scale than ever before and more and more members of the medical and pharmaceutical professions got to know about him and his work. No doubt they felt threatened. What if it transpired that Brian could heal AIDS? What if he could go around the world healing hundreds, or even thousands of people? What would happen to the doctors, nurses and pill makers of the world, who depend on the continuance of diseases for their livelihood? What if there were no more new viruses to discover and the world population became healthy? Although this was a very unlikely scenario, it became clear to me that many people would want to stop Brian and other healers like him. There are always those who do not want to upset the status quo, who like things to continue just as they are. How many people in the history of the world have been murdered to stifle progress and change? It would be impossible to count. And yet, even as harbingers of progress were assassinated throughout history, the new order still inexorably marched on, even if the killers had managed to delay it for a few months or years. Thus I believed that Brian's abilities as well as my own were now part of the inheritance of the human race and if we were no longer able to exercise our gifts and offer a cure to those who were ill, then perhaps someone somewhere would carry on the work we had started. Once a piece of knowledge or a new item of information is established, it becomes everyone's possession and privilege and right, whether they are consciously aware of it or not.

So I phoned Andrew to share my thoughts on this matter with him; I hoped he would understand. I felt he was still skeptical about the possibility of healing with energy, but he listened attentively. He was pleased that his letter had been well received. He wanted me to know the outcome of the investigation so far.

"Come with me to a New Year's Eve party," he said. "There is something I want to tell you." A new year would be starting in six days. A new year without Brian. A new year, so completely different from the one I had just experienced.

"All right," I said.

We were at his friend's house and there were a lot of people there. There was dancing and drinking and a lot of food. Everyone seemed so happy that the year was coming to a close. Was I the only person there who wanted to hold on to the memories of the year that had just gone by? Was I a party pooper? Was I being unreasonable? I tried to let go and think of the future and dance with Andrew and enjoy myself, but it simply was not possible. So I helped myself to champagne until I felt giddy and the future seemed less grim.

Twenty minutes before midnight I decided I needed to freshen up and take a look at myself in the mirror. I asked the hostess where the bathroom was and got directed upstairs—second door on the right. I closed the door and sat down on the bathtub to catch my breath and cool off for a moment. I was not looking forward to the new year, but I also had no desire for the old one to linger. In fact, I felt I was in no man's land, not quite sure where my life was heading at the moment. I remembered Grandmother's advice to decide what I wanted. Well, I wanted the impossible—I wanted Brian to be alive. So how do you deal with such a want? How do you un-want something? I walked up to the sink and splashed my face with cold water. Above the sink there was a mirror and as I straightened up and looked in it, I could see a young woman with a flushed face and fear in her eyes.

"What are you afraid of?" I asked the girl in the mirror out loud. The answer came to me quickly: I am afraid of loneliness. That's what I was afraid of. And then something strange happened. I could see in the mirror that the door to the bathroom had opened and before I had time to say it was occupied I was stunned into silence, because I could have sworn that it was Brian who had walked into that bathroom. I rapidly turned around to come face to face with James, Brian's brother. Funny, I had not noticed the similarity before but now I could clearly see that they were indeed brothers—the same height, the same dark hair, the same shape of the face. James didn't wear glasses and there was a difference in the look in his eyes. There was something wild, almost wolf-like about them. He locked the bathroom door and took a step in my direction. My heart started beating faster with fear.

"What are you doing here?" I asked

"I could ask you the same question," he said.

"I was invited by a friend," I replied.

"Already? So soon after Brian's death?"

"It's none of your business," I said emphatically.

"I thought I saw you go upstairs," James changed the subject.

"Why can't you leave me alone?" I asked.

"I want to apologize for that night at Brian's apartment. I wish you had stayed."

"You were drunk."

"Well, I'm almost sober now. How about I make it up to you?" He took another step forward and was now much too close for comfort.

"Take one step closer and I'll scream," I said. I had my back against the sink and there was nowhere to escape to.

"You wouldn't do that," he said. "You wouldn't want to ruin the party now, would you? How about you and I make up? He put his arms on my shoulders and I immediately pushed him back. He took a step back and I managed to move away from the sink. I was standing next to the bathtub now.

"I will scream," I assured him. I could tell he did not believe me, because he started moving towards me, smiling, as if he was dealing with a stubborn child. He reached towards me and grabbed hold of my blouse. I got hold of his wrists but did not have the strength to pull his hands off my clothes. I decided that I would scream and had just opened my mouth when he managed to free his right hand and covered my mouth with it. I used my freed left hand to start hitting him on the chest and I was really starting to panic. James was ignoring my efforts, as if my punches were totally ineffectual. He pulled me towards him, pulling at the fabric of my blouse, so that the two top buttons popped open. He then withdrew his right hand from my face and squeezed me even closer to him by placing his freed arm around my back; he then pressed his mouth against mine. It all happened so quickly. I squeezed my lips together and at the same time I released his left wrist, grabbed hold of his shoulders and tried to push him away with all my might. He took one step back and looked at me with a strange menacing crooked smile on his face, but he was still holding my blouse in his left hand while his right hand had moved to my left shoulder. I was trying to assess how to escape this situation when suddenly there was a knock on the door and someone was turning the handle. James dropped both hands by his side and I managed to quickly take advantage of the fact that his attention was drawn to the door, so I slipped by him and made a dash for the exit. I unlocked the door and opened it—I was so relieved to see Andrew standing there.

"What happened to you?" he asked. "Are you all right? I was beginning to worry—you were gone for so long!" I walked out of the bathroom and into the upstairs corridor, closing the bathroom door behind me. I didn't want him to see that I was in there with James. I quickly buttoned up and straightened my blouse.

"I wanted to freshen up before the New Year begins," I said.

"Well, it's almost midnight now," Andrew said. "Let's go downstairs and have a drink." He took my hand and led me downstairs to the living room where there were about fifty people having their glasses filled with champagne. Someone had turned the radio on and we listened to the countdown as the last sixty seconds of the old year passed slowly into history. Someone handed us both a glass filled with the bubbly liquid.

At midnight we raised our glasses and as the clock struck twelve, there were kisses, good wishes and more drinks. Andrew kissed me and held me tight. His embrace made me feel warm and secure.

"Will you marry me?" he asked. I was still shaken by the experience in the bathroom and I could feel the safety and companionship that Andrew was offering me with his proposal.

"Yes, I will," I said. He kissed me again and left me for a moment to refill our glasses. What have I done? I thought but soon dismissed the fear that had crept into my mind and decided that marriage was a good idea after all. Andrew was a great dancer and I believed he loved me, and that seemed really important at the time. He soon returned with our glasses filled and as we toasted the New Year yet again, out of the corner of my eye, I could see James walking through the room towards the door. I looked back at Andrew and thought with relief that I needn't be afraid of James or anyone like him ever again.

A few days after January first, when I returned to Grandmother's house from work, she was lying on the sofa, obviously in pain. I looked at her in surprise, because I had never seen her lying down during the day. She looked pale, with dark circles under her eyes.

"What's the matter? "I asked.

"I'm not well," Grandmother replied. "You need to take me to the hospital." I noticed her voice was slurred and she had difficulty talking. I phoned for an ambulance immediately.

"They're asking what are your symptoms," I said. "An ambulance is on the way."

"Tell them it's a stroke," she replied, and I noticed I had difficulty understanding what she was saying. "I have chest pains and my left arm is going numb." She closed her eyes. I relayed the information to the woman on the other end of the phone. "The ambulance will be there in five minutes," she said.

I put the receiver down and pulled a chair up to the sofa and sat down next to Grandmother. I held her right hand in mine and said, "Hold on Grandmother, help is on the way."

"It's all right," Grandmother reassured me in a whisper. "I'm not going yet. But my time is coming and there is nothing you can say or do that will stop me from going home." She smiled and for a moment I thought she was looking better.

The paramedics arrived promptly and within minutes they had Grandmother on a stretcher and were carrying her down the stairs and into the waiting ambulance. I climbed in the back of the vehicle and accompanied her on the ride to the local emergency room. It felt strange to be riding in the back of an ambulance so soon after the incident with Matt.

After a couple of hours of waiting, while the doctors were performing a series of tests on Grandmother, my mother arrived, as always, in a hurry and in a panic.

"What's happening?" she asked, her eyes darting all over the waiting room, as if she was trying to gather information from the walls, the furniture and the nurses' station.

"Grandmother had a stroke," I told her. "She's in good hands and the doctors are looking after her, doing all kinds of tests. She said she's not going to die. Not yet, anyway."

"I'll go and get a cup of coffee," Mother said, and walked down the corridor towards the hospital cafeteria. When she got back, we sat together in the hospital waiting room, telling each other stories about Grandmother's extraordinary healing powers and clairvoyant abilities.

"It runs in the family," Mother said. "It skipped one generation because you both have these extra sensory abilities, but I don't." She looked disappointed. "It's a gift," she said emphatically. "At first it worried me when you started predicting the future, but now I understand that you can help people. There are things we cannot change, but we can always change our attitude in a challenging situation and the way we think about ourselves and our future." I was surprised to hear her say that. She must have noticed my surprise, because she added, "I am a late learner, but I do appreciate the fact that there are people like Grandmother and yourself who can help others deal with their misfortunes." I thought of Brian and how the world was missing one of its greatest healers. Perhaps he could have helped Grandmother now. But it was too late.

"I have a lot to learn," I said quietly.

"Haven't we all?" Mother confirmed and then repeated, "Haven't we all?" in a softer voice.

A few days later Grandmother was transferred from the intensive care unit into a room of her own. She became more stable and we were able to visit her in the hospital.

A week later Grandmother returned home and I became her primary care giver. My mother arranged for a nurse to come in once a day, to wash her and help her with anything she might need while I was at work. We fell into a routine and I spent more time with her than ever before. I was glad I could pay back for at least some of the care and attention she had lavished on me during my childhood years when my parents were traveling around the country from one consulting job to another. And for the valuable lessons she had given me in recent months, lessons that had already changed my life for the better.

Ten days after she returned from hospital, Grandmother started to feel better. She was eating more and she even began occasionally getting out of bed and walking around the house with the help of a cane. She still had some difficulty talking, but I could understand her. One day, when I came back from work and was making her something to eat, she asked me to sit beside her and began to explain: "Never underestimate the gift of language," she said. "It allows you to communicate with other people, but more importantly, it allows you to talk to yourself and tell yourself your own story. Your future, as well as your present and your past, depend on the stories you tell yourself. Many things might happen to you in your lifetime—the good, the bad and the indifferent. It only becomes good or bad when you tell yourself that it is.

"So it is important how you speak to yourself and what you allow yourself to connect to. Remember that language is energy and that the words you think, speak or write carry a charge. It depends on you what kind of frequency you load into these sacred packages that are called nouns, verbs, pronouns and adjectives, to send into the world. Every letter, every sound, every syllable is a unique expression that can either heal or inflict, cheer someone up or depress them, cause them to stop and think about themselves and their life in a new way, or to continue along old habitual patterns." She paused and I could tell she had some difficulty speaking. I waited for a moment, and she continued. "Language is a sacred gift from the gods, added to over the centuries by prophets, poets and orators. The library in Alexandria might have been destroyed, but the contents of all the books in all the libraries of the world that have ever been written still exist. They are written into the planet's energy fields and you can connect to the information and inspiration contained therein." I could tell that she was becoming inspired, because the atmosphere in the room changed and I could feel a charge, and the space around her bed became electric and bright.

"All oral traditions that have never been written down are also alive today," she continued. And all the books and poems that have not yet been written are also there, ready to be received and translated into language. That's why it is so important to make room for what is new and to be in service to higher powers and forces that would want to speak to the human through those faculties that are able to listen. You have always had the gift of clairvoyance, so it is your sacred duty to listen to that voice in your head that guides you and leads you. It is your spirit talking to you, and your spirit is connected all the way up the levels of creation, all the way to God. So remember to listen, my child, and do not become too self-absorbed or take yourself too seriously. Every petty worry, or argument, or moment of boredom is time away from service and from the higher levels of human endeavor that you should be studying and attempting to reach."

She paused again, then looked at me with that intensity of hers, and passed on one more vital piece of wisdom. "When I am gone," she started and when I tried to protest, she held out her hand to stop me and continued. "Let me finish," she said and I decided to keep quiet. "When I am gone, there will be another teacher to help you reach the next level. I don't know when he or she will come into your life, but look out for him, because when you are ready, he will appear. I have completed my tasking with you. This is your last lesson from me."

I looked at her in surprise and she responded, "No, I am not leaving yet, but my teaching days are over and I need to prepare for my next life."

I could tell she was tiring, as the gaps between her sentences became longer, and she was closing her eyes at regular intervals. "I must rest now," she said, "so leave me alone, and I will sleep."

With that she closed her eyes once again. I waited for a couple of minutes, but she did not open them again and her breathing became regular—I could tell she had fallen asleep. I tiptoed out of the room and closed the door behind me.

Over the next couple of weeks my time was taken up by working, looking after Grandmother and going out with Andrew. Andrew was good to me—he took me to shows, to concerts and his favorite restaurants. I grew fond of him and he taught me about food, wine and foreign countries. He spoke three languages—English, French and German—and he seemed to know a lot of interesting people. We were always bumping into friends of his, many of whom were actors, writers or television personalities. I still missed Brian terribly and in my mind I would compare Andrew to Brian, which was very unfair to Andrew.

When Grandmother was taken ill and I promised my mother that I would take care of her, it meant that I stayed in the house most evenings and weekends. Sometimes my mother would come over to relieve me so I could go out and have a break. But even while shopping or going to the movies with Andrew, I worried about Grandmother and wanted to make sure that she was given the best care possible.

During those long winter evenings Andrew would sometimes come over, often bringing with him a special treat from one of his favorite grocery stores or restaurants, like a baklava from the Greek bakery around the corner or an aged camembert from the cheese counter at the expensive deli that I rarely frequented, due to their high prices.

Grandmother liked Andrew; he was courteous and pleasant, and always asked about her health. However, she did not talk with him about healing or clairvoyance or spirituality. Somehow she knew that he was not interested in universal law or the unseen worlds. Sometimes we would watch television together—our favorite programs were the reality shows and we would sometimes try to assess the competitors' characters and bet on who would win.

Chapter Twenty-three

The Open Door

Soon after New Year's Eve I put the thought of marriage aside as I needed to take care of Grandmother. Work became more demanding because without Brian on the job, the deliveries became more disorganized and my new boss—an older man who had worked as one of the dispatchers for five years—did not seem to have the energy to keep the delivery machine well oiled and effectively planned. I tried to help out as best I could, working extra hours and making as many suggestions as I felt prudent to do, but we kept falling behind and then scrambling to make up for lost time.

Grandmother was not getting better and she made it very clear to my mother and me that she believed her end was coming and that she was still alive because she needed to tidy up her affairs so that when the time came, there would be no loose strings or unclear instructions to sort out by those she would leave behind. Her lawyer visited her a few times during those cold winter days in January and every time I would come into her bedroom to bring them both a cup of tea or a sandwich, the conversation would cease until I left the room again and closed the door behind me.

A day before my grandmother died, she told me she wanted to speak with me. She asked me to make sure we were alone and she spoke to me in hushed tones; it felt like she was imparting an important secret. She held my hand, as if she was afraid she would slip away before finishing her thought.

"Never be afraid of death," she said. "It is a change of state. In fact, it is a birth, for you will be born where you are going, just as your birth was really a death, for you died to where you came from." Then she smiled and added, "Of course you still have time. But my time is up. I will leave you when you are ready to face the truth that the time of my departure has arrived."

"Don't say that," I started to respond, but she stopped me from continuing my thought.

"I know it is my time," she said, "and I am happy to leave this world. I fulfilled the final task I needed to do."

"What is that, Grandmother?" I asked.

"I needed to pass on the wisdom I had acquired during my lifetime before my departure. You represent the fulfillment of my final tasking."

And so it came to pass that my mother and I were sitting by my grandmother's bed when she decided to leave us. I do believe it was her decision to leave us at that time, and that she was well aware of the moment of departure when it finally did arrive. Not only did she predict the day and hour, but she had made sure that all her affairs were in order and that we were ready to say our goodbyes.

A week after her funeral I was clearing out my grandmother's desk and I came upon some papers she had left in the top drawer. Amongst them was a notebook with my name on it. I opened it onto the first page and began reading:

> Now in my eighties, I feel like a spirit waiting to be born. When a woman is pregnant, before the quickening at mid-term around the twentieth week, the spirit comes near and hovers, waiting to enter the fetus within the woman's womb. As I near my departure, I feel that while still alive on this Earth, I am at the same time waiting to be born elsewhere, hovering around my next incarnation, whether it is to be in this world all over again or whether this time I will be called

into service elsewhere. Wherever it is to be, I feel it is my calling and I am already projecting into my next life. I can feel it, I know it and it is influencing everything I can still do in this life. Teaching you is part of my taking leave—I have the responsibility of passing on what I know to the next generation, or to be more precise—my lessons are skipping a generation, as I was unable to teach my own children in this way, but have found a listener in you, my child.

I wish I had more time to tell you more and to share some deep hidden mysteries with you, but this is a beginning and it will have to suffice for now. Armored with these fragments of an ancient teaching, you will surely find your next teacher, when the time is right. So be brave, be fair and always search for the truth of any situation, regardless of whether it is beneficial to you or not. The truth will always set you free and allow you to look in the mirror every day without regrets.

Two weeks after the funeral Grandmother's lawyer phoned me and told me that I had inherited her house and a small amount of money. The rest of Grandmother's savings was divided between my mother, her sister Daisy and my brother Steven. My mother also inherited a few of the family portraits that hung in Grandmother's living room and bedroom, as well as some jewelry, an old fur coat and her mother's silverware. Everything else was left to me, so unexpectedly I became the proud owner of a three-bedroom house.

A week later Andrew moved in to Grandmother's house. I gave him Grandmother's room because I did not feel ready to take over the space in which she had suffered and spent her last days, struggling with pain and preparing for death. I stayed in the spare bedroom—it seemed simpler that way. Together we repainted the master bedroom and got rid of Grandmother's king-size wrought iron bed. I gave away her old dressing table and just kept the pine chest of drawers and bedside table. I repainted both items of furniture so that they matched and looked like new. Andrew brought with him some clothes, a single bed, a small table and a large armchair—the room now had totally changed its nature and atmosphere—it was more austere and sparse, and exuded a masculine atmosphere. The last thing to do was to change the flowery curtains, so I went out and bought some material in brown and beige stripes, to match the armchair; I also made a bedspread to match.

Andrew and I thus became roommates and although we were unofficially engaged, we had still not slept together. We kept our respectful distance and fell into a routine of working long hours, sharing a meal in the evening and then either watching television, reading or going out to a movie. It felt like we had known each other for a long time; our dealings were harmonious and respectful, though there wasn't a lot of passion sparking between us. I know Andrew was waiting for me to get over Brian's death and the grief I felt after Grandmother passed away, and I just wanted to continue as we were; it felt comfortable and familiar in a new sort of way. Maybe this was how couples who had been together for a long time felt—no need for a lot of words.

However, all that changed on Valentine's Day. I came back from work and there on the dining room table was an enormous bouquet of red and white roses in a pink vase. I could smell the scent of food as it wafted in from the kitchen. I also noticed that the table was set for two and that there were candles scattered around the room, throwing flickering shadows onto the walls. I proceeded into the kitchen and there was Andrew, wearing an apron and oven gloves, bent over the oven as he was checking what appeared to be a large roast chicken.

"Dinner will be ready in ten minutes," he said as he closed the oven door, stood up and took off the oven mittens. "Would you like some wine?" he asked and I noticed two glasses of red wine already poured, waiting for us on the kitchen table.

"Sure," I replied.

"I thought it was time to celebrate our engagement," Andrew said. "And what better time to do so than on Valentine's Day?" He handed me a glass of wine and we clicked glasses. "Here's to our future," he said.

"To us," I added, taking a sip of wine. "It's nice," I commented.

I felt overwhelmed by his kindness and consideration. How I longed to just take the two glasses of wine, place them on the table, throw my arms around his neck and kiss him, so that at last we could become true partners at many levels, including sexual. But I restrained myself and decided we needed to talk first.

"So what's for dinner?" I asked, smiling.

"Chicken, rice and a salad," he replied.

"OK, let's eat," I announced. "What can I carry to the table?"

"You just sit down and enjoy your wine. I'll bring in the food." So I picked up the wine glasses, walked into the dining room and sat down at the table. The places had already been set and the candles created an intimate atmosphere. Nevertheless, I couldn't help thinking of Grandmother every time I sat at her table. I thought perhaps we should buy a new table. Andrew soon followed me into the room, carrying a tray with the chicken on a platter and a bowl of rice; the salad had already been placed in the middle of the table.

"Help yourself," he said as soon as the food was in place and he was sitting down opposite me.

"Thank you for the surprise," I said.

"You're welcome."

We had another sip of wine and I helped myself to some food.

"I think we need to talk about our relationship," I said. "We are sharing this house and we said we would get married, but we haven't agreed what kind of relationship we want it to be."

"What do you mean?" Andrew asked. "I want to get married and have kids," he said. "I want an ordinary life."

"Well, that's where we differ," I said. "I want more than that. I want to understand why I am here and what this life on planet Earth is all about. When my grandmother was alive, she told me many things and I have many questions about this life and the next one, too. I want to understand more."

"I am a simple man, Barbara. I can look after a family and I can be a reliable husband and father. I don't know about the next life but I do know about this one. So take me, as I am." He reached into his pocket and pulled out a small box, which he placed on the table in front of me. When I opened it and looked inside, the diamond in the ring caught the light from one of the candles and reflected it in a rainbow of brilliant colors. I looked at Andrew and for the first time since Brian's death I felt that maybe I could be happy again.

We took our honeymoon in Hawaii, using my Halloween award voucher—it seemed a great idea to have our special time together paid for by Andrew's company. We flew to Honolulu where the company had booked a hotel on Waikiki beach. It was the ideal place—we walked on the beach, climbed to the top of Diamond Head volcano and visited the Arizona Memorial at Pearl Harbor.

One day after hours of extensive walking Andrew wanted to sit down on a bench on the beach and watch the sunset from there, but I was determined to explore the colorful International Market opposite the beach. He said he would be fine and suggested I took my time while he enjoyed watching the beautiful Hawaiian sunset. As I walked into the market, I spotted a sign that said Personal Readings by Clairvoyant. I had never met another clairvoyant and I was wondering about my future, so I decided to enter behind the curtain, which was slightly open, indicating that there wasn't a client visiting the clairvoyant at the present time. I first peered inside and saw a blonde lady with an open, pleasant face. I decided to go inside. She indicated for me to sit down at the table opposite her, she drew the curtain closed behind me, introduced herself as Angela and started a clock that I think was designed for bridge players, to measure the time of each move. She sat back down behind the table and picked up a deck of tarot cards.

"Is there anything specific you would want to know?" she asked.

"I want to know about the future," I said. She began shuffling the cards, then suddenly she stopped.

"Did someone close to you die recently?" she asked.

"Yes, in fact two people, one after the other," I replied and I felt a wave of sadness come over me and I felt sorry for myself, yet again.

"There's an older woman here beside you," Angela said. I could feel her presence as well; I could even smell her scent of lavender and musk, the same scent that still lingered in the closets and drawers in her house.

"It's my grandmother," I said. "She passed away this winter."

"Well, she's here and she has a message for you." I looked at Angela in surprise.

"What is it?" I asked.

"She wants you to know that she loves you and she is looking after you from the other side." I felt the tears welling up in my eyes. "There's something else," Angela was concentrating. "She wants you to know that you will meet a teacher who will be very influential in your life. He will take you to the next level of initiation, beyond the level to which she was able to guide you." I felt a tear roll down my cheek. I brushed it away.

"That's her all right," I said.

"And there's someone else," Angela said. "A young man."

"Yes, that's Brian," I said. "He passed away last year," I added.

"There is something he is not happy about," she said. She concentrated for a moment and then asked, "Are you engaged or did you recently get married?"

"Yes, I'm on my honeymoon here in Hawaii."

"He is indicating that there will be some trouble with this marriage," Angela said.

"Oh?" is all I could bring myself to say in response. It just didn't make sense. Angela continued, "But it will cause you to grow spiritually." She asked me to cut the cards and laid three of them out.

"This is very interesting," she said. "You have a lot of talents and the cards are indicating that you have a lot to give. However, you need to find the best way to pass on your skills and to help people. It will not be an easy journey, but it will be exciting and unique."

"What kind of talents?" I asked.

"I think you are a healer and a medicine woman, but you don't know it yet."

"I do sometimes predict the future and see the past," I admitted.

"That is a sign that what I am telling you is true. But you must find ways to help others. That is what we are here for; we must interact and share our gifts."

"I do want to but I don't know how."

"You will. You will," Angela said. Our half hour was coming to a close. "You are not an island. Just as you are here to help others, you will be meeting people who will help you and show the way. There will be a teacher and he will guide you towards your next steps. So be patient and look out for those people who are on your frequency." Angela turned the clock off. I recognized the last sentence as something Grandmother would have said.

"You are a lucky girl," Angela concluded. "You have people on the other side who care for you very much and will always look after you. You have unique talents and abilities and you have a very interesting life ahead of you." She gathered the cards together and smiled, indicating that the interview was over. "In the meantime, enjoy your honeymoon," she said.

I thanked her and left the booth. As I stood in the middle of the market, under an old, enormous bunyan tree, I paused and reflected on what had just occurred, with many people passing by. I closed my eyes and whispered, "Brian, take what is yours and thank you for your guidance. Grandmother, take what is yours and thank you for your love and wisdom." I waited for a moment and I felt that I was being received. The grief and the pain caused by the fact of losing two people who had been so close to me subsided for the first time since their demise. I felt I was free again, as I slowly walked across the street to join Andrew who was still sitting on a bench and gazing at the horizon, admiring a pink and gold picturesque Hawaiian sunset.

Epilogue

No Returns

When I looked back, I could not believe how much life had changed within one year. In twelve months I had found a new job, fallen in love and lost two of the people I felt closest to—Brian and Grandmother. I had a falling out with my friend Alice and I had learned about the worlds of energy and behavior from Grandmother's lessons. It had been a roller-coaster ride, but I felt I was now ready to begin.

Looking through my notes, I realized I had a whole collection of lessons that my grandmother had taught me. She was now gone and would never again be able to pass on any of her wisdoms, which were original, unique and each one was one of a kind. It was then that I thought of sharing them with others and that is how the idea of this book was born. If I could put them together and report them as they happened, then perhaps my grandmother's wisdoms could be of interest or even of use to others, helping them on their journey through life, as they no doubt were trying to understand others and to deal with them without conflict (or at least with as little misunderstanding as possible) and to good effect.

In my life up to this point I had found dealing with others to be the most difficult challenge that I had ever had to face. Almost like a test—you learn to deal amicably and successfully with one person, thinking that everyone should be as reasonable and straightforward as you think you are, when along comes someone else who changes all the rules and behaves in a totally unpredictable and not easily explainable manner.

And so as I complete this journal, I wonder what is in store for me and for the world in the years to come. I am very fortunate to have the love and support of my friends and family, and to have been given the gift of clairvoyance and healing. I hope to find ways to honor the memory of my grandmother and pay back for this incredible gift I have been given, called life.

I complete this account of my personal development lessons with my grandmother by quoting a poem that I found in her papers.

You Can Never Return

You can never return,
Because if you do, it will be a different city, a different place.
Childhood voices are silenced
The store downstairs no longer sells sporting goods;
It is a café instead.
The children's faces are unfamiliar
And even the fat boy across the street
    has married and gone away.
Where are you, my childhood memories?
In my mind, where they will stay
Alive, as long as I live.
The next generation are growing their own
Which in time will also be displaced.
As life evolves, I am moving on to my next destination.
I feel it, it beckons.
So do not cry for me,
I am on another shore
Awaiting the boat that will carry me home.

I distinctly felt these words were written for me and again, I sensed Grandmother's presence, which brought with it a certain settlement and closure. I could clearly feel this was her final goodbye, to me and the world.

And thus ends the story of my spiritual training with Grandmother, who was always like a first angel of my life, informing me in my formative years and shaping me so that I would be ready for the second angel of my development, yet to come.

In-Tuition

Moments of Discovery

In-formation; Moments of Realization is the first of the three-part series, *The Tri-Angel Way,* tracing the adventures of a young woman in search of meaning in her life. The second part in the trilogy, *In-Tuition; Moments of Awakening* is available from major online booksellers, such as *www.Amazon.com, www.Borders.com* and *www.BarnesandNoble.com.*

To give the reader an opportunity to flavor this next adventure, we attach the first chapter of this book, for your reading pleasure.

Part three of the trilogy, *In-Sight; Moments of Being* is currently in preparation and is expected to be published by the end of 2009.

Chapter One
The Discovery

I really didn't mean to know. I wished I could reverse the onslaught of time and be ignorant again. I have no idea what caused me to put my hand into his jacket pocket as I took his suit to the cleaners. I never look through his pockets; it's the kind of thing you read about in novels, but if two people trust each other, you don't need to … Who am I kidding? I would so much like to think of myself as a sophisticated wife, secure and happy, trusting and loving. But suddenly all that wishful thinking was shattered in one brief moment as I stood in front of the counter and the lady asked me whether I wanted to check the pockets before I left the suit to be cleaned. It wasn't even my idea, as if the whole thing was a terrible joke played out by fate and everyone else, while I remained like a puppet, whose strings were being pulled by some invisible hands.

So there I was, jacket in one hand and that dreaded hotel bill in the other—I must have been quite a sight, seeing my name on a bill —Mr. and Mrs. Johnson—for a room at a place I had never been to. My mind was racing—September sixth, what day of the week was that? I couldn't think. I put the jacket back on the counter, took the receipt, even managed a smile and a "thank you" and dashed out of the door. I almost ran to the car, let myself in, threw my bag onto the passenger's seat and sat there, slowly gathering my thoughts, resting the bill in front of my eyes, using the steering wheel as a pulpit.

I didn't want to know on the one hand and I could have easily torn up the offending piece of paper and thrown it out of the window, pretending that this was not really happening. But there was also a great curiosity to know more. Who is she? Where did they go? What was the name of that hotel? were questions that were rattling around in my head, demanding answers. I carefully scrutinized the bill—The Golden Dusk Hotel. Hotel. Never heard of it. Certainly not a major chain or group of hotels. In a way that was a relief; it wasn't somewhere where we had been together, say for dinner or afternoon tea. And even as I looked, I was playing out scenarios in my head: The Confrontation and The Questioning. This was a drama with tragic-comic undertones with the final result being separation and divorce. Then there was the Playing Ignorance spy-thriller, trying to find out more, hiding around corners, opening letters, searching drawers and pockets for more evidence.

Mr. and Mrs. Johnson at the Golden Dusk Hotel—one night, breakfast and two phone calls. Even the phone numbers were on the bill. One was our home—he had phoned home—and one was to the office. Both numbers were so familiar to me, probably etched in my memory forever. The date—September sixth. When was that? I couldn't think; it was more than six weeks ago. It couldn't have been a weekend; I could account for every one of them. My mind was racing. I had a small diary in my bag—I pulled it out. Dentist appointment—that was the first thing I noticed about Tuesday, September sixth. Then, in small letters it said underneath: Andrew away at conference. The same writing appeared within the box for the previous Sunday and Monday as well. A three-day conference. He was away for three days. That's right! I remembered now. I sighed and leaned back in the seat, as floods of memories from those three days rushed in. I could clearly see little snapshots of life at home, the things I did during those three days. And then I pictured the faces of his colleagues, the ones that I knew, who were supposed to have gone too. And then the one thing I did not want to submit to came in as an avalanche of doubt and suspicion: Who was he with? Who could it be? In my mind's eye I searched a gallery of portraits—faces of friends, people we knew, people we met. Women, friends, colleagues.

It was useless; I didn't know. It could be anybody; it shouldn't be anybody. Who knows how a man thinks? Sitting here is not going to solve anything. I needed to think this through. I needed to talk to somebody. I needed time.

I started the car and slowly drove towards home. I took my time as I tried to gather my thoughts. There were so many things I wanted to do—I wanted to run away, to confront him, to hire a detective to follow him and then I wanted to forget all those ideas and do nothing at all, to pretend nothing was happening so that life could carry on as before. But, of course, I knew it couldn't. I knew it never would be the same again.

When I got home, the house felt empty. I paced around the place, checking messages, making myself a cup of tea. I couldn't sit still, I didn't know what to do. As always, when at loss, I dialed Anne's familiar number. She was home. She answered the phone. Now what do I say? She picked up that something was wrong. After all, we knew each other well.

"Are you all right?" she asked.

Tears flooded to my eyes, as I answered, "No, I'm not. Can I come over?"

She always liked a good drama. "Sure," she said, "come right away."

On my way over to Anne's house I became subject to two mental processes, both related to and dependent on each other. The first was a great value and appreciation for the normality of things, and a further longing for life to be boring, mundane, uneventful, continuous and secure. I also felt the beginning of a realization that all that had now changed and that nothing would be the same ever again. I couldn't even begin to think about the future, for my whole life, as I knew it, stood in front of me in ruins now and I had no idea how to go about repairing it.

Then, in my desperate quest for some sort of solace or comfort, I found my mind racing through the various books I had read and films I had seen, in search of a similar scenario. I was sure this was a stereotype situation, very banal and a veritable template for many cheap paperback stories, which I used to consume voraciously when

I was a teenager. And yet, for the life of me, I couldn't remember what ought to happen next according to any one of them. And then, suddenly, I remembered and it almost caused me to stop the car in the middle of the traffic. Of course, the wife doesn't find out till later, but it is always her best friend who is having an affair with her husband! Of course, Anne! How could I have not spotted it before? I'm going over to her place to pour my heart out and she will be mocking me because she already knows all about it. No doubt she will then urge me to get a divorce so she can have him all to herself! I quickly scanned in my mind all the times we had been out together, the three of us, and how well Anne and Andrew used to get on, how pleased I was and relieved that both of my favorite people enjoyed each other's company. What a fool I had been.

And then a further thought came into my head and that was that perhaps the hotel bill was left in his pocket on purpose, so that I would find it, demand an explanation and file for a divorce. Perhaps it was part of a plan, all thought out and premeditated to place the ball in my court, for me to make the decisions. Perhaps not completely consciously, but as part of a plan nevertheless.

In the meantime, I was nearing Anne's home and I needed to decide what I was going to tell her, how I would be with her and what would I give her the satisfaction of hearing. Before I had time to really think about it, I was parked outside her house and before I even had time to lock up the car, she was standing in the doorway waiting for me to reach her at the top of the porch steps. As I walked toward her, I could see that she knew right away that something was the matter—she knew me too well. There was no point in pretending any more. I didn't want to anyway; I needed to talk to someone. And if it was her, then she would need to deal with her own guilt and decide whether she would be honest with me or not. I didn't care any more. It needed to come out into the open.

Anne put the kettle on to make tea, as she always did when I visited her. As soon as we sat down together in her living room, she asked, "What is the matter?"

I immediately blurted out, to my own surprise as well as hers, "Andrew is having an affair!"

"Really?" she sounded genuinely surprised, but not shocked, and the next thing she asked was, "How do you know?"

So before I knew it, I was telling her the whole story, which wasn't much of a story, really, for all there was to report was the discovery at the dry cleaner's and that's it, with a few more speculations, indignations, surprises and bewilderments on my part. She seemed very sympathetic and quiet, with a few questions that I had already thought about, like, "When looking back, isn't there anything else you can see that now seems suspicious? Like unexpected business trips or unexplained expenses?"

Well, sure there was, but that's the way Andrew was anyway and that was the nature of his job—traveling a lot, spending generously during his trips and then claiming back expenses—it was all very difficult to keep track of. Money in, money out. I always saw myself as the policeman standing in the middle of a busy crossroads, directing the traffic, but never holding on to much in the process and never really investigating where the traffic was coming from or where it was going. As long as it was there, I had places to send it; as long as I could pay the bills and the mortgage for the next month, I trusted that the next bit would come in somehow so that we could continue. And so far it always did.

"Nothing more unexpected than usual," I replied, thinking hard, but not able to relate to anything suspicious or out of the ordinary, like an exotic perfume or unfamiliar scent.

"What about the classic one, lipstick on his collar?" Anne said, pouring another cup of tea. I couldn't control it and despite my grief and confusion, I burst out laughing.

"Oh, please," I said, indignant, though I knew I had no right to be after what had happened so far. "He would never do that."

"That's what every wife in your situation always says. But it does happen because it's one way of letting you know," Anne said, now turning into a psychologist. I could almost see her in a white coat with a pad and pencil in her hand. "Another, of course, is to leave a hotel bill in his coat pocket."

This thought took me by surprise. Not because I hadn't thought of that already, but because I didn't expect her to come up with it. I pretended to be ignorant or naïve or both.

"Are you saying that he did it deliberately?"

"Well, not necessarily consciously or deliberately," Anne explained, obviously pleased that I was taking her seriously. "But something in him wanted you to know, otherwise he would not have left that bill there. I believe," she added, with an air of authority, "that if someone wants to do something but doesn't know how and hesitates for too long, then their sub-conscious mind will find the opportunity to do it on its terms, whether the person agrees to those terms or not."

"Oh, Anne, you mean he wanted me to know so that I would take the initiative and walk away from our relationship? Or perhaps decide that I can forgive him and carry on? Is it that he can no longer live with the lie and the guilt?" I did not wait for an answer to all these questions that were spilling out, one after the other. "So what should I do? What would you do in my situation?" I asked rather pathetically, putting myself hypothetically in her care, sipping the comforting warm liquid in this otherwise unfamiliar new territory.

"I don't know," she hesitated. "What do you want to do?" she asked, emphasizing the word 'you.' And when I hesitated, taking a moment to reply, she continued, "I see three options here, depending upon what you want and what you are prepared to live with, or not prepared to live with, as the case may be. First, and the most dramatic, is to move out and file for divorce right away. The other extreme is to ignore the whole thing and carry on as if nothing has ever happened. But I don't think you would want to do that," she added, with a hesitation in her voice. "The third possibility is to confront him, talk it through and see if you can work something out, providing, of course, you both want to and are able to, after what has happened."

She's right, I thought. That leaves me two options: to say something or to shut up. Well, I knew that all along. I didn't need her to tell me that! Suddenly I felt resentful. How come she is so ordered and well organized, pontificating about what to best do? I thought and my suspicions grew stronger than ever. I started to feel like a hypocrite, sitting there with these thoughts knocking about in my head. I felt I had better leave.

"You're right," I said out loud to her. "It's simple, really. I just need to think it through and make a decision. Thanks for the tea." I stood up. My change of mood must have seemed abrupt to her.

"Where are you going?" she asked, responding to the sudden haste.

"I must get home. Just look at the time!" I said, glancing at my watch. It wasn't late at all and I knew Andrew wouldn't be home for some hours. If only I could listen in to her telephone conversations the moment I walked out the door. I felt sure she would be phoning him immediately to warn the perpetrator that they had been found out. We kissed on both cheeks, as we always did and said our goodbyes. I noticed her perfume—expensive, no doubt.

Back in the car, I dialed Andrew's office. "I'll put you through," said the receptionist and immediately I could hear the busy signal. The receptionist's voice came back on. "His line is busy. Do you want me to put you through to his voice mail?"

"No, it's all right, Anita. I'll talk to him later."

There it was—another proof, another piece of evidence. All right, I would take it all the way. I stopped at the nearest phone booth and looked up the hotel in the telephone book—the Golden Dusk. I phoned their office and asked for the address of the hotel. I was going to get to the bottom of this. Once I had the address, I worked out that it would take me about an hour to get there. I still had enough time to drive there and back before Andrew would come home. I dropped in to the house on my way and rummaged around in the box of photographs, where I found a picture of Andrew, Anne, Nick (Anne's current boyfriend at the time) and me, taken during last year's vacation in France. There we were in a vineyard in Provênce, tasting the grapes. How sun tanned and happy we all looked! How ironic! But it was a good, close up shot and you could clearly see Anne's features on it.

It didn't take me long to get out of town and the hotel was not difficult to find, as it was advertised on a billboard on the main road and was located at the edge of a small village, with a forest and a chain of green hills stretching out behind it. Set in its own grounds, it was very picturesque and clearly well cared for, with outdoor swimming pool, landscaped gardens with fountains, flowerbeds and a golf course. It had that quiet, stately atmosphere that makes you slow down and feel you have all the time in the world.

Once in the large foyer, which made you think you were in the tropical colonies, I walked up to the reception desk. An attentive clerk asked me if he could help me.

"I want to check something," I said, suddenly feeling self conscious and awkward. I pulled out the photograph. "I would like to know if this woman was booked in to your hotel on the night of September sixth."

The man looked at the photograph, then at me, incredulously.

"Madam," he said, "there are three hundred guests every night in this hotel. They come and they go all the time." As he spoke, a bellboy appeared behind the desk and as he reached for the key to one of the rooms, he craned his neck, trying to catch a glimpse of the picture. The clerk looked at him admonishingly and handed me the picture back.

"I can't possibly remember," he said and added, "sorry," in a tone that sounded final and clearly marked the end of the conversation. I felt crestfallen and stood there for a moment, not knowing how to proceed further. The clerk then leaned over the counter and added in a hushed voice, "Unless this is part of an official investigation, we pride ourselves on our discretion. We do not disclose guests' details to anyone."

"I understand," I replied as I put the photograph away. "Thank you for your time," I said, turning away and feeling that it wasn't all right at all and that I had just wasted my time. I slowly walked to the door.

As I left the hotel and made my way towards the car, I saw a figure approaching me from the side entrance to the hotel. It was the bellboy whom I had seen earlier behind the desk.

"I saw the picture," he said, as he approached me, "and I remember the girl," he added quickly, as if trying to hold my attention before I walked away. "She was here," he said firmly.

I opened my purse and pulled out a twenty-dollar bill.

"How can you remember?" I asked, handing him the banknote.

"I only remember because that was the day of my sister's wedding," he said, taking the money and putting it into his pocket with the speed of a true professional informer. "And I was due to be best man, so I was in a hurry to leave work. It was the end of my shift and I was really off duty, but those were the last guests that I was escorting to their rooms. You see, John, that's the guy who had the next shift after me, was late and I was filling in for him while he was getting changed into his uniform. I remember because we had an argument about it, but the manager asked me to stay on for half an hour longer, so I did. That lady—the one in the photograph," he added, "was being very fussy, asking me questions about the place, about meal times, pool times, gym times, even though it's all written down in the brochure. Then she got me to shift the suitcase from the stand to the bed, checked out the bathroom, the closet and the tea service. I remember her because I was almost late for my sister's wedding."

"You have an extraordinary memory," I said while thinking that it sounded just like Anne—fussy and very particular. She was, after all, a Virgo. I was convinced it had to have been her. Once again I pulled the photograph out of my purse and handed it to the bellboy.

"Are you quite sure?" I asked.

"Yes ma'am, I am certain," the boy said. "I hope that will be all. I've got to go now. I'm still on duty." He brought his two fingers up to his cap in a kind of salute, pivoted on his toe and began walking back to the entrance of the hotel.

I was left there, standing in the middle of the driveway, still holding that photograph from a year ago. So it is her, was all that kept reverberating through my head. It's her. Suddenly, in my mind Anne was the villain, the false friend, the husband stealer, cold and destructive, cruel and uncaring—the vamp, the femme fatale, the family breaker.

About the author:
Joanna Infeld is an international speaker, writer and workshop facilitator. To find out more about her and about upcoming events, check out her website, www.RainbowWoman.com.

www.ingramcontent.com/pod-product-compliance
Lightning Source LLC
Chambersburg PA
CBHW021046090426
42738CB00006B/206